Mawson's Last Survivor

The Story of Dr Alf Howard AM

Anna Bemrose

First published 2011

National Library of Australia Cataloguing-in-Publication entry:

Author:	Bemrose, Anna.
Title:	Mawson's last survivor : the story of Dr Alf Howard AM / Anna Bemrose.
ISBN:	9781921920189 (pbk.)
Subjects:	Howard, Alf, 1906-2010. British, Australian and New Zealand Antarctic Research Expedition 1929-1931 Scientists--Australia--Biography Antarctica--Discovery and exploration--Australian.
Dewey Number:	509.2

Typeset in Perpetua 12pt.

Cover Design: Boolarong Press

Cover Images: Iceberg (iStockphoto)
Scientific personnel of BANZARE (1929-30) on deck of the *Discovery*. Mawson Collection, South Australian Museum [R 263]

Published by Boolarong Press, Salisbury, Brisbane, Australia.

Printed and bound by Watson Ferguson & Company, Salisbury, Brisbane, Australia.

For Alf

CONTENTS

Foreword

BY

Tim Bowden AM

Few men have packed more high adventure and scientific achievement into a long life than Alf Howard. Anna Bemrose's friendship with Alf has inspired her to share with us his remarkable 104 years on our planet with this meticulously-researched and intriguing biography.

As Alf told Anna, 'The idea of stopping work abruptly never appealed to me … the point is, the brain doesn't just switch off on a particular date'. So said the man who, at the age of 97, was still programming computers and mentoring research students in the Department of Human Movement Studies at the University of Queensland in 2003.

Already highly qualified as a chemist and hydrologist in 1929, Alf Howard sailed on both Sir Douglas Mawson's BANZARE (British, Australian and New Zealand Antarctic Research Expedition) voyages in 1929, and 1930. Australia's ambitious claim of 42 per cent of the Antarctic continent is largely based on these two voyages, which explored the coastline of Greater Antarctica from Enderby Land to the west and as far east as George V Land, including Commonwealth Bay the base camp for his AAE (Australasian Antarctic Expedition) of 1911-14.

The BANZARE voyages, using Scott's old ship *Discovery*, were modern and innovative voyages, where science was given equal weight to flag planting and proclamation intoning. *Discovery* carried a Gipsy Moth float plane, used to glimpse great mountain ranges and interior features of Antarctica never before seen by man.

Alf Howard was in the forefront of the science of oceanography, taking part in sampling (among many other achievements) the chemistry and biology of the Southern Ocean in a series of observations from the south east coast of Tasmania to the Antarctic continent—work not built on until the 1970s when the Australian Antarctic Division began its present oceanography program. Like all ships designed for the ice, *Discovery* had a rounded hull, and as Alf told me in an interview for the ABC in 1993, 'she rolled like buggery', which made winching up deep sea trawls a frightening experience, let alone processing the results in an on-board laboratory during 45 degree rolls. But this work went on continuously which irritated the acerbic Captain J.K. Davis, who fretted about burning up his precious supplies of coal in the interests of science.

The so-called Heroic Era of Antarctic exploration is supposed to end in the early 1920s, but I think the BANZARE voyages should be included, with a wooden sailing ship and its company braving the extremes of ice, blizzards and extreme cold for so many thousands of miles. In that sense Anna Bemrose has brought these voyages vividly to life not only through Alf Howard's vivid recollections, but the use of other diaries. The irrepressible Frank Hurley sailed on both voyages not only chronicling their adventures with still and movie film, but performing his usual practical jokes—like making smoke appear to come from his ears by a series of concealed tubes.

I have yet to read a more compelling account of what it was really like to voyage on a near-as-dammit 'Heroic' Antarctic expedition. The reader can smell the tobacco-fug in the wardroom, crunch the coal dust between their teeth and feel the queasiness induced by *Discovery's* unforgiving motion as well as sharing the comradeship of this robust and dedicated cast of characters.

But the Mawson voyages were only the beginning of Alf Howard's remarkable life. Ahead was his career with the fledging CSIR (later CSIRO) and pioneering work in food preservation during World War II. Always seeking to study in new disciplines–let's mention psychology, statistics and computer programming in passing–after his 80th birthday, there were four more voyages to Antarctica (and two to the high Arctic) culminating in a three month circumnavigation of Antarctica on board the Russian icebreaker Kapitan Khlebnikov just after his 90th birthday. And there were European and African travels as well.

I was privileged to meet him and interview him about his BANZARE experiences when he was coasting through his eighties. Anna Bemrose, living in Brisbane, was able to get to know him extremely well until his death, at 104, in 2010. What an innings. And now this splendid book to help remember Alf Howard, small in stature, but a giant in every other way.

PREFACE

One could catch a glimpse of him crossing the University of Queensland campus with a knapsack on his back and sporting a cloth hat. A small-built frame, slightly bent, a sprightliness in his gait that revealed sure-footedness, determination and focus of destination. In summer: long-sleeved shirt and tie, Bermuda shorts and knee-high socks, replaced in winter with long trousers and zipped casual jacket; always dapper and smart. His white hair, moustache and spectacles conjured up images of Albert Schweitzer and David Livingstone.

In 1990, in a university newsletter, there was a photograph and article about my mystery explorer! Dr Alf Howard AM was preparing to revisit Antarctica for the first time since his return as a scientific member of the 1929-31 British, Australian and New Zealand Antarctic Research Expedition (BANZARE), led by Sir Douglas Mawson in Robert Falcon Scott's old ship the *Discovery*. How wonderful it would be to meet him; Antarctica had always been a destination of fascination for me.

Weeks passed and one day he boarded the same bus en route to university; it was packed. He disappeared somewhere in the front, I was near the back door. I recognised him from the photograph and when the bus arrived I quickly alighted and waited for him to appear. 'Excuse me, would you be Dr Alf Howard?' He doffed his hat and smiled, 'I am indeed.' So began a long treasured friendship.

A few years ago when the idea of writing a book about Alf came up, he was only too delighted to engage in conversation about his life–especially his voyages with Mawson.

ACKNOWLEDGEMENTS

THANK YOU to everyone who has contributed to the production of this book:

The team at Boolarong Press for their professional expertise.

Shirley Howard, Alf's niece, for a wonderful day in Camberwell visiting her uncle's childhood home, school and scout den, and for making available personal letters from her uncle and offering other valuable assistance.

The Australian Geographic Society and Dick Smith for their support in the early stages of research for this book.

Tim Bowden for his Foreword and for his support throughout this project.

Sally Douglas, daughter of BANZARE aviator Eric Douglas for her enthusiasm since the beginning of the project and for sharing original and personal material from her father's papers.

Ian Jobling, Mark Pharaoh and Robin Shorthose for reading sections of the manuscript and for their valuable comments.

David Simmers, son of BANZARE meteorologist Ritchie Simmers, for kindly posting his father's diaries from New Zealand.

School of English, Media Studies and Art History (EMSAH), The University of Queensland, for their ongoing support.

Alf Howard's friends and colleagues generously participated in this book by granting interviews, communicating by letter, email or telephone, and giving other significant assistance: Philip Barnaart, Jan Black, Tim Bowden, Andrew Brooks, Les Brownlie, Sheila Bryce, Michael Bryden, David Carstens, Tim Cassidy, Lesley Chase, Craig Engstrom, Ian Fletcher, Peter Gambetta, Fred Grau, Shirley Greer, Cam Griffin, Ian Jobling, Jack Kefford, Syd Kirkby, Tom Larsen, Ralston Lawrie, Liz McBain, Doune Macdonald, Ingrid Mcgaughey, Shirley McKeon, John Morrison, John Splettstoesser, Ray Specht, Margaret Steinberg, Jeff Pittam, Graham Pryde and Robin Shorthose.

Research for this book could not have been completed without the resources, permissions and time offered by archivists, keepers of collections and personnel in libraries, museums and Antarctic institutions. Australian Antarctic Division: Wendy Pyper, Andie Smithies and Graeme Watt; Canterbury Museum, Christchurch, New Zealand; Centre for Environment, Fisheries and Aquaculture Science (Cefas), Lowestoft, England: Sarah Turner; City of Boroondara Library, Melbourne; Commonwealth Scientific and Industrial Research Organisation (CSIRO) Archives, Brisbane: Meryn Scott, Discovery Point, Dundee Heritage Trust, Dundee, Scotland: Gill Poulter, Niall Cooper and Ann Malone; Meteorological Service of New Zealand (MetService) Library: Penny Bull; Marine Biological Association of the United Kingdom, Plymouth: Kathy Broad; Mitchell and Dixson Libraries Manuscripts Collection, State Library of New South Wales: Tracy Bradford and Edward; South Australian Museum: Mark Pharaoh, Senior Collection Manager, Mawson Collection; State Library of Queensland: Linda Pitt and Margaret Mowberry; State Library of South Australia, Adelaide; Scott Polar Research Institute, Cambridge; Unicopying, St Lucia: Bill Mouritz; University High School, Melbourne: Kate Marquand; University of Melbourne Archives: Kathryn Wood; University of Queensland: Social Sciences and Humanities Library — Document Delivery: Alison Stewart and the Fryer Library.

The Amity/Bupa staff at New Farm, and in particular Judy Laqua, for the care given to Alf.

Timeline

ALF HOWARD

1896	Alfred Samuel Howard marries Amelia Caroline Welsford. Clarence born 20 November 1901.
1906	30 April, Alf Howard born Canterbury, Melbourne.
1912-24	Camberwell State Primary School 888, Gardiner Central School, and the University High School, Melbourne.
1914	First official registered Wolf Cub in the First City of Camberwell Scout Group.
1922	Awarded the King's Scout Badge.
1924-27	Bachelor of Science, University of Melbourne.
1928	Master of Science, University of Melbourne. Awarded Kernot Scholarship.
1929-30	Chemist & hydrologist on the 1st BANZARE voyage led by Sir Douglas Mawson on the *Discovery*.
1930-31	Chemist & hydrologist on the 2nd BANZARE voyage led by Sir Douglas Mawson on the *Discovery*.
1931-2006	Sharing BANZARE with schoolchildren.
1931-41	Chemist with CSIR in Griffith, NSW.
1934	Married Elizabeth Beck.
1942-48	Transferred to CSIR Division of Food Preservation, Sydney.
1949-71	Officer-in-Charge of CSIRO's Cannon Hill's meat research laboratory in Brisbane.
1964	Fellow of the Royal Australian Chemical Institute Inc.
1968	Degree of Doctor of Philosophy at the University of Queensland (UQ).
1970	Fellow of the Australian Institute of Food Science and Technology Inc.
1971	Retired from the CSIRO.
1976	Bachelor of Arts Degree (UQ).
1980	Bachelor of Arts Degree Hons. (UQ).
1981-82	Research consultant & part-time lecturer in statistics Dept. of Psychology (UQ).
1983-2003	Honorary statistical consultant & computer programmer Dept. of Human Movement Studies (HMS), UQ.
1984	Study tour to Greece with HMS students.
1986	80th Birthday.

1991 Revisits Antarctica & Mawson's hut on board the *Frontier Spirit*. In the same year visits Antarctic Peninsula, South Georgia, Ecuador Galapagos Islands and Easter Island.

1993 Hon. Degree of Doctor of Science (UQ).

1994-96 Travels to Japan, Mediterranean Sea & Pacific Ocean music cruises; Kuril Islands & Kamchatka Peninsula.

1996 90th Birthday.

1996-97 Three-month circumnavigation of Antarctica on board the icebreaker *Kapitan Khlebnikov.*

1998 Order of Australia (general division AM).

1999-2003 Travels to Madagascar, Seychelles & Reunion; Kenya Safari & Tanzania; Ballet tour to Scandinavian capitals, London & New York; Kimberleys cruise; Canadian Rockies & Alaskan cruise.

2000 Senior Australian of the Year award.

2001 Australian Geographic Society gold medal for lifetime of adventure.

2006 100th Birthday.

2010 104th Birthday.

2010 4 July, passing of Alf Howard.

HISTORICALLY-RELATED ANTARCTIC EVENTS

1772-75 Captain Cook circumnavigates Antarctica in the HMS *Resolution* & HMS *Adventure*.

1872-76 *Challenger* Expedition led by Charles Wyville Thomson.

1882-83 First International Polar Year.

1898-1900 Carsten E. Borchgrevink's *Southern Cross* Expedition.

1901-04 Robert Scott's *Discovery* Expedition.

1901-03 *Gauss* Expedition led by Erich von Drygalski.

1901-09 *Nimrod* Expedition, led by Ernest Shackleton.

1910-12 Roald Amundsen's *Fram* Expedition.

1910-13 Robert Scott's *Terra Nova* Expedition.

1911-14 Australasian Antarctic Expedition led by Douglas Mawson in the *Aurora*.

1914-17 Imperial Trans-Antarctic Expedition, led by Ernest Shackleton in the *Endurance*.

1921-22 Shackleton-Rowett Expedition, led by Ernest Shackleton in the *Quest*.

1925-27 *Discovery* Investigations.

1929 29 Nov., Admiral Richard E. Byrd became the first pilot to fly over the South Pole.

1929-30 First BANZARE voyage on the *Discovery* led by Douglas Mawson.

1930-31 Second BANZARE voyage on the *Discovery* led by Douglas Mawson.

1932-33 Second International Polar Year.

1932-36 *Discovery* laid up in the London Docks.

1933-39 Lincoln Ellsworth — *Wyatt Earp* Expedition.

1937-54 *Discovery* used by Sea Scouts in London.

1943-45 Operation Tabarin, led by Lt. James Marr.

1947 December, Heard Is. station established.

1948 March, Macquarie Is. station established.

1954 Mawson station (Australia) established.

1954-79 HMS *Discovery* used as a drill ship for the Royal Navy Volunteer Reserve on the Thames.

1957 Davis station (Australia) established.

Scott Base (NZ) established.

1956-58 Commonwealth Trans-Antarctic Expedition, led by Vivian Fuchs during the International Geophysical Year (IGY)): 12 countries involved in Antarctica, more than 40 stations established and numerous research projects and expeditions realised, which led to the development of the Antarctic Treaty in 1959.

1959 Australia took over former USA Wilkes station.

1979 April. *Discovery* handed over to the Maritime Trust as a Royal Research Ship.

1984-85 Project Blizzard documents the state of the Mawson's Hut site.

1984-87 In the Footsteps of Scott led by Robert Swann.

1986 *Discovery* returns to Dundee aboard the floating dock ship *Happy Mariner*.

1988 Casey station (Australia) officially opened.

1992 *Discovery* on permanent display as centrepiece of Dundee's main attraction 'Discovery Point'.

2006 Jan.-Mar., *Aurora Australis* BROKE–West Marine Science (Baseline Research on Oceanography, Krill and the environment).

2006 *Discovery*'s Odyssey wing–covering the 1929-31 BANZARE voyages–officially opened at Discovery Point, Dundee, Scotland.

2007-2008 International Polar Year.

Part I

Invitation to Adventure

June 1929

Alf Howard boarded the train for Fremantle to sail on the SS *Orvieto* bound for Toulon, with London his immediate destination. The last 48 hours had been a whirlwind:

> I was working in the Melbourne University's chemistry laboratory when I was visited by Sir David Orme Masson[1] who was on a committee organising local requirements for Sir Douglas Mawson's proposed expedition to Antarctica later that year. Masson indicated that the purpose of the expedition was essentially to survey the coast and examine the off-shore waters for temperature, salinity and the content of nutrients, which could be correlated with findings of the density of marine life. I can still recall Masson's words: 'Howard, are you interested in going as the expedition's chemist and hydrologist? If so, you will need to leave for England as soon as possible.' Naturally I jumped at the opportunity and was immediately dispatched to London to learn the required analytical techniques.

However, Albert Cherbury David Rivett[2] — a member of the founding committee — felt strongly that Sir Douglas should see 'each man whom it is proposed to appoint to the staff': 'In the case of Howard, the young chemist who has been recommended, I should hesitate myself to take the responsibility for putting him in,' wrote Rivett; 'Probably quite a short interview with him would lead you to make a more accurate estimate than anyone else can do regarding the likelihood of his fitting in well under the somewhat trying conditions on board ship.'[3]

After an exchange of correspondence, Rivett fast-tracked the issuing of a passport and arranged a brief meeting between Sir Douglas and Alf in Adelaide while the train was being coaled for the long haul across the Nullarbor Plain. Mawson's view of the youngest member to join his scientific team was positive: 'The Chemist Howard. I have just seen him while passing through Adelaide, and have given him a letter of introduction to [John King] Davis requesting Davis to introduce him to Dr. Stanley Kemp and to Mr. Townsend of the Hudson Bay Co. He seems a good style of man and I think should do well.'[4]

> Like most of my peers I was familiar with *The Home of the Blizzard* and presumed Sir Douglas planned to map the coastline between the areas mapped by his Eastern and Western parties and probably continue westward beyond Gaussberg. I believe I was basically correct, but soon learnt that national politics were involved. The British authorities were worried about reports that the Norwegians were operating whalers and research vessels near the areas chartered as Enderby Land and Kemp Land back in the 1820s by ships of the British Enderby Company. The British wished to establish sovereignty over the area and anything to the east to which they could make claim and therefore welcomed Sir Douglas' proposed expedition. They made available the SY *Discovery* — Scott's old ship — which had been in service in the Falkland Islands, but had just been replaced by a steel vessel, the *Discovery II*. Sir Douglas had appointed Davis as Captain and the British supplied the three mates, two engineers and the radio operator as well as the crew. They also made available [James W.S.] Marr, a marine helminthologist, who had worked on the *Discovery* in the Falkland Islands and was an expert in the operation of deep-sea research equipment. New Zealand was invited to join the project and supplied the meteorologist and ornithologist, thus creating the British, Australian and New Zealand Antarctic Research Expedition — BANZARE.[5]

As the train chugged across the endless treeless landscape, Alf could at last relax a little and reflect on the amazing recent turn of events. He had celebrated his 23rd birthday on 30 April and was about to embark on an adventure that would turn out to be the catalyst for everything that followed.

*

Immediately after accepting Masson's invitation Alf went to the family home in Stanhope Grove, Camberwell to share the news with his father, Alfred Samuel Howard, and his older brother, Clarence. He had fond memories of Clarence taking him to the local primary school on the handlebars of his bicycle and of evenings when the family gathered around the piano while their mother, Amelia Caroline, played and sang the popular tunes of the day.

> I believe my father had a very big influence on the way I developed. He was a country lad from Beechworth, northern Victoria, and won a scholarship that took him to Melbourne's Technical College where he studied chemistry and geology. He had a lot of books, which were all handed over to me, so that probably influenced me from quite an early age. I became interested in mathematics and then of course when I went to high school I concentrated largely on mathematics and chemistry. I had a chemical set that my father passed

on to me; there were no instructions and I think he left it to me to play around with and see what I could do. So, from that point of view he was responsible for the way that I developed as a youngster through primary school, secondary school, in fact until I went to uni.

Alf Howard BSc, University of Melbourne, 1927

News reached Mr Sharman, then Principal of Melbourne's University High School (UHS), that one the school's old boys had been selected to go south with Mawson, prompting a 'special assembly' to be called to mark the occasion:

> We are sure that everyone connected with the school will be pleased to know that Alf Howard, an old boy of the UHS, has gained the honour of being chosen to accompany Sir Douglas Mawson on his expedition to the southern polar regions. The school feels some of the reflected glory, in having had as a pupil a man of the type of Alf Howard. It will be understood that in an expedition of this nature, the choosing of the men is a matter of the utmost importance. They must possess brains as well as nerve and pluck.
>
> We were able to persuade Alf to come up on the platform at a special assembly, while the school sang "The Best School of All". Mr Sharman then presented him with a school badge, which he will take with him as a mascot. Alf replied with his usual modesty, and confessed that it was the influence of this school that caused him to take his university course. He retired amid thunderous applause. It is gratifying to think that by the performances of such old boys as Alf Howard this school has gained a name that any school might well envy.[6]

Besides scholastic success and being elected a UHS sixth-form prefect in 1923, Alf played in the school's tennis and football teams. In tennis it was noted that 'Howard's service has shown improvement, and his overhead work is sure and steady,' while in football, according to the school's 'football critique,' 'Howard is a most useful change ruck. He always manages to come through well.'[7]

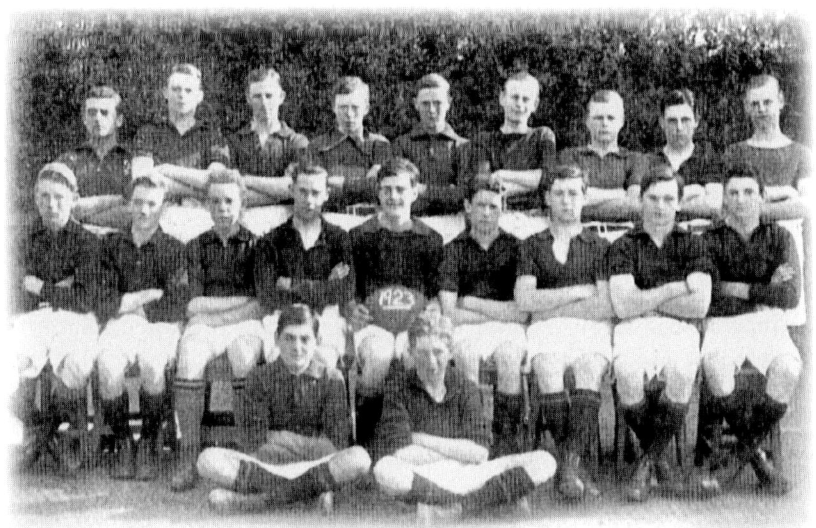

Alf (back row, far left), University High School rugby team, 1923

*

The old steam engine rattled along the tracks towards Perth; with each turn of the wheels Alf's childhood and high school days were becoming hazy memories in the trailing vapour as pieces of the expedition's jigsaw started to fall into place. His appointment had only been announced in Melbourne on 15 June at a meeting of the BANZARE committee members – Sir David Masson (Chair), Sir Douglas Mawson, Sir Edgeworth David,[8] Dr A.C.D. Rivett, Commodore Stevenson, Mr J.H. Sheehan and Dr W. Henderson.[9]

> It was decided to appoint Mr A. Howard and to send him to London without delay in order that he might work in the laboratories of the Hudson Bay Company with a view to obtaining special training. The question of whether he should leave London on the *Discovery* or proceed later to Cape Town and join the *Discovery* there was left open, as it was not known what period would be necessary to enable him to do the special work with the Hudson Bay Company.

> It was decided that his remuneration on the expedition should be at the rate of £300 a year to begin from the date of his embarkation for London, that he receive an advance of £50 on his pay, and that he be allowed £10 for expenses on the vessel while proceeding to London and £1 a day while in England, and that the cost of travelling in England while on the business of the expedition be paid by the expedition.[10]

Recorded at the same meeting were the appointments of the plankton expert, James Marr, who would be seconded from the British Government; the survey officer, Commander Morton Moyes, who would be paid by the Navy Office while serving the expedition; and the photographer, Captain Frank Hurley. Yet to be confirmed were the positions of medical officer, physicist, taxidermist, wireless expert and the aviators.

Preparations for Mawson's forthcoming expedition were being followed by the press and Alf's appointment was noted in the *Sydney Morning Herald* of 22 June as well as in Melbourne's *Argus* of 11 July, by which time Alf had boarded the SS *Orvieto* in Fremantle.

> Mr Alfred [*sic.*] Howard, a young Melbourne University graduate, has been recommended by the Federal committee as a member of the expedition that Sir Douglas Mawson will lead to the Antarctic at the end of this year.
>
> Mr Howard, who is 23 years of age, has been engaged for two years in research work in the chemistry school at the University of Melbourne. He obtained his Master of Science degree in March 1928 and has already proved his ability in research work, and has made some original contributions on problems of organic chemistry. He has had a full training in physical and general chemistry, and this has qualified him for the work that he will be called upon to undertake in the Antarctic. Mr Howard will investigate oceanography, studying the composition of the sea water (which has an important bearing on the food supply of fish).[11]

On her return cruise in June 1929, Orient Steam Navigation's SS *Orvieto* had a cargo of approximately 350 crew and 1300 passengers. Due to last-minute arrangements to send Alf to London there was no berth available until Fremantle. Many passengers had already boarded the ship in Brisbane, Sydney, Melbourne and Adelaide, now she was steaming towards Colombo, Suez, Port Said and Toulon.[12]

> I recall the passage across the Indian Ocean as being relatively smooth and enjoying a bit of tennis and other sports on deck. We docked in Colombo for a few hours so I joined a tour to visit two popular beach resorts. After a spot of lunch in a guesthouse overlooking the beach at Mount Lavinia we went over a

nearby coconut plantation. In Negombo, I was particularly fascinated by one of the Buddhist temples and the impressive ruins of a Portuguese fortress. There was also time to have a look at the local fish market; it was quite amazing how so many people and so many colourful varieties of fish could fit into what appeared to be a relatively small area.

Going through the Suez Canal was memorable — an extraordinary engineering feat. While we didn't disembark in Suez vendors came to the ship in small boats to sell their crafts. We passed the statue of Ferdinand de Lesseps[13] and had a few hours in Port Said while the ship was taking on coal. After the Canal, the ship entered the Mediterranean Sea, then passed through the Strait of Messina between the foot of Italy and Sicily. We were close enough to Stromboli to see molten lava jettisoned from its crater and flowing into the sea. Later that same day we crossed the Bay of Naples and could make out Vesuvius looming in the distance. There were a few hours to look around Naples before continuing to Toulon where I left the ship. I lashed out and went to Hyères by taxi to explore the coast; that was the most extravagant thing I did during the voyage as I had a limited number of gold sovereigns.

Alf backtracked to Toulon, then on to Marseilles where he caught a train to Paris. When he alighted at the Gare du Lyon there was barely enough time to cross the city to the Gare du Nord for the Calais connection with the Dover ferry. Alf was impressed by the famous white cliffs and as it was Sunday decided to visit Dover Castle, stay overnight and take the train to London the following morning.

On arrival at Victoria Station I took a taxi over to Australia House to check the accommodation arrangements. Going up the stairs on my way to meet Captain Davis with Sir Douglas' letter of introduction in hand, I bumped into a chap who turned out to be Ritchie Simmers, a New Zealander, who had just arrived and had been appointed as the expedition's meteorologist. He left New Zealand about the same time as I left Perth, but went via the Panama Canal. We immediately struck up a friendship. The point was that he and I spoke the same language as physicists, whereas most of the others were biologists. The meeting with Davis went well and he told me that the *Discovery* would soon leave the West India Dock and berth at the East India Dock from where she would set sail for Cape Town. I was to go to Plymouth the following week and spend a fortnight at one of the analytical laboratories, which was the whole point of my travelling to England. I remember having a bit of trouble with people who didn't know how to handle sovereigns, and later went to a bank suggested by Australia House to put the remainder of them into an account.

I walked and walked around the streets of London and thoroughly enjoyed it, but the highlight was finding my way to the West India Dock to have a glimpse of the *Discovery*, which would be a floating laboratory and home for me and the other scientific members once we all arrived in Cape Town from various departure points. It wasn't possible to look around, but I could see there was much activity on deck getting her ready for the first stage of the voyage south. She looked a stout little ship and I couldn't wait to be on board for her departure from Table Bay rigged as a barque with fore, main and mizzen masts under full sail.

With time in hand before heading for Devon, Alf was able to catch the last days of the Third World Scout Jamboree being held from 29 July to 12 August on a 450-acre site at Arrowe Park in Upton. More than 50,000 scouts attended from all corners of the globe, attracting over 300,000 visitors, making the 1929 Jamboree the largest ever.[14] 'I would say a highlight for me was meeting up again with Hoadley from Victoria who was sort of in charge of the Australian contingent; he had been a member of Wild's Western Party on Mawson's earlier expedition,' recalled Alf. 'It rained on and off while I was there turning Arrowe Park into a veritable quagmire. Nevertheless, spirits were high and we visited each other's camps. The Indian camp, with totem-like poles at its entrance, was quite outstanding, as was the "Eiffel Tower" built by the French contingent, and everybody seemed to be talking about the visit of the Prince of Wales, attending the Jamboree in scout uniform.'

Alf, 3rd right, at Scout Corroboree in Sydney, 1922

Alf's interest in the scouts dated from 1916 when at 10 years old he became the first official cub — cub registration certificate No. 9 — in the First City of Camberwell (*Melba's Own*) Scout Group; his brother Clarence was the first cubmaster:[15] In 1922, Alf, Clarence and four other members from their troop attended the First Australian Corroboree of Boy Scouts in Sydney.[16] That same year Alf was awarded the King's Scout Badge.

On hearing about his polar appointment, Alf's old scout camping companions sent him a letter of congratulations signed 'Fenton Mattingly', which he did not receive until he returned from the first BANZARE voyage in April 1930: '… On behalf of the Forrest Rover Crew I wish to congratulate you on your appointment as chemist to Sir Douglas Mawson's expedition to the Antarctic. … They take it as an especial honour that one of the crew was selected, but fully recognise that it was due to your own individual good qualities. … We sincerely hope the Antarctic will give you a freezing reception, but not sufficient to adversely affect your research work …' [17]

*

Overlooking Plymouth Sound, the laboratory of the Marine Biological Association (MBA) was first opened in June 1888. Besides a permanent staff of scientific researchers, the MBA made available a number of working places for visiting research workers from universities in the United Kingdom and overseas. The laboratory provided accommodation for visitors, which included 'cubicles, separate rooms, or bench space with adequate fittings for biochemical and physiological work, the use of all ordinary glassware, chemicals, and apparatus of a general nature.'[17] The laboratory also supplied animals, plants or water samples required for any investigation. Alf's accommodation for the week cost 30 shillings, and in the MBA annual report for 1929 an entry records that 'A. Howard, Mawson Expedition (Hydrography), occupied a table in the laboratory during the year.'[18]

> The training was intensive and turned out to be invaluable for the work I was appointed to do during the expedition. On my way to the Fisheries Laboratory in Lowestoft, on the other side of the country near Norwich, I stopped for a few hours in Bath to visit the Georgian buildings and the Roman baths. I would say that my training in water analysis at the Fisheries definitely complemented my investigations in the Plymouth laboratories.

It was now September and Alf's colleagues in Lowestoft invited him to tour the Lake District for the weekend before returning to London. They took him to Grasmere, Windermere and Ullswater, and then to Ruskin's School in Hawkshead. Alf made the most of every opportunity before going south, and on the 6 September, barely a fortnight before boarding the SS *Armadale Castle* in Southampton, he was in Calshot near Dover for the 1929 flying boat/seaplane Schneider Cup Competition. The actual race took place in the Solent between the mainland and the Isle of Wight, with the trophy winner reaching a top speed of 328 mph in a Supermarine 6 during the 150-mile course.

Three Ships — Destination Cape Town

At a reception given on board the *Discovery* by Captain Davis and the expedition's committee on 27 July 1929, just prior to her departure from London, more than 200 Australians inspected the famous ship placed at the disposal of Sir Douglas Mawson by the British Government for the Antarctic expedition he would lead from Cape Town on his arrival there from Australia in October. Visitors included Admiral Skelton — who supervised the building of Scott's ship, and the Australian polar explorer, aviator, submariner and photographer — Sir Hubert Wilkins.[1]

Details of the final preparations for the expedition were being filtered to the *Sydney Morning Herald* among other tabloids of the day: 'At least ten Australians will be included in the expedition which Sir Douglas Mawson will lead. More than 1000 applications were received for positions on the scientific staff. ... Forty tons of provisions will be taken on board at Cape Town, where the Australian and New Zealand members of the staff will join the *Discovery*.'[2]

*

On 1 August 1929, 'in driving rain and with half a gale blowing,' the *Discovery* slipped away from the East India Dock soon after 8 am, two hours earlier than expected, to make her way down the Thames then to her first port of call — Cardiff. 'Groups of people cheered the beflagged ship and shouted "Good luck". When just clear of the dockhead the tow-rope snapped, and the Thames current drove the *Discovery* against the quay. There was a sound of rending timber, but the old ship was unscathed. The dock came off worse. Further trouble was averted by dropping an anchor till a new tow-rope was run. Her Captain, John King Davis, is a grizzled veteran amongst a youthful crew.'[3]

Davis left London with a company of men totalling 27 and two members of Mawson's team: the expedition's photographer and cinematographer,

Captain Frank Hurley, and marine biologist/zoologist expert, James William Slessor Marr. Hurley, who had stepped aboard the *Discovery* at 6.30 that morning, noted: 'Old Father Thames appeared more sombre than ever in a grey mood of fog and rain. Atop in the rigging, I took farewell photographs. ... In addition to the ship's officers and crew, two of my old comrades from the 1911 Mawson Expedition are voyaging as far as Cardiff. They are Blair and Hodgeman.'[4] For Hurley the cabin accommodation and cuisine was 'comparable with many a passenger liner. ... Old jokes grow new again and tales of previous expeditions fill a happy hour after the evening meal.'[5]

On the Sunday there was time for Hurley to help Marr open his cases and stow his gear in lockers and to learn the rudiments of operating the echo-sounding equipment. The eve before arriving in Cardiff much merriment filled the wardroom when old favourites such as "Pomona" and "Drink to me only with thine eyes" were sung to the accompaniment of the chief engineer playing the flute, the second engineer the mandolin and the wireless operator the violin.[6]

The *Discovery* arrived in Cardiff at 10 am on 5 August and immediately proceeded through the docks to the Crown Preserved Coal Company Jetty to await her turn with ships from all over the world to load briquettes; it was a bank holiday so all work on the waterfront was suspended. Hurley painted the scene in his diary: 'The waterways are ever busy with barges and quaint watercraft coming and going. ... The elegant masts of the *Discovery* tower above the rows of gantry cranes and seem to look down in disdain upon those coal cargo carriers. In her festive dress of fresh paint she looks as much out of her environment as an elegant lady surrounded by a motley of grimy tramps.'[7]

The following morning Hurley and Hodgeman went into Cardiff and were surprised to find it so clean and agreeable. 'We made a few purchases and enjoyed the experience of spending sixpences at Woolworths.' Back on the *Discovery* Hurley wrote: 'As usual many visitors assailed the ship prying into cabins and corners as if in search of treasure. During the evening I developed a large batch of accumulated plates and find my darkroom space inadequate. In the absence of the analytical chemist I am commandeering some of his area.'[8] This was the chemical laboratory where Alf, once he joined the ship in Cape Town, would be working. Hurley was sharing the same space as Alf, and to reach his darkroom he first had to enter the laboratory and cross the room to the door of his comparatively small developing area. Nevertheless he was impressed that the chemical and biological laboratories were 'commodious and equipped with the most modern scientific apparatus, which also applies to the dredging and deep-sea trawling gear.'[9]

The vital coaling of the *Discovery* in the Roath Dock took nearly five days to complete. This same dock had been the coaling place for most ships heading to the polar regions and had berthed such other famous vessels as the *Aurora*, *Nimrod*, *Terra Nova* and the *Endurance*. Although few people were permitted to go aboard, visitors lined the dockside each day to watch the loading process and the activities on deck. The briquettes were stacked 'on small trolleys from the Crown Company's works 100 yards from the jetty and moved along a raised track to the cranes. One lift and the trolley and briquettes ... [were] lowered on to a platform alongside the ship.' Owing to the inaccessible position of the bunkers, loading the coal briquettes — which had to be manhandled — became a lengthy, laborious and a particularly noisy process as they slid down the chute and into the hold.[10]

Early 10 August, large crowds gathered on the wharf to farewell the *Discovery* on her way to Cape Town. As Hurley noted there was the usual ritual: 'The tug alongside, the casting off of the moorings and the passage through the docks to crowds cheering, whistles tooting and dipping flags,'[11] as she left Cardiff with her crew and the 'inevitable stowaway.' The incident was reported in the London *Times* the next day and actually witnessed by Hurley:

> While moving down Channel, Marr and I examined all likely and unlikely places for stowaways. While removing the cover from a boat on the bridge, to my surprise I discovered a human being cuddled up between the boat thwarts. I hauled the lad out, a poor, weak, dirty-faced little chap of some 14 years and handed him over, not without some feelings for the little woebegone urchin, to the Captain. I was pleased to hear 'J.K.' speak kindly in reply to his question: 'I want to go to sea, Sir.' Had he been of more sturdy physique and mature years, J.K., who has a tender leaning for lads who display grit and deep-sea inclination, would have added him to the ship's complement.
>
> The boy was sent off when the pilot boat put off for the shore. I questioned the lad and found his name to be Leslie Sutton of Cardiff, occupation newsboy. Fair weather favoured our departure and we proceeded down channel without another incident other than an occasional vessel saluting us with ensign and whistle.[12]

The 16 days at sea between *Discovery*'s departure from Cardiff and her arrival at St Vincent in the Cape Verde Islands passed with everyone on board stowing the 13 kilo coal briquettes in every possible nook and cranny of the vessel on top of normal duties. Time too for Hurley to explore the best positions on the rigging for adventurous photographic angles and to assist Marr unpack his cases and 'learn the method of operating the echo-sounding gear.'[13] There were other cases being unpacked as Captain Davis told a reporter on arrival in Cape Town: 'Some time after leaving England the cook was opening a case of flour in the galley when an envelope fell out. It contained six shillings and a message wishing the expedition success, and had been sent by some of the employees of the firm [Colman's] that presented us with our flour'.[14] He also mentioned a potential gourmet treat that never appeared on the menu: 'We had a vision of turtle soup one day, when we sighted a turtle asleep on the surface. Unfortunately the turtle swam away before we could lower a boat.'[15]

*

'The exploring barque *Discovery* is now hurrying southward through the NE trades with all sails set, aided by the same steady winds which 400 years ago carried Columbus across the Atlantic. We shall arrive all going well at St Vincent, Cape Verde Islands, on August 26th where we take 100 tons of bunkers.'[16] When Captain Davis sent this press communication to Univalser, Fleet Street, London, the ship's position was at Lat 25N Long 40W and had just been overtaken by the motor steamer *Dunster Grange*, which beside the *Discovery* under full sail must have presented an interesting picture — illustrating the earliest and latest means of propulsion. In the same press release, Davis commended Hurley and Marr for 'spending most of their time assisting with all sorts of routine jobs from pulling on braces and setting sail to trimming coal.'[17] 'We are due at Cape Town early in October where all look forward to meeting our leader Sir Douglas Mawson and his party. When we leave there the real business of the expedition will begin. What the future has in store for us who shall say, it is sufficient for us that if success is ours we may be the first intruding mortals in a new land.'[18]

*

In Australia, Mawson was busy finalising arrangements for the expedition before joining members of his scientific staff on the SS *Nestor* in Adelaide. In a letter to Dr W. Henderson in Canberra just weeks before his departure, Mawson, unlike Davis' positive acknowledgment of his leader's imminent arrival in Cape Town, expressed concern regarding the master of the *Discovery*: 'Unfortunately Capt. Davis has messed up a lot of arrangements I made when in London. I am very annoyed with him for this, for he has introduced very unnecessary complications into our equipment. Davis has not yet realised, I fear, that I am in command of the Expedition, and that he is there to carry out my instructions.' Mawson did, however, appear to be more than satisfied with the generous donations being received for the expedition: 'Since arrival in Adelaide I have been going ahead with the completion of the Expedition equipment such as is not arranged for in England. There has after all been a very good response from manufacturing firms in Australia. There will be quite £1,500 worth given in the aggregate, and we shall not buy more than a few hundred pounds worth at the most, probably about £200.'[19]

*

The Union-Castle Mail Steamship Company's twin-funnelled SS *Armadale Castle* had been sailing between the United Kingdom and Africa for 26 years when Alf Howard and Ritchie Simmers boarded her in Southampton on Friday, 20 September. Simmers noted in his diary that earlier the same day he and Alf met in London, took the 11.20 am train from Waterloo Station, sorted out their cases on the wharf, and embarked just before the ship 'sailed at 4 pm sharp and passed down the Solent.'[20] Besides their own trunks and cases Alf and Simmers were entrusted with important 'files of papers' sent to them by R.G. Casey, then High Commissioner for the Commonwealth of Australia in London, which would be given to Mawson on their arrival in Cape Town:

> (a) Lists of vouchers for Naval Stores delivered to *Discovery* just prior to sailing, to be receipted and returned to London. (b) Wireless: opinions re optimum times of sending. (c) Amendments and addenda to relevant naval charts, since *Discovery* sailed. (d) Aeroplane wireless, full description with plans, in duplicate. (e) Additional information re echo-sounding gear, asked for by Captain Davis by wireless. (f) Later particulars re distribution of Expedition photographs. (g) Copies of correspondence and telegrams re additional insurance of expedition personnel. (h) Copies of telegrams re South African Government and expenditure at Cape Town.[21]

Mentioned in the same communication from Casey to Prime Minister Bruce in Canberra was a list of 'expedition stores', which were 'being despatched by the *Armadale Castle*, in charge of Messrs. Simmers and Howard.' For Alf the voyage to South Africa was memorable:

There were just Simmers and I from the expedition's scientific team on board the *Armadale Castle* and I think we made the most of the cruise down to the Cape. We took on more passengers in Cherbourg, but there was no sightseeing until we dropped anchor in the harbour of Madeira's main town — Funchal.

Hordes of traders in their boats surrounded the ship all jostling, shouting and promoting their goods: baskets all shapes and sizes, chairs, as well as beads and some pieces of hand-made lace. Young boys shrieked out loud that they would dive for a penny — in all it was total bedlam. Tender boats ferried us across and we had time enough to look around the town and see a little of the interior of the island. The sensation of sitting in a wicker toboggan with two guides in white traditional uniform and straw hats running alongside as we hurtled down the very steep cobbled streets is one I have never forgotten. We visited the fish and fruit market, walked in the splendid City Gardens, and I do recall being surprised at the time to see so many cars in the main square. Basketware would be no use in Antarctica so I bought a few stamps and took some photos.

A couple of days out from Madeira there was much hilarity on board when the baby attendants and maiden aunts fancy dress event took place. Of course we all got a dunking in the pool afterwards whether we were dressed up or not.

Other distractions, such as deck game competitions, tennis, dog derbys, dancing every night and the two Eriksons with their gymnastic and acrobatic routines, helped to pass the time on the long route down the west coast of Africa. 'What a conglomeration of nationalities,' recorded Simmers, 'Belgian, German, Russian, French, Dutch, Italian and Swiss to my personal knowledge.'[22]

Soon after the ship passed the Cape Verde Islands on 27 September Alf and Simmers sighted 'a huge shoal of porpoises — hundreds and hundreds of them.' The obvious excitement of drawing closer to Cape Town is evident in Simmers' 6 and 7 October entries:

Packed ready for Cape Town tomorrow. Rather excited at thought of nearness to the final scene of the preparations. ... Getting nearer. I wonder if anyone will be down to meet us. Will we have trouble passing the Customs? Entrance is entrancing — Table Mountain without a doubt provides a good background for what looks to be a very clean but spread-out city. As we sneaked in we passed thousands and thousands of shags–the water was literally black with them. The wait in Table Bay Docks before being permitted ashore seemed interminable but in the end Alf and I charged off and along to the *Discovery* which had arrived on Saturday and was moored just ahead of us.[23]

The *Discovery* in Cape Town flying the Australian flag, October 1929

The *Discovery* arrived just two days ahead of the *Armadale Castle* on Saturday, 5 October and those on board, as Alf recalled, were surprised to see both Simmers and himself: 'When we wandered into the wardroom it was quite obvious that Simmers and I hadn't been expected for another week. No wonder everyone seemed rather alarmed as apparently Australia House in London hadn't let them know of our arrival date.' A message had in fact been sent via the British Wireless Marine Service on 21 September addressed: 'Master *Discovery* from Casey' informing Captain Davis that 'South African Government offer pay cost overhauling of *Discovery* at Cape Town as well as coal required' and alerting that 'Simmers & Howard sailing *Armadale Castle* 20th September carrying aeroplane wireless and certain scientific stores for expedition.'[24] 'The point was that we were the only two members of the expedition sailing on the *Armadale Castle* as most of the scientific team were with Mawson on board the *Nestor* which was still on its way from Australia to South Africa,' explained Alf; 'it was all a little overwhelming to be at last on Scott's famous ship and to be in the wardroom with such acclaimed Antarcticans as Davis and Hurley.'

Simmers was also awestruck when he first set foot on the *Discovery*: 'What a feeling to be on the old bus at last. How clean and spic she looks in comparison with her appearance in London. Alf and I had lunch on board the *Armadale* and tea on the *Discovery* — our first meal on board — will the food always seem as good, and for how long will we have a table cloth? In the evening we went ashore for a look round then home to the *Discovery*. Fancy calling it home already and we haven't slept on her yet.'[25]

*

At noon on 9 September 1929 the Blue Funnel Line steamer SS *Nestor* left its berth in Sydney with two members of Mawson's team: Commander Morton Moyes, surveyor/cartographer, and Harold Fletcher, assistant zoologist. Sir Edgeworth David was there to farewell them with gifts of Rudyard Kipling's *The Day's Work* before 'the ship moved away from the wharf and slowly steamed out into the harbour.'[26] More scientific staff boarded the *Nestor* in Melbourne: the medical officer, William Wilson Ingram, the aviators, Flight-Lieutenant Stuart Campbell and Pilot Officer Eric Douglas — seconded from the RAAF, and the assistant zoologist, Mr R. A. Falla.

The *Nestor* would carry a special consignment of scientific instruments to Cape Town from the Commonwealth Meteorological Bureau consisting of a mercurial barometer, thermograph, a self-registering anemometer, and a barograph. Australian manufacturers gave a large consignment of foodstuffs which included: 48 cases of dried fruits, 57 cases of butter, 12 cases of powdered milk, 15 cases of sheep tongues, 10 cases of tea, 26 cases of cheese and brawn, 14 cases of canned vegetables and 16 cases of plum pudding. A delivery of two cases of clothing, two cases of rubber boots, two cases of oilskin coats, four cases of blankets and 40 pairs of skiing boots were also donated to the expedition.[27] Heavily laden, the ship left Melbourne on 14 September.

Clearly, Mawson had spent time working out the best ship to transport the cargo of equipment and foodstuffs donated by manufacturers for his Antarctic expedition: 'These items I am instructing manufacturers to forward for shipment as best suits them at Brisbane, Sydney, Melbourne or Adelaide. However, there will be no necessity to have a collecting depot in each of these towns; my instructions are to the manufacturers to ship the goods, suitably branded … to the wharf at which the *Nestor* is loading, the goods to arrive at the wharf two days before the vessel calls. … I am also arranging with them space for the cased goods we are taking to the Cape.'[28]

Wednesday, 18 September, Sir Douglas and his chief biologist, Professor T. Harvey Johnston, boarded the *Nestor* in Adelaide for her voyage to Fremantle. Except for Hurley and Alf, the Australian contingent of expedition members was now together for the first time. Eric Douglas recorded that they crossed the Great Australian Bight in choppy seas averaging 10 knots and arrived in Fremantle early morning of 23 September with enough time to fit in a few hours of yachting on the Swan River, as the ship did not sail until the following afternoon.[29]

According to the *Nestor*'s 'Sports and Entertainment Programme' the BANZARE team were on the committee responsible for organising Deck Tennis, Dances, Concerts, Cricket and Race Meetings. Elected to the role of Chairman was Sir Douglas; Hon. Treasurer: H.O. Fletcher Esq; with Comdr. M.H. Moyes, RAN, E. Douglas and R.A. Falla elected as Members.[30]

By 1 October the ship was halfway across the Indian Ocean on her way to the Port of Durban. Douglas commented that the ship's average run each day was 310 miles, the sea was sometimes moderate, sometimes choppy and that the vessel was often followed by albatrosses; '8th Oct. Arrived Durban 6.50 am. Very fine day; Ship to coal today; Town about as big as Perth. Fine ocean beachfront. Went to show at night'; '9th Oct. Had a ride in a rickshaw, visited the Aero Club and the yacht clubs. Went for a run inland with Doc [Ingram], Stuart and Fletcher. Very interesting country; had a surf and then back to the ship. Ship left Durban 7 pm. The lights of Durban look well; fine lighthouse and breakwater; good tug boats.'[31]

The SS *Nestor* entered Table Bay at 8 am on 13 October. As the ship steamed slowly across the bay, Fletcher was on deck with the other expedition members for their first sight of the *Discovery*, which was to carry them 'south to battle against the Antarctic gales and blizzards. When she was sighted there was a general feeling of apprehension. Completely dwarfed by nearby overseas ships she appeared to be very small for the task ahead.'[32]

A Cargo of Infinite Variety

Cape Town's waterfront was a hive of activity, and during the period before Mawson's arrival Alf was able to have a good look over the vessel that would take him south as well as fitting in some sightseeing: 'Simmers and I had about a week on the *Discovery* before Mawson and his crowd got there. I suppose I was showing off a bit as almost immediately I went up on one of the masts and then came down on one of the ropes. I'd done my little show so from then on everything was OK.' Gymnastics had been one of Alf's preferred hobbies since he was 12 when his father set up a horizontal bar in the garden. He soon joined the local gymnastic club with his brother Clarence where they practised rotations and push-ups on the roman rings, somersaults off the end of the horse and climbing a rope that hung from the ceiling. The bars were his favourite: 'On the horizontal it was doing rotations around the bar. I was never able to do the complete circle, but liked doing somersaults sitting on the bar and then throwing yourself around and landing on your feet. You could do almost anything you felt like on the parallel bars.' Alf's strength and agility would serve him well not only on board the *Discovery* but, throughout the years ahead.

Alf on board the *Discovery* in Cape Town

Alf's shared cabin with aviator Eric Douglas was at the end of the wardroom, adjacent to the chemical laboratory. There was still time to find out where everything was and make sure all his scientific equipment was in place: 'As far as the chemical work was concerned everything was there, but both Simmers and I needed gimbal tables. We needed the tables to be about three foot square and were lucky enough to have the necessary material casts, which made it possible for the carpenters to make them. The point was there was nothing I could do until we got under way with regard to doing any of the tests.'

The main event in the city was the opening of the first Table Mountain Aerial Cableway on 4 October by the Mayor of Cape Town, the day before the *Discovery* berthed at No. 1 Jetty. Within 24 hours of settling into their new quarters Alf Howard and Ritchie Simmers, having located their baggage and bade farewell to the *Armadale Castle*, headed for the lower station to make the five-minute ascent to the top of Table Mountain in the tin-roofed, wooden-sided cable car. Alf recalled the steep cable ride: 'There was no sensation of movement and you could just make out the tops of the pine trees as the car silently skimmed above them. I remember it being very misty and the view being rather limited in all directions. Soon we were in full sunshine with the perpendicular face of the mountain almost within touching distance. Once the mist cleared the panoramic views from the 1000-metre summit station were breathtaking.' Making the most of their first look around on shore, Alf and Simmers took a leisurely stroll in the city and were impressed by the architecture of the parliament, library, museum and university buildings and by Cape Town's main oak tree-lined avenue. The heavy rain that greeted them on their arrival showcased the city's botanical gardens at their best. There was time for 'a bite in a tea room — and very good too' before returning to the ship

*

Wednesday, 9 October 1929 and still another four days before Mawson and the rest of the scientific staff would arrive. Determined to leave Cape Town on 19 October, Captain Davis, realising that the *Discovery* was too heavily rigged for her small crew, made arrangements to make her easier to handle in the stormy Southern Ocean. The procedure was reported in the *Cape Times*: 'A gang of men from the Harbour Department were busily engaged yesterday morning in getting the necessary gear ready while the crew of the vessel were clinging to the main topgallant yards unbending the square sails. The main topgallant yards of the research ship *Discovery* are to be sent down and landed on shore, and it may be that the topgallant mast may be landed as well.'[1] Davis in an interview with the *Cape Argus* remarked: 'She'll be easier to handle when we get those yards down. I want her the same as the *Aurora*. Everything will be ready by the time Sir Douglas Mawson reaches Cape Town. We'll coal tomorrow.'[2] True to Davis' plan, at 6 am on 10 October the *Discovery* moved to another berth to be coaled. The process of coaling was a new experience for Alf: 'Coal chutes suddenly seemed to be everywhere on the vessel, even a couple passing below the wardroom to a stowing area beyond. We were having a bite of breakfast when they started to pour the coal and what a hell of a racket it made as it crashed and banged its way through. We couldn't hear one another and the ear-splitting noise really put one's teeth on edge.' Any space on the ship's decks and below was used to temporarily store the expedition's most precious cargo, and as some of the scientists had not yet arrived their cabins as well as the upper and lower laboratories were not off limits.

The following afternoon Simmers and friends of his in Cape Town invited Alf to join them 'for a drive round the whole show.' The outing culminated with a visit to the home of Cecil Rhodes, Groote Schuur, and the memorial to him on the outlying shoulder of Table Mountain. 'Rhodes certainly did know how to furnish this old Dutch home,' noted Simmers. 'In the library is a priceless collection of Latin translations, Greek too and ordinary standard works — all typewritten. Wandered round then went up to the Rhodes Memorial which is situated in a commanding position overlooking the extensive Cape Flats right over to the two oceans — Indian and Atlantic.'[3] Alf was impressed by the grandeur of the memorial with its statue of Physical Energy: 'I was struck by the crouching lion sculptures leading to the monument; quite an impact after seeing lions in the brick amphitheatre-like enclosure near Rhodes' home.'

*

The *Discovery* would leave Cape Town with ample provisions for a two-year voyage. Tons of preserved foods were already on board, which included tinned meat and quantities of pemmican — a composition of fat and dried beef — as an emergency back-up. While British manufacturers gave BANZARE a substantial amount of equipment and clothing, 'in some cases articles had to be obtained outside the Empire. From Lapland were procured reindeer skin boots and from Norway wolf skin sledges and skis. Certain Alpine equipment was purchased from Switzerland.'[4] Once the *Nestor* arrived the foodstuffs and equipment on board destined for the expedition would have to be immediately transferred to the *Discovery*.

Stores going on board the *Discovery* in Cape Town (Photo: Frank Hurley)

Promotions for products donated to the expedition appeared in newspapers on both sides of the world. In Melbourne, an advertisement for REX Foods in *Table Talk* listed the 2½ tons of their wares donated to the expedition below a drawing of a crowned pig pulling a sledge filled with hams, bacon and smallgoods over a polar landscape.[5] A large advertisement in the *Argus* with a photograph of the *Discovery* in full sail proclaimed that 'in deciding on Diamond Batteries for the scientific apparatus those in charge of the expedition acknowledge the supremacy of these famous Australian Batteries.'[6] 'SOUTH WITH SHELL' boldly stood out in the *Cape Times* drawing of the *Discovery* breaking the ice with an endorsement by Sir Douglas: 'Everyone in South Africa has shown us great kindness, and not least has been that of The Shell Company. All the petroleum products in use on the *Discovery* — lubricating oils for the engines, paraffin, spirit for the aeroplane — are the products of the Shell Company. I am fully satisfied that they will stand up to the extreme conditions of the South.'[7]

*

Seven o'clock on Sunday morning, 13 October, Sir Douglas Mawson and his party were greeted on the *Nestor* by Davis and Hurley, and 'after formal introductions and exchanges of *Discovery-Nestor* happenings, the colossal miscellany of baggage was duly assembled ashore for customs clearance.'[8] As the cabins allotted to Moyes, Ingram, Fletcher, Campbell, Douglas, Falla and Johnston were still being used as temporary storage spaces until all cargo was in place, arrangements were made for them to stay at the new Carlton Hotel. Sir Douglas did not leave the ship until 9 am, when he went aboard the *Discovery*.[9]

Before embarking on a round of interviews, lectures and dinners hosted by the Mayor of Cape Town and other institutions in the days before departure, Mawson's first priority was to meet his team in the wardroom at the end of which hung a portrait of Captain Robert Falcon Scott. For Alf, who had briefly met with Sir Douglas in Adelaide on his way to Perth, it was an exciting gathering as now he would again meet the BANZARE Commander as well as the other members of the expedition:

> Of course I already knew Simmers quite well as we had met in London and voyaged to South Africa together and we also went on a number of trips in and around town. Hurley and Marr were friendly and very helpful, and by this time I had met Captain Davis again and some of the officers and crew. I believe my first impression of the scientific mob from the *Nestor* was that they were a cheery bunch. However, I clearly recall that from the moment Sir Douglas entered the wardroom he was in control. I would say, without exception, we all felt honoured and humbled to have him as our leader.

Simmers noted the meeting in his diary: 'Sunday saw the arrival of Sir Douglas — he'll do me as a leader and from wardroom remarks he'll do the rest. Now I understand better that historic march of his. In a few minutes after arrival he had control, or to me seemed to have control. With him were the other seven members and they seem a particularly felicitous choice.'[10]

Each moment of Mawson's six days in Cape Town before going south was filled with checking every detail of the expedition. Stanley Melbourne Bruce, the Prime Minister of Australia, communicated instructions to Mawson the day before his arrival clearly stating that scientific investigation and territorial acquisition were to be the main objectives of the expedition:

> You will use your best endeavours to make a hydrographic survey of the coast and its contiguous waters between the western extremity of Queen Mary Land and Enderby Land at 45° / 40° east, such survey to comprise the correct location and charting of coasts, islands, rocks and shoals.
>
> On such lands or islands ... you will plant the British flag wherever you find it practicable to do so, and in doing so you will read the proclamation of annexation ... attach a copy of the proclamation to the flagstaff, and place a second copy of the proclamation in a tin at the foot of the flagstaff. ...
>
> During the course of the expedition you will carry out to the best of your ability all scientific work and investigations which it is practicable for you to do in respect of all the matters falling within the competence of the scientific staff which has been selected to accompany you, comprising, amongst other things, meteorological and oceanographic observations and investigations concerning the fauna, notably whales and seals, of the seas and lands visited by you.[11]

The emphasis on proclaiming new lands was perhaps to some extent a result of articles in the South African and British press, which questioned Norway's presence in the same unknown sector of east Antarctica where the *Discovery* was bound. On 8 October 1929 — the day that the *Nestor* arrived in Durban — Mawson was greeted with an article in the *Cape Argus* headed 'New Race to the Antarctic Starting?' and one in the *Cape Times* entitled 'Have the Norwegians a Secret?' A media frenzy followed, with one article commenting that the presence of Norwegian vessels and soon Mawson's *Discovery* expedition in the same unexplored regions of Antarctica 'recall[ed] the epic race for the South Pole between the same two nations, resulting in the success of Amundsen and tragic deaths of Scott and his companions.'[12] Three days later a short article in the Norwegian press appeared in the *Cape Argus*:

> The small whaler, *Norwegia*, has been exploring for two years, during which time material of high scientific value had been collected. It was proposed that this work be continued, including the study of whales. The purpose of the expedition is not to search for new land, but if uncharted unclaimed land is found the Norwegian flag will naturally be hoist. International rules will be strictly observed, and all interested parties will be able subsequently to discuss the matter in a friendly spirit.[13]

'The *Norwegia* set out some days previously in company with a large factory vessel aboard which, so rumour has it, are two large seaplanes', noted Hurley.

'The mission and destination of these ships is indefinite, though rumour again whispers that the objective is the neighbourhood of Enderby Land and their purpose is to discover and lay claim to as much territory as possible in the interests of Norway. Exactly what part of our programme sets out to do for Great Britain!'[14]

*

The image of the sturdy *Discovery* dwarfed by the great liners in port remained embedded in Alf's memory: 'Well, she stood out despite her size. For one thing there was her massive hull and the unusual rig with the crow's nest at the top of the main mast. She certainly sparked a good deal of curiosity. Also, there was the fact that she had been built for Scott and this was not the first time she had dropped anchor in Table Bay.' On 3 October 1901, the *Discovery* — under the command of Captain Scott, leader of the 1901-1904 British National Antarctic Expedition — had docked overnight at Cape Town to take coal on her way to Antarctica via New Zealand.[15]

During the *Discovery*'s two weeks in Cape Town additional items of equipment from blankets to test-tubes arrived for her holds which were already well stowed. Space also had to be found for boxes, bales, barrels and bundles brought by the *Nestor*. A little disarming must have been the sight of dockside workers carrying cases of dynamite up the gangway; this handle-with-care cargo would if necessary be used to blast channels through the ice along the Antarctic coastline. Reassuring was the fact that the *Discovery* was carrying more complete scientific equipment than any previous expedition into polar seas and was also equipped with an X-ray plant on board.[16]

Except for the crew and scientific team about to sail on her the *Discovery* was open only to those who had special permits. The BANZARE vessel was now the focus of universal curiosity, and as Frank Hurley observed, people flocked to the docks to see her and 'to peer at the men privileged to voyage on her. The sightseers! What a grotesque colourful anomaly! Well-dressed citizens: beauty and elegance strangely mingled with dusky coons and belles clad in clashing hues; grimy labourers in rags, bags, tatters, remnants of wartime apparel. This human menagerie appeared to be thoroughly enjoying the free show.'[17]

Hurley jotted down his first impressions of the scientific team: 'A keen, eager group of young scientists selected for their specialised knowledge in the various branches of the Expedition's operations who, I felt, could be relied upon to cooperate and carry through many other branches of activity which they might be called upon to perform.'[18] 'The crowded hours of our brief stay,' wrote Hurley, 'sufficed to enable most members of the scientific staff to become infatuated with the charms of Cape Town — scenic and feminine. For my own part, various activities precluded me from indulging, though I admired both from afar.'[19]

ılı

The general hustle and bustle dockside and on board signalled the day before departure. Carpenters were hammering together a pen that 15 sheep would occupy amidships, the expedition's launch was receiving a coat of paint and lorry after lorry arrived on the quay with stores. Ingram noted that 'the final preparations for a great expedition seem chaotic. Every member of the scientific staff finds at the last moment that something essential to his department has been forgotten and they all keep darting into town to get bolts and screws, glass tubing, glass slides, hair clippers and such like things.' Ingram also made the observation that 'Captain Davis was everywhere personally supervising the work. He had made up his mind to leave at a certain hour and he was goading everyone to activity so that he could leave to the minute, as indeed he eventually did.'[20]

Davis gave his crew shore leave every night during their stay, which was mentioned in the *Cape Times*: 'In no single case has this latitude been abused. ... The crew of the *Discovery* are a fine body of men who have made an excellent impression in Cape Town.'[21] The crew had worked long hours on board preparing the ship with port officers and workmen lent by the Union Government. Together they had rigged the *Discovery* as a barquentine,[22] strengthened the bridge, made the decks shipshape and given her a general overhaul. Davis had only praise for the port authorities: 'If this had been South Africa's own expedition to the Antarctic, nothing more could have been done for us in Table Bay Docks. ... The safety of all on board a ship like this depends largely on the quality of the work done. *Discovery* is leaving Cape Town in first-class order.'[23]

On the eve of departure Alf received an unexpected gift. After having spent the morning at the University of Cape Town's physics laboratory helping Ritchie Simmers set up and check out his pyrheliometer and actinometer,[24] he returned to the *Discovery* to find a basket of tropical fruits and a large tin of sweets in his cabin. Printed on a card, with neither address nor telephone contact, were the words 'BON VOYAGE ALF FROM UNCLE SAMUEL.'[25]

Officers and crew of the *Discovery* at Cape Town. Captain Davis (middle front), Frank Hurley, 2nd row far left, James Marr, front row, far right. (Photo: Frank Hurley)

Part II

South With Mawson

on the

British, Australian and New Zealand Antarctic Research Expedition

1st BANZARE Voyage

from Cape Town, 19 October 1929 to Port Adelaide, 1 April 1930

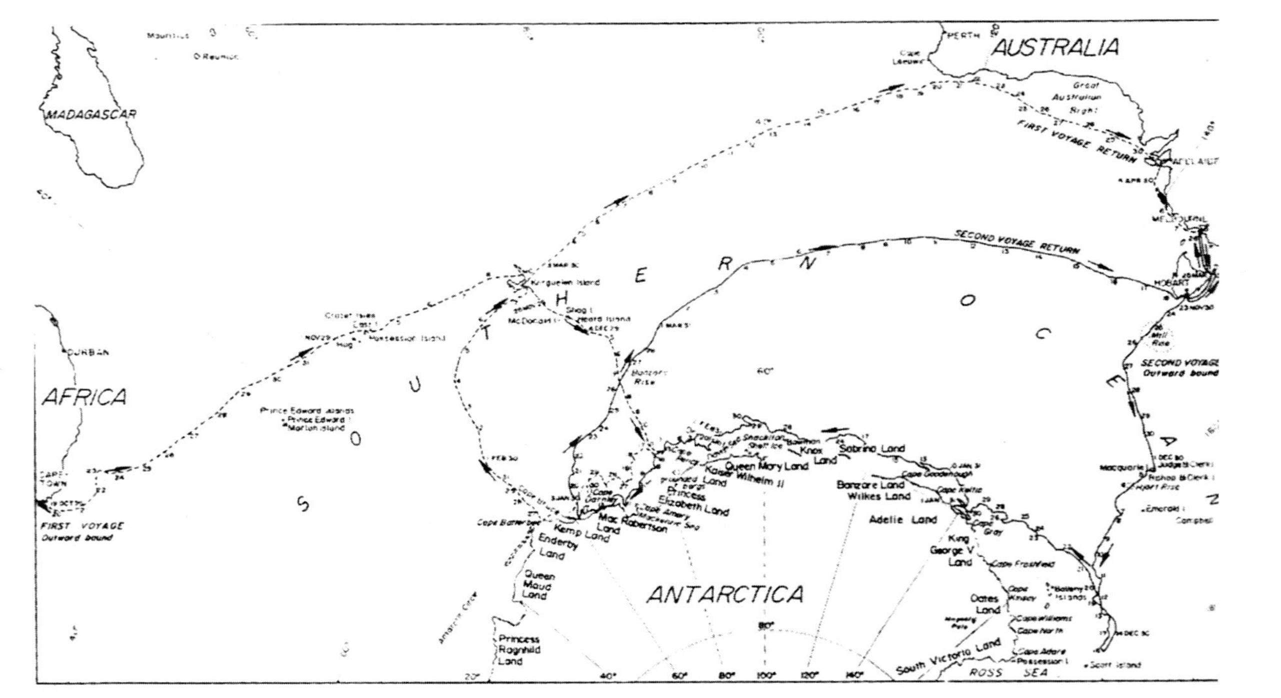

Map tracking the BANZARE voyages in the *Discovery*

SY *Discovery*, A Stout Little Ship

The *Discovery* received a rousing send-off from Cape Town as the gap widened between ship and shore. Vessels in dock saluted her departure with three blasts of the siren as the tugboat drew her away from Jetty No. 1 at 10.05 am on 19 October 1929. 'Sir Douglas Mawson, wearing a cloth cap, blue coat, and blue flannel trousers, appeared on the bridge at that moment. He was smiling happily. When the crowd on the quay gave three cheers and sang "Auld Lang Syne," Sir Douglas led the cheering in reply. From the forecastle-head a group of Australians shouted their "Coe-e-e-e".'[1] All on board were at work as the vessel made her way through the dock entrance. Flags were dipped, the cheering continued. Aloft, Hurley captured the departure on his cinecamera. Because the light breeze made it impossible to leave as a barquentine, the famous ship steered out past Green Point on her long voyage to Antarctica,[2] flying the burgee of the Royal Thames Club and the Australian ensign.

Despite past adventures in the south it was a nostalgic moment for Captain Frank Hurley as the *Discovery* passed through the docks: 'A small group gathered on the extremity of the outermost pier, waves and cheers to human limit. To me this small group is a symbol, a punctuation, at the termination of civilization which stays emotions with an abrupt stop and makes one ponder — not over past chapters, but the blank pages of the future.'[3]

On board Ritchie Simmers was obviously excited: 'All the ships in harbour saluted us as we made our stately way out. Oh boy but I bet she rolls and even though the sea was smooth — almost oily in fact — she rolled more than the *Armadale Castle*. But it was grand and I must say I enjoyed the creaking of timbers which I'm afraid will get into my blood if creaking can get into one's blood.'[4]

Mawson recorded that the *Discovery* 'steamed half-speed till 4 pm when off Slang Kop where compass tested (swung) and tests made of direction-finding apparatus. ... We had intended dressing scientific staff in grey flannel pants and cardigans but in unpacking cardigans found to be all one size (7) and poor fits. The pants from Cape Town were poor — too short in body. So we dressed in grey pants and blue blazers.'[5] That evening Ingram jotted down his sentiments:

> It was to me surprising that at the last minute the people of Cape Town should have become so enthusiastic. Although the *Discovery* had been in port over a fortnight no attempt had been made by any official body to entertain or get to know the members of the expedition. Not that we expected it but the apparent great enthusiasm shown on the last day was marred by the fact that practically no one on the ship knew a soul on shore. At the last moment Sir Douglas Mawson called for three cheers for the people of Cape Town, and we gave them readily enough, if only to show the inhabitants of that delightful part of the world that we could, if given an opportunity, get to like them very much.[6]

South with Mawson — Sitting in front: A. Howard. First row, L to R: G.E. Douglas, J.W.S. Marr, Prof. TR.H. Johnston, Dr W.W. Ingram, R.G. Simmers, Sir D. Mawson, Com. M.H. Moyes. Back row, L to R: H.O. Fletcher, R.A. Falla, S.A.C. Campbell (Photo: Frank Hurley)

A plethora of good wishes from Rear-Admiral Edward Evans, commanding HM Australian Squadron, and the Earl of Athlone, then Governor-General of the Dominion of South Africa, were published in the *Cape Times* on the day of departure. This last message read: 'Princess Alice and I are so sorry not to be able to entertain you at Cape Town, and wish you, and all on board, every success in your interesting expedition — The Governor-General.'[7] Sir Douglas was very pleased with the message he received from Prime Minister Bruce, who 'conveyed his best wishes and said that the people of the Commonwealth looked forward to welcoming back to Australia in 1930 "all you who so gallantly volunteered to face the hazards of the Antarctic in the interests of science and exploration." '[8]

*

The *Discovery* may have 'appeared to be very small for the task ahead,' but the old ship was a legendary stalwart, and as Scott wrote in the *The Voyage of the Discovery*, she was 'the sixth of that name and the heir to a long record of honourable service, and, what was equally important, of fortunate service, as the name *Discovery* seems never to have been associated with shipwreck or disaster':

> The first made no fewer than six Arctic voyages from 1602 to 1616 to the regions of Hudson Bay and Baffin Bay, on one of which she was commanded by the famous navigator William Baffin. The second also voyaged to Hudson Bay in 1719. 'Discovery' No. 3 took part in Cook's third voyage in 1776. 'Discovery' No. 4 was Vancouver's ship when he discovered the insularity of the land which is named after him. 'Discovery' No. 5 took part in the 1875 expedition to the Arctic.[9]

Constructed in Dundee for Scott's 1901-1904 National Antarctic Expedition, the *Discovery* was built almost entirely of wood except for the fastenings. 'She was designed by Sir William Smith with a full hull form and tumblehome and was unique, having a lifting propeller and rudder, but able to be steered and steamed if she lost her Rudder Post.'[10] Her frame was mainly of English oak, the beams on the main deck of pitch pine, with Canadian elm used largely for the planking below water and pitch pine above water. Three and a half inch thick Riga fir was used for the inner bottom planking while Dantzig fir was chosen for the decks. 'The forefoot was of the most solid construction, with special ice protection generally of oak timbering extending to about 5 ft. above the load water line. ... Beams and heavy diagonal timbers, all of oak, were introduced in the lower part of the vessel at the forward end to withstand ice pressure.'[11]

Despite *Discovery*'s overall length of only 198 feet and extreme breadth of just 34 feet, she was a solid vessel and had survived two winters icebound in McMurdo Sound on her 1901-1904 maiden voyage under the command of Captain Scott. Sold to the Hudson Bay Company in 1905, *Discovery*'s accommodation arrangements were changed so she could transport supplies to the Hudson Bay Trading Post and return with furs. During World War I she was used to carry food and munitions for the French Government, then in 1916 was refitted and went south to pick up Shackleton's crew of the *Endurance* who were stranded on Elephant Island, but she had already reached Montevideo before hearing of their rescue. After two years in London's West India Docks the *Discovery* was purchased in 1922 by Crown Agents and modified for use as the world's leading oceanographic survey ship. She was now registered in the Falkland Islands, which would be her base for the 1925-1927 *Discovery* Investigations, from where she carried out the first research into the life and ecology of the whale.[12]

Alf and indeed most members of the scientific staff had never been on a steam yacht before, and certainly not one designed for the ice like the *Discovery*, which was one of the last three-masted wooden ships to be built in the United Kingdom. For Alf the sense of history attached to this polar vessel would grow as the voyage south progressed: 'I don't remember any particular feelings that the *Discovery* was something different as I had had no previous contact with ships. I think from my general reading I knew a sailing ship was like that. I believe, from my point of view, when I got to Cape Town this was just a ship, and later on a ship with an extraordinary history.'

All aboard were soon made aware of how the *Discovery* behaved in the open sea. Alf's recollections were that

> It rolled like the blazes — a roller of the worst kind. Well it was rolling all the time but there were balustrades everywhere to hang on to so from that point of view the rolling was just part of it. Sometimes she would roll until the yards nearly touched the water; on these occasions personal belongings would fly from top bunks clear out of cabins into the wardroom and all night long there would be an endless rattle of pots and pans. It took some of us a few days to find our sea legs and there were a few absentees at the breakfast table. I recall there being a couple of occasions when I couldn't make it.

Five days out from Table Bay Mawson reported that the 'ship rolled heavily all night, wind keeping at force 5. ... Ship making about 6.5 knots with all sail. Noon position Lat 38° 09′S, Long 23° 48′E. Birds include Cape Horn Wandering Albatross, Mollymawk, Sooty Albatross, Mother Carey's Chickens, and several other varieties of petrel.'[13] By 23 October several members of the scientific staff had succumbed to the ship's motion and in particular the medical officer, Dr Ingram.[14] When Ingram recovered from his first attack of *mal de mer* he soon discovered that their 'gallant ship was no ocean greyhound. Some days she averaged a little over three knots and her best effort was seven knots in one day.'[15]

For Hurley, the *Discovery* was a well-manned ship: 'The officers and crew appear to have been well chosen. Particularly the former, young men who are keen, enthusiastic and eager,' he wrote. 'The only dour fact is that of the master – Capt. Davis, an excellent fellow at heart, whom I fear deems it derogatory to exhibit his true self which he seeks to hide behind a stern guise. Davis, however, is perhaps one of the most capable ice navigators living — a seaman to his finger tips with a profound knowledge of ships and men.'[16]

Within days of leaving South Africa arrangements were being put into place for two sittings as the wardroom table could only seat twelve and there were the officers and the twelve-man scientific team to accommodate. The meal hours were:

Breakfast	1st sitting	8 am
	2nd sitting	8.30 am
Lunch	1st sitting	12.30 pm
	2nd sitting	1 pm
Afternoon tea – no special sitting		3.30 pm-4 pm
Tea	1st sitting	5.30 pm
	2nd sitting	6 pm

Light supper at 9.30 pm.

Hurley and Marr, having been on the vessel since she left London in August, were by this time 'on diplomatic terms with the stewards and enjoyed a mug of tea at 7.15 am.'[17]

The wardroom with its multiple uses as a dining room, social gathering point or space to sort out biological and marine findings, measured approximately 26 feet by 14 across. When the ship was reconditioned for the *Discovery* Investigations some minor modifications were made to the wardroom accommodation on the main deck which 'extends from the forward end of the boiler room to the after end of the petty officers' and crew space, and contains 10 cabins.' These were the cabins for the scientific staff, the doors of which opened out into the wardroom. Both the cabins and the wardroom were 'comfortably furnished in polished mahogany.' At the forward end of the wardroom accommodation on the port side was Alf's chemical laboratory, where Hurley had to pass through to enter his small darkroom. 'The furniture of the wardroom consists of a large central table with swivel chairs, a bookshelf, slow combustion stove and small upright piano. An electric fan is fitted at the after end to assist ventilation.'[18]

However, as recorded by Scott on his 1901-1904 voyage, the temperature of the wardroom accommodation could at times be very uncomfortable because 'the coal-space or bunker under the wardroom ... was only shut off from the engine-room by a steel bulkhead, and consequently it became extremely cold and communicated its temperature to the wardroom. This difficulty would not have arisen had the decks of the living spaces been thoroughly well insulated.' This turned out to be the case on Mawson's BANZARE. Scott also noted that 'daylight was admitted to the living-spaces through central skylights and small round deck lights. There were no portholes or sidelights in the *Discovery*.'[19]

On the upper deck was a large teak deckhouse between the fore and main masts; at the forward end of it was the chart room and at the after end was the large biological laboratory where Fletcher, Johnston, Marr and Falla sorted and analysed their specimens. Adjacent to the lab was the wireless cabin where Williams with two separate Marconi wireless sets, each of 1½ kW capacity, received news from outside as well as successfully wiring the progress of the *Discovery* via ship-to-ship/ship-to-land communication to the rest of the world.[20]

Among the first messages of goodwill to be transmitted to the ship was one sent on 20 October 1929 from King George V. From London on 21 October the British Official Wireless advised the press that: 'His Majesty the King has sent the following message to Sir Douglas Mawson who sailed in the *Discovery* on Saturday from Cape Town on the expedition to Antarctica: "The Queen and I send you and all the members of the Expedition our best wishes for your success and safe journey".'[21]

*

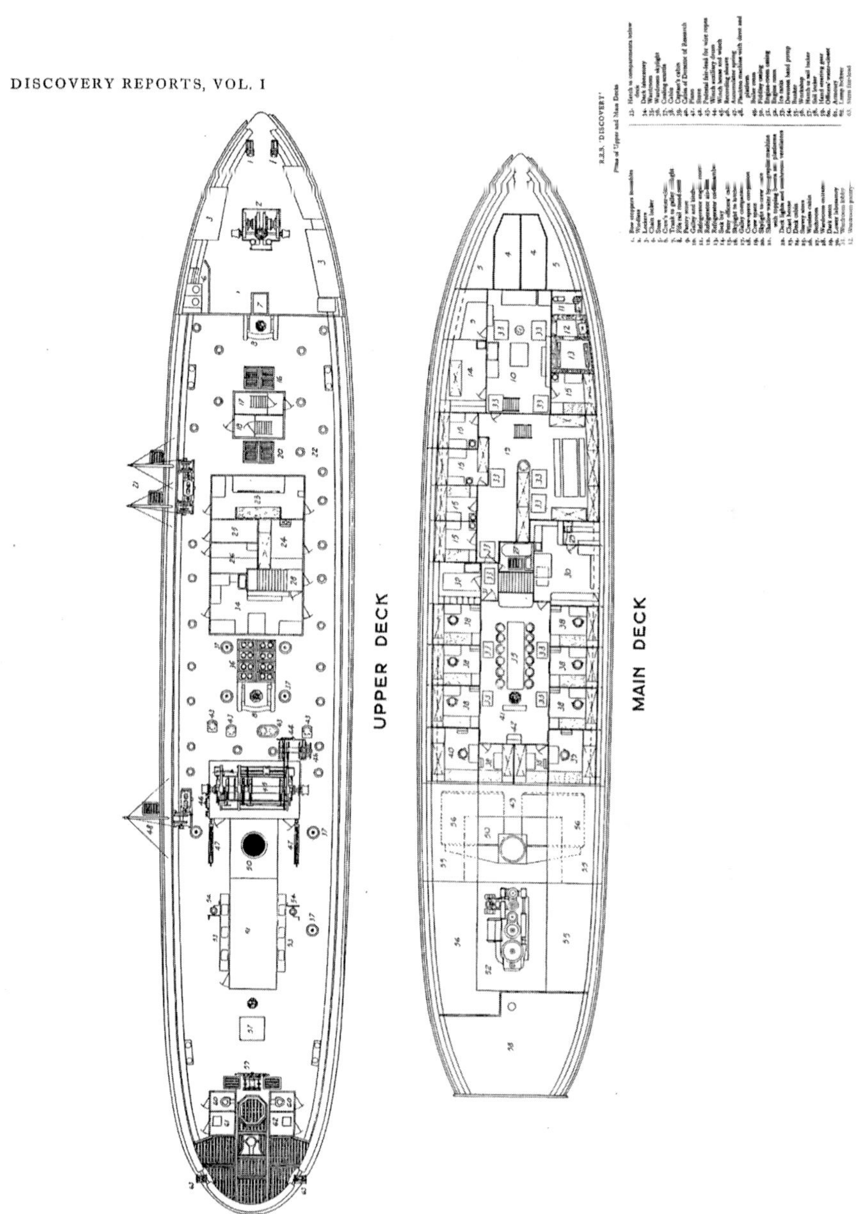

Plan of the *Discovery*'s Upper and Main Decks

Less than five months had passed since Alf was invited to go south with Mawson, and now after crossing the Indian Ocean on the *Orvieto* and the Atlantic Ocean on the *Armadale Castle* he was on Scott's old ship in uncharted waters of the Southern Ocean. All on board were now a long way from the 'real' world and it would be days before Sparks (Williams) received a wireless message informing them of the Wall Street Crash on 'Black Tuesday', 29 October 1929, which devastated world economy and signalled the beginning of the Great Depression.

Eight days out of Cape Town and unaware of the global economic panic, *Discovery* was fighting against the Agulhas Current, an unfriendly stream, to stay on course for the Crozet Islands.[22] Commander Morton Moyes, the cartographer, noted that 'during one day with the wind on the port bow we logged 119 miles but the current knocked us back 40 miles. How the old ship revelled in that wind and the breaking waves it brought along. Like a swimmer dives under the crest of a surf, the *Discovery* seemed to dip her bows, for the heavy seas to curl up over the port rails.'[23]

Sir Douglas observed 'extraordinary flocks of whale-birds [prions] about, apparently feeding and migrating to SE.' Further jottings in his diary on 28 October indicate that while the crew were busy keeping the vessel as steady as possible the scientific staff was already at work:

> Seas increased to 6-7 from WSW and wind 6-7 from SSW. A wild night. Ship rolled heavily, much water taken on board. At midnight wind eased and during day came from WSW. Temperature fell today. Echo-sounding at 12.45 pm in 42° 22′S and 34° 16′E gave 2912 fth [fathoms]. Noon position 42° 20′S and 34° 10′E. Campbell went back to his own cabin. The ventilators to cabins leak no matter what is done. Very uncomfortable drips developed in heavy weather, some in middle of my bed from other cause than ventilators. Sheep getting in a bad way with so much wet and cold. They get lucerne hay and some quaker oats in their water. Whale-birds numerous still. A squid washed on deck during night — likely to be one of those which jump out of water mentioned in encyclopaedia.

Campbell and Doc Ingram had caught influenza in Cape Town, and while Ingram recovered from the flu only to succumb to seasickness, Campbell was diagnosed as having a touch of pleurisy and confined to bed.[24] Unfortunately 'a few of the live sheep had a bad time with the slippery decks and had to be killed, "to save their lives" as the cook put it.'[25] Mawson's reference to the encyclopaedia is interesting as Alf recalled that 'quite often in the evening Sir

Douglas would introduce a topic for discussion at the dinner table. It didn't take long to figure out that he not only had a complete set of the *Encyclopaedia Britannica* in his cabin, but that he appeared to be working his way through it systematically.' There certainly was no shortage of reading material on board the *Discovery*. The ship's inventory listed more than one hundred books destined for the ship's library, which covered a wide range of subjects such as: philosophy, drama, poetry, history, biography, travel, fiction, popular science, as well as dictionaries and the *Encyclopaedia Britannica*. 'Of course there was a long queue to read Scott's *Voyage of the Discovery*,' said Alf. 'I seem to remember reading *Moby Dick* soon after we left Cape Town. At the time I probably picked it up because I thought we'd be seeing a lot whales down there.'[26]

The *Discovery* was now battling the seas of the roaring forties. Alf described the experience: 'I had never seen or felt such high seas before and the decks were constantly wet due to the heavy rain squalls. Of course there was the persistent rolling of our good ship and so we were all given an issue of oilskins and some warm undies before we reached the Crozets.' Moyes noted that everyone 'worked under cover from the rain, carpentering, mending nets and otherwise preparing for operations. Day succeeded day with no change except that rain gave way to hail and sleet.'[27] Ingram specified the allocation of tasks: 'Hurley had specialised in gimbal tables and fish traps, Mawson in setting up and repairing nets and gear, Simmers in taking hail meteorological observations, Douglas in getting the motor boat in order, Moyes in taking daily bearings and sightings, Falla and Fletcher in observing the bird life in our trail, myself in attending to Campbell who had developed pleurisy from which he happily rapidly recovered.'[28] During this period Mawson recorded: 'Hurley very busy constructing gimbal tables for sounding purposes and in helping Howard rig out the lower laboratory.'[29]

*

On the 15th day out of Cape Town the Crozet Islands were sighted and there was much anticipation of a landing the following day. 'Alf and I are to do a dip circle determination in preparation for which we have been ruling off forms. Capt. Hurley has set Alf and me a good example in lab tidying and now it is glistening after liberal applications of oil and white paint. The zoologists in particular are in for a busy time and I don't know how they are ever going to lump all their gear ashore,' wrote Simmers. That evening 'Sir Douglas gave a very interesting talk about the coast between Adelie Land and Erebus and about old times at Cape Royds etc.'[30] What intrepid tales of adventure could be told by Sir Douglas, Captain Davis, Captain Hurley, Commander Moyes, Kennedy and (Scout) Marr — each one of them a link with the heroic era of Antarctic exploration.

Overhauling the net equipment. L to R: Howard, Moyes and Campbell
(Photo: Frank Hurley)

Sailing with Legends

Two groups of islands and some 20 pinnacle rocks make up the Crozets, which are sprinkled over the southern Indian Ocean for nearly 100 kilometres. The *Discovery* dropped anchor in American Bay on the north-east coast of Possession Island, which was the site chosen by the French explorer Marc-Joseph Marion du Fresne when he discovered the islands on 24 January 1772.

'We were naturally looking forward to a landing after nearly two weeks on the roller-coaster. Sir Douglas decided that we should go ashore in the afternoon and so the launch was lowered as well as the pram [dinghy], which was used quite a bit during the expedition for difficult landings. I must admit we looked a bit of a motley crew,' recalled Alf. 'The scientific members … arrayed themselves for the shore. "Arrayed", I write, because of our bearded warlike aspect, the guns we carry and the fearsome sheath knives belted about most waists,' wrote Hurley. 'To the uninitiated, a sub-Antarctic island must be approached with caution. Collectively I have never beheld a more piratically attired group of scientists, nor a gang more calculated to scare wildfowl and penguins, than those who clambered over the ship's side and awkwardly down the rope ladder to stumble into the motor boat.'[1]

*

Captain James Francis Hurley was no newcomer to sub-Antarctic islands or indeed to the Antarctic continent. Already an established 'commercial photographer' in Sydney by the age of 26, Hurley wrote to Mawson 'offering his … services as photographer and kinematographer' to the 1911-14 Australasian Antarctic Expedition (AAE).[2] He was the AAE's official photographer and worked tirelessly under arduous conditions from December 1911 to March 1913 taking photographs and movie footage, which was assembled as *Home of the Blizzard* and shown to full houses. He again went south in early 1914 on the *Aurora* with Captain Davis to bring Mawson and his companions home from Commonwealth Bay. Later in the same year Hurley was assigned photographer to Sir Ernest Shackleton's 1914-16 Imperial

Trans-Antarctic Expedition, a gruelling expedition that could have ended in a disastrous loss of human lives. Hurley's photographs and film *In the Grip of Polar Ice* record for all time the agonising end of their ship *Endurance* as it was slowly crushed and destroyed by the pack-ice and the crew's 22-month ordeal and heroic struggle for survival. At the invitation of his old friend and leader Sir Douglas, Hurley was once again sailing with companions from earlier Antarctic expeditions and now creating a photographic and cine record of the BANZARE.

'We were all eager to go ashore,' said Alf. 'It became obvious that our first island landing was going to be a chilly one. Snow covered the hills and reached down into the valleys. The beach ahead of us was long and quite wide and we could see hundreds of sea elephants. As we drew closer we could not believe the dreadful scene being played out before us. A group of men were slaughtering bulls, cows and even new-born pups.' Moyes, who had been elected to keep a record of the first voyage, described the scene: 'A sealing ship [*Kilfinora* from Cape Town] had anchored shortly before our arrival and already the sealers were busy. Male seals were shot, and baby seals killed with axes before all were stripped of skin and blubber, leaving a frightful picture of slaughter in the place of a charming scene of peace and rest.'[3] Getting the scientific staff ashore with their equipment and Hurley with his cameras on to the motor launch and then into the pram proved challenging as Mawson's jottings reveal: 'Anchored motor launch about 100 yards off the breaking beach. Went ashore in number of parties by pram. Had some difficulty in surf but got all hands and gear off safely, though everybody's legs wet — sea boots filled.'[4] Sir Douglas also took note of the interesting flora, fauna and geology of the island, which presented a welcome change after having been at sea for 15 days:

> Valleys vegetated heavily, very peaty and boggy in bottom. Nice stream running into the bay. Teal duck along water courses. Penguins, chiefly Gentoo, at frequent intervals, rookery of nellies 2 m to east. Giant Albatross nesting at intervals in isolated nests on the vegetated slopes — striking nests, with moat surrounding them. Doc arrived with Davis. Collected vegetation and rocks. ... Simmers and Howard late arriving to get off to ship, as delayed in magnetic dip and force determination–cold wind and snow make it difficult for them. We had difficulty boarding *Discovery* as she was so far out to sea — big swell about her. ... Very difficult hoisting launch in davits.[5]

Ingram holding a young albatross in the Crozet Islands
(Photo: Frank Hurley)

Alf remembered the first dip circle determination of the expedition with Simmers:[6] 'It was freezing and we were both really at a loss as to how we could do a good job with an instrument neither of us had seen before.' Simmers recorded similar sentiments: 'I'll never forget my initiation into the mysteries of the dip circle determination. A windy, exposed spot, a cutting wind, learning to use an unknown instrument, frequent squalls of hail and snow and finally a frantic Hurley ordering us to pack up immediately and go to the boat as it was 7.20 and we were due back at 7. Half frozen, our fingers refusing to work, grumbling that why should we have to stop just before we finished a determination.'[7] With improved weather conditions overnight they returned to complete the dip the next morning: 'Immediately Alf and I went up to our spot and by 12.30 had completed a full determination of dip and intensity with only two breaks for snow and hail. A lunch of bread, butter and cheese made wonderfully good by a morning's work in the bracing air.'[8]

'Each evening during our time in the Crozets,' recalled Alf, 'the wardroom table was covered with an old cloth on top of which large sacks with a mixture of insects, mosses and rocks were emptied for us and particularly for the biologists to sort out.' For Hurley 'the dining table resembled a section of a richly verdured Possession Island meadow. … They are searching the tangled mass blade by blade and leaf by leaf for tiny springtails, diminutive spiders, beetles, slaters and other lowly insects. I am afraid I cannot enthuse over these microscopical bug hunts.'[9] 'However,' continued Hurley, 'I cannot but help admire the arduous zeal and indefatigable patience with which these professional gentlemen indulge in this strangely profound occupation which appears to hold as much glamour for them as lion stalking does for me'![10]

Sorting specimens from the Crozets. L to R: Marr, Ingram, Mawson and Harvey Johnston (Photo: Frank Hurley)

'We were jolly tired at the end of each day collecting specimens as the terrain was hilly and the ground was like one big bog. There were some periods of sunshine, but for the most part it was damp and cold and I hadn't seen or felt snow before,' said Alf. 'It was also during our time in the Crozets that I saw my first iceberg. Bob Ingram and Fletcher had sighted a couple from a high point of the island, but my initial sighting of one of these floating majestic ice sculptures was unforgettable.'

*

Discovery raised anchor early 4 November setting sail for the Kerguelen Islands. Mawson's entry the next day confirmed the changing seascape: 'Course S 51° E. … Ship proceeding under full sail at 4½ knots. Three icebergs passed during early morning watch. … Australian ski boots distributed to staff and ship's officers, bluchers to crew. "Lofty" Martin cannot find a blucher big enough, so we have to give him a No. 11 ski boot.' With the colder weather setting in Sir Douglas distributed some of the Jaeger clothing, which included heavy woollen lumber jackets, heavy shirts and trousers, heavy undergarments, oilskin coats, heavy socks, short and long finger mitts and balaclavas.[11] 'Jaeger supplied the equipment in three sizes: large, large-medium and large-small,' recorded Hurley. 'Sir Douglas, who believes in "roominess", seems to have modified the usual acceptance of these terms. The result is that most of the garments are of a generous fit. The scientific magnifying glass will be useful to locate Howard, our smallest member, amid the overwhelming folds of the smaller size.'[12] Alf reflected on the 'roominess' of the Jaeger clothing: 'I think Sir Douglas must have ordered all clothing with only himself in mind. Being of small stature everything I tried on was far too wide and much too long. Some of the garments were so thick that I had to use thread and needle reserved for mending the nets. I wouldn't say that my sewing skills would have won me a blue ribbon, but somehow or other the stitches held fast.'

On 6 November 'light snow fell in evening' and on the 7th the ship was 'taking water fore and aft.'[13] It was all action stations on board: 'Marr, Fletcher and doctor busy rigging trawls. Campbell and Douglas getting winch ready. Johnson and Falla still busy packing specimens. Two more sheep killed … Only 3 out of the 15 now left. … Many telegrams received through the *Verbena* at Simonstown. A long cable from Sydney Station got through the *Gloucester*.[14]

News of the expedition's movements was first transmitted by Sparks (Williams) to the nearest ship, then to shore, and finally to the various contracted media outlets. The first news Alf's father and brother would have had of the expedition since its departure was a snippet in the Australian newspapers on Monday, 11 November:

> **THE DISCOVERY**
>
> Report from the Crozets
>
> CANBERRA, Sunday.
>
> The exploring ship *Discovery*, which left Capetown on October 19, conveying the British, Australian, and New Zealand Antarctic Research Expedition, arrived at Possession Island in the Crozets, on November 7. Sir Douglas Mawson reported 'all well.'[15]

The *Discovery* had reached Possession Island on 2 November, but it was not until 7 November that Mawson cabled a message advising *Discovery*'s arrival in the Crozets, by which time the ship was well on her way to the Kerguelen Islands.[16]

As Commander of the expedition, Sir Douglas carried out the tradition of raising a glass to sweethearts and wives on Saturday nights, as well as on birthdays, festive occasions and to celebrate other important events. Yalumba's famous 4 Crown Port was the chosen toast on these occasions as it had also been for Mawson's 1911-1914 expedition. The Yalumba Vineyards at Angaston generously donated 10 cases of their celebrated port for the first voyage, which was delivered on board the *Nestor* in Port Adelaide and traversed the Indian Ocean with Sir Douglas.[17] BANZARE would be Mawson's third and final scientific expedition to Antarctica, and lifting his glass to toast occasions such as Williams' birthday on 10 November must have brought back memories of similar times in the hut at Commonwealth Bay.

*

Alf was sailing with legends, but none more so than his leader, Sir Douglas Mawson. The famous photograph of Mawson in balaclava on the Australian $100 dollar note — which remained in circulation until 1996 — was in fact taken with his BANZARE team on board the *Discovery*. He was a member of the 1907-1909 British Antarctic Expedition led by Ernest Shackleton on the *Nimrod* where he first met John King Davis, then the ship's Chief Officer. Together with Shackleton and Edgeworth David he made history by being in the first team to climb Mt Erebus in March 1908. During the same expedition Mawson, David and Alistair Mackay claimed to be first to reach the magnetic South Pole on 16 January 1909.

Mawson turned down an invitation to join Robert Falcon Scott's fatal 1910 *Terra Nova* Expedition, choosing to raise funds and lead the 1911-1914 Australasian Antarctic Expedition (AAE) to King George V Land and Adelie Land in east Antarctica with Davis as Master of the steam yacht *Aurora*. As the purpose of the AAE was to chart this virtually unexplored territory the expedition split into small parties to explore on foot. Just five weeks from the base hut at Commonwealth Bay tragedy struck Mawson's party when Belgrave Ninnis disappeared down a deep crevasse with a team of Greenland huskies and the sledge carrying most of the food. Mawson and Xavier Mertz turned back for the long haul home, but shortage of food forced them to eat the sledging dogs in order to survive. It is believed that Mertz fell ill from the toxic levels of vitamin A in the huskies' livers and died leaving Mawson to make the gruelling return journey to base alone. Exhausted and famished, he too nearly lost his life in a crevasse; through sheer mental strength and courage he dragged his poisoned body over more than 160 km of blizzard-swept ice and snow to the safety of the hut only to see 'a speck on the north-west horizon.'[18] It was the *Aurora*, which had waited a month for Mawson's return, but was forced to leave Commonwealth Bay to relieve Frank Wild's party on the Shackleton Ice Shelf. Another year passed before Davis could return to take the leader and the rest of his wintering party home. While the journey proved tragic Mawson's party had travelled more than 1000 kilometres in east Antarctica collecting geological samples, discovering massive glaciers and mapping the coastline. Sir Douglas' epic journey was described as 'the greatest story of lone survival in polar expedition history.'

*

Tuesday, 12 November 1929 and the *Discovery* was at last ready to drop anchor in the Kerguelen Islands after high seas, snow squalls and plunging decks the day before had forced her to run north with the gale. Mawson described the approach:

> By 7 am came into tangle of kelp, hundreds of acres of it. … Called all hands —scientific staff on deck when we entered kelp. … We got through the kelp all right and ran down the coast in improving weather, soon entering Royal Sound. … Everywhere penguins and diving petrels were sporting in the placid waters. A small whale or whales spouted occasionally along our course. It was a very fine view indeed as we passed by one island after another, through the narrow and eventually up to the jetty at Jeanne d'Arc Whaling Station.

The first days in the Kerguelens proved to be backbreaking: 'To supplement our coal supplies briquettes had been dumped for us at Jeanne d'Arc. The jetty was rather dilapidated and there were a number of deserted wooden buildings on shore—the remains no doubt of a one-time busy whaling station that had obviously been abandoned for many years,' recounted Alf. 'Crew and scientists were soon put to work tossing the 25 lb briquettes from one to the other all the way to the bunkers. Of course the coal was always a question. The point was that once we reached the ice we had to have enough coal to get us out. This was of great concern to Davis.' As captain and second-in-command of the expedition the safety of the crew and scientists was paramount to Davis, who already had a long and successful seafaring career behind him before he took the *Discovery* to the icy frontiers of the Earth.

The *Discovery* at old whaling station Jeanne d'Arc, Kerguelen Island (Photo: Frank Hurley)

*

John King Davis was conceivably the greatest ship captain of the 'heroic' era of Antarctic exploration. Two years after having completed his seaman's apprenticeship on the iron ship *Celtic Chief* he was recruited by Ernest Shackleton as chief officer of the *Nimrod* for the 1907-09 British Antarctic Expedition, during which voyage he became friends with Mawson. On a subsequent relief voyage for that expedition he was appointed ship's master. 'Captain Davis is the most experienced navigator of Antarctic seas living,' wrote Sir Ernest in 1913, 'he's an expert on oceanographical work, especially in sounding and dredging in deep waters ... He successfully navigated *Aurora*, landing Dr Mawson at his winter quarters through the stormiest oceans and one of the worst ice seasons ever recorded.'[19]

Mawson invited Davis to be second-in-command on his 1911-14 Australasian Antarctic Expedition (AAE) and master of the *Aurora*. Early January 1912, after having landed Mawson at his Commonwealth Bay winter quarters, Davis took the *Aurora* 1200 miles west discovering the Davis Sea and Queen Mary Land and landing Frank Wild and his party–which included BANZARE's Moyes and Kennedy–at the Shackleton Ice Shelf. During the AAE, Davis made five notable voyages gathering scientific data on the Southern Ocean as well as playing a pivotal role in establishing and relieving the wintering bases at Commonwealth Bay, on the Shackleton Ice Shelf and Macquarie Island. In a rare interview for *The Age* in 1959 Davis said: 'This was my main life's work. It was a three-year assignment filled with the most extraordinary vicissitudes.'[20]

After conveying troops and horses to Egypt and England during World War I, Davis was once again navigating the Southern Ocean in October 1916 as commander of the Ross Sea Relief Expedition, 'mounted to rescue Shackleton's "shore party" left at McMurdo Sound to support their leader's epic but ill-fated attempt to cross Antarctica from the Weddell Sea. After being marooned for two winters with inadequate supplies and equipment, its members reached New Zealand in the *Aurora* on 9 February 1917.'[21]

*

Discovered and named after the French navigator Yves-Joseph de Kerguélen-Trémarec in 1772, the Kerguelen Archipelago with its heavily glaciated main island and approximately 300 islets lies on the Antarctic Convergence where the cold waters from the Antarctic mix with the warmer waters of the Indian Ocean. Kerguelen's climate is harsh, with wind gusts, rain and snow most of the year, its birdlife and marine mammals abundant, as the BANZARE scientists soon found out.

With coaling completed there were a few days to collect samples of Kerguelen's flora and fauna. In all, 212 tons of coal was loaded at Port Jeanne d'Arc into *Discovery*'s depleting bunkers. The crew and scientific staff shovelled most of it on board, and were helped on two occasions by the men from the sealing ship *Kilfinora*, which had recently arrived in port. The *Discovery* — low in water with its heavy cargo of coal — left the anchorage and 'steamed down the middle of Island Harbour and anchored close to the kelp off Grave Island.'[22]

Moyes noted that the 'difference between the surface of the mainland and that of the numerous islets which studded the channels was very striking.' A few pairs of rabbits set free from HMS *Challenger* in 1874[23] had multiplied, resulting in scant vegetation on the main island. The islets, however, were densely covered with vegetation which included the Kerguelen cabbage. 'Burrows of Diving and Blue Petrels and Prions were numerous. … Teal were also plentiful along the rivulets winding down from the uplands and Doc Ingram, Simmers and Howard brought on board a very fine "bag" as a welcome change of diet.'[24]

*

Commander Morton Henry Moyes had known Sir Douglas since his university days in Australia. He successfully applied to join Mawson's 1911-14 AAE as the meteorologist for the Western Party under Frank Wild. Moyes took part in a number of sledging journeys during 1912, but is best remembered for enduring nine weeks alone in the winter quarters hut on Shackleton Ice Shelf while the rest of the men were sledging. 'The loss of a sledge delayed the group's return and Moyes endured nine weeks of anxious solitude.'[25] He was appointed navigating officer of the *Aurora* under the command of Captain Davis and sailed from New Zealand to the Ross Sea in December 1916 to rescue marooned members of Shackleton's Trans-Antarctic Expedition. Davis had rejected Moyes as a ship's officer for the 1929-30 BANZARE voyage, however, Mawson fully aware of his scientific skills in various surveying and recording tasks, requested him to join the scientific staff as survey officer.

Another veteran of the early Antarctic expeditions was Alexander Lorimer Kennedy, who joined the scientific staff as magnetician on the second BANZARE voyage. He too was a member of Mawson's 1911-14 AAE and served as cartographer/magnetician with Wild's Western Party on the Shackleton Ice Shelf. Kennedy's duties entailed a great deal of night work and it was necessary for him to set up his equipment in an igloo to avoid contact with anything metallic that would influence the readings. When 'it was Kennedy's term night … the work [kept] him in the igloo from 10 pm until 2.30 am.' Wild recorded the official opening of the igloo built by Kennedy and members of the Western Party to be used as a magnetic observatory: 'On the afternoon of the 30th, the magnetician invited everyone to a tea-party in the igloo to celebrate the opening. He had the place very nicely decorated with flags, and after the reception and the formal inspection of instruments, we were served with quite a good tea. The outside temperature was -33°F and it was not much higher inside the igloo. As a result, no one extended his visit beyond the bounds of politeness.'[26]

As the Kerguelen archipelago offered a choice of good anchorages the scientific staff was able to take the launch and explore some of the smaller islands. On one of the islands Mawson noted that he sighted only 'one female sea-elephant and part-grown young on beach … illustrates that sealing and penguin massacring has been on a vast scale on this island.'[27] 'We took it in turns to go ashore,' said Alf, 'as there was always plenty to do on the old ship. One afternoon the biologists and geologists went specimen collecting while Marr and I concentrated on getting the deep-sea equipment ready; Marr was an expert in this field. We hit it off straight away.' Both had been scout patrol leaders; Marr with the First Aberdeen Troop and Alf with Melbourne's First City of Camberwell (*Melba's Own*) Scout Group.

*

Often referred to as Scout Marr, James William Slessor Marr was chosen by Sir Ernest Shackleton from thousands of volunteer scouts to accompany the *Quest* Expedition of 1921-22 to explore the coastline of Coats Land in the Weddell Sea and some of the rarely visited South Atlantic islands. Engine trouble in the early stages of the voyage forced Shackleton to change route and the *Quest* headed for South Georgia via Rio de Janeiro where Sir Ernest fell ill. Less than three weeks later Shackleton died in his sleep from a heart attack on board the *Quest* in Grytviken Harbour on 5 January 1922. Marr expressed the loss in his book: 'To the last he retained his old courage and good cheer; then in the chilly solitudes he went hence, mourned by all as trustworthy leader, loyal shipmate and wise counsellor. … A great man had left us, and the ship was lonely.'[28]

Marr's invitation to take part in the 1925 British Arctic Expedition came almost immediately after he was awarded a BSc degree in zoology. Just before and after joining Mawson's 1929-31 *Discovery* voyages, Marr took part in three expeditions to Antarctica on the *William Scoresby* in 1928-29, and on *Discovery II* in 1931-33 and 1935-37–voyages set up by the '*Discovery* Investigations' organisation in order to study the biological resources of the Falkland Islands Dependencies and in particular the biology of Southern whales.[29]

*

By 23 November Davis was keen to move on but cautious because of the low barometer reading: 'Our time here has not been wasted as we have been able to get the ship cleaned up and ready for sea quietly. ... As soon as the weather, or rather the barometer, shows signs of settled weather we shall get under weigh. ... It would be folly to rush out into a SE Gale with the ship as deep as she is at present and with so much coal on deck.'[30] However, Mawson's diary entry of 24 November expressed frustration rather than a sense of accomplishment:

> I am extremely disappointed to be going south from Kerguelen without being able to conduct a full oceanographic programme. ... Work at Kerguelen reduced to very little by constant friction with Davis. Scientists spent time largely re-sorting equipment and coaling. On account of very small coal capacity of *Discovery* have had to allow winch house and deck to be filled with coal, and until used cannot tow net or dredge. Hope soon after Heard Island to be able to start full scheme.

Davis was on constant alert to avoid a number of partially hidden rocks in the many fjord-like channels and was 'glad to get away from Kerguelen safely.' The 243-mile passage in force 4-5 winds ended up being relatively smooth compared to the 'expected gale.'[31] Heard Island was sighted at dawn on 26 November, and anchor was dropped in Corinthian Bay. Sir Douglas selected the shore party: 'Dr Ingram, Commander Moyes, Prof Johnston, Pilot Douglas, Fletcher, Falla, Capt F. Hurley, Marr and self. Campbell had to remain on board to overhaul echo-sounder, Simmers and Howard to carry on their work.'[32]

On The Plank, Into The Lab

Discovery's approach to Heard Island was slow as she battled the elements in a heavy swell. The island (53° 01′S 73° 23′E) is recorded as being continuously buffeted by gale-force winds and lashed by treacherous seas, a fact that Mawson noted as being 'beneficial in limiting the massacre of seal and penguin life.'[1] The stratovolcano Big Ben — its steep slopes heavily crevassed with glaciers running into the sea — peaks at 2700 metres and dominates this isolated outpost discovered in 1853 by an American, Captain John J. Heard, on board the freight ship *Oriental*.[2] Photographs document that the Union Jack was raised during the BANZARE visit, however, on 26 December 1947 the Australian flag was planted and an official proclamation signed by Stuart Campbell, declaring that '… His Majesty's Government in the Commonwealth of Australia intends forthwith to continue the occupation of these Islands and to administer them as Australian Territories,' was put in a canister buried beside the flagpole. The transfer of Heard Island from Great Britain to Australia was legalised by an 'exchange of notes' in 1951.[3]

For Alf, Heard Island was the real beginning of the oceanographic studies. 'We arrived at dawn and after breakfast the launch was lowered with provisions for a few days. It would be fair to say that Simmers, Campbell and myself were a little disappointed having to stay onboard. We took turns to go up to the crow's nest and follow the shore party until they made a successful landing on the other side of the isthmus.' Simmers noted that 'shortly before lunch a launch party returned with stories about elephant seals, penguins, and the Admiralty Hut.[4] Sir Douglas wasted no time as he brought back his first load of rocks. Early in the afternoon the second official party left and we are now left with a comfortable amount of elbow room.'[5]

Heavy snowfalls and gale conditions on the second day caused *Discovery*'s anchors to drag, forcing Davis to put out to sea thus leaving the shore party marooned. Moyes described how cramped conditions were in the old 10-foot-wide hexagonal hut at Atlas Cove:

> The rations we had brought ashore 'for a few days' soon disappeared, but we were able to live 'off the land'. The lower slopes of the hills were occupied by various tribes of penguins ... and these kindly supplied us with eggs. The hut had four pairs of bunks and a 'bogey' stove. There was very little space for nine men with their gear and apparatus, but we soon stowed our belongings and set out on our various duties. ... The party on shore found plenty to do and the only worry was how to find room for the specimens which Harvey Johnston and the other collectors brought home each day.[6]

While the stranded contingent had to wait until Davis felt it safe enough to return to Corinthian Bay there were some memorable moments recalled Alf: 'Of course they had stories to tell on their return like the time Hurley cracked a couple of dozen Gentoo penguin eggs for an omelette; and they spoke of more than one instance when a three to four-ton bull elephant seal tried to push its way into the hut.' A first attempt to rescue the land party had to be put off as the seas were still high. Moyes recorded the perilous launch trip from Atlas Cove to the *Discovery*:

> Our equipment and numerous tins and cases of specimens were awaiting the boat's arrival and we were soon chugging out to sea. It was a trip no one would like to do again. The waves dashed over the open launch, sleet blew strongly in our faces, and down the necks of those who carried out the necessary bailing operations. Fortunately the engine responded to Eric Douglas' skill and care and Sir Douglas standing in the stern, steered the craft well out past the reef and turned her skilfully into Corinthian Bay. The *Discovery* was rising till the keel was almost showing to sink again for the waves to reach the rails. As the launch rose with the waves, a couple of men would throw themselves across the rails to be dragged on board, while others handed up tins and cases before the launch swung away to the trough again. As the launch was emptied, two seamen sprang aboard her before she moved away, ready to shackle on as she surged upwards, and with a line of men on the tackle, the launch was held fast and hoisted on board, as once more we put to sea.[7]

Davis expressed both relief and exasperation as the ship pulled anchor and slowly moved away from the island into a north-westerly wind and a high sea just after midday on 3 December: 'We are indeed lucky to have got the whole party on board. ... We were at the island for a week. A few soundings, some information as to the NE side of the coast and that is all.'[8]

The break on and in the vicinity of Heard Island had been a welcome change and the biologists returned to the ship loaded with specimens for their collections, some of which unexpectedly arrived on the wardroom's breakfast table one morning: 'We were to have boiled penguin eggs,' wrote Simmers, 'when lo and behold in came boiled skuas eggs each containing a chicken. Someone had sent the wrong lot of eggs to the cook and what we had was a private collection which the Dux[9] was taking home. There were two penguin eggs of which I was lucky enough to have one.'[10]

*

Alf's own work really started the day before arriving at Heard Island with the taking of surface temperatures by means of the Lumby Sampler. These had to be taken by him every four hours, and every 12 hours he collected samples for salinity and routine analysis. There was, however, some relief as Simmers took over the early morning observation. Although the bucket-like Lumby was heavy and cumbersome it was 'a robust, reliable instrument' reported Alf. 'In spite of being caught between the ship's side and ice on several occasions, the sampler stood up to the heavy conditions. … The samples were taken a little forward of midships and well forward of any engine-room discharges. In good weather the Lumby towed steadily at or within a few feet of the surface, depending on the ship's speed.'[11]

As the expedition's hydrologist and chemist 'A. Howard was responsible for the taking of sea-water temperatures and the collection and chemical examination of sea-water samples,' wrote Sir Douglas:

> This was a never-ending task. He worked very long hours daily, mainly occupied with the chemical examination of the very numerous sea-water samples obtained. Except in calm weather, the rolling of the vessel rendered difficult the delicate operation involved in the chemical examination of those waters. Howard is therefore to be congratulated upon the extensive series of determinations he ultimately achieved and the unabated enthusiasm and great care with which he prosecuted the task.[12]

Masson was no doubt impressed with Alf's record at the University of Melbourne when he recommended him for Mawson's team. His student card lists courses in pure maths, mixed maths, physics and chemistry for his Bachelor of Science, which was conferred in 1927, as well as French and German. In 1928 Alf received his Masters degree in chemistry and shared the Professor Kernot Scholarship in the University's School of Chemistry. However, 'as the other student sharing the Kernot Scholarship was unable to fulfil the conditions as to research and demonstrating, it was resolved in the circumstances that the whole of the emoluments should go to Mr Howard if he were able to fulfil the conditions.'[13] 'I did take up the scholarship and then worked as an industrial chemist at Dunlop,' said Alf. 'I soon realised that I didn't want a career in industry and as my father was keen to get away for a break both Clarence and I threw in our jobs and joined him on a cruise up the east coast and through the Indonesian islands. When I returned I applied for a postgraduate Commonwealth Scholarship and was soon back at the university working on organic chemistry.' Alf's early scientific contribution to Australian science is noted in Joan Radford's *The Chemistry Department of the University of Melbourne*:

> Alf Howard had held one of the University's research grants for MSc in 1928 for work on the synthesis of pyrones. In 1927 he had worked jointly with Davies and Dann on the hydrolysis of nitro-bromo-styrenes. But his duties in Antarctica were very different in character. He was to test seawater for temperature, salinity, pH, phosphate, silicate, nitrate, nitrite and dissolved oxygen. Most of the sampling was done by Howard himself, often in difficult conditions, from surface and vertical sections. Almost three thousand samples were taken and analysed at sea. ... But checking and final chemical analyses were made at the University by Howard, after his return from the second expedition in 1931. ... Though this early Antarctic work is known by comparatively few chemists, and its location not readily accessible, the venture should be remembered with respect by Australian chemists as their first serious chemical participation in Antarctic science.[14]

With his training at the marine biological stations in Plymouth for temperature analyses and in Lowestoft for the sampling of surface waters, Alf was equipped for his dual role in the team to work with instruments for marine hydrology and carry out the required chemical analysis of the sea-water samples.

Over the two voyages approximately 114 vertical stations were worked and more than 1500 surface samples were collected. Taking water samples from the surface to a depth of 400 metres with the Nansen-Pettersson water bottles was a potentially dangerous task for Alf as he stood on an outboard iron-grate, no more than one metre by 70 centimetres, with just a wire rope to protect him from falling into the often-turbulent Southern Ocean. The necessity to use a boom and outboard platform with the deck machine was due to *Discovery*'s high bulwarks and the pronounced inward inclination of the upper part of her sides. The final BANZARE reports underline the potential harm to the water instruments in rough seas, which equally applied to Alf's safety during these operations:

When in a heavy swell there was considerable danger of the water bottle crashing against the ship's side after it emerged from the water, and thus breaking the enclosed thermometer. With practice, and by careful co-operation between the winch operator and the man on the outboard platform, it was possible to make the bottle leave the water just as the vessel commenced to roll to port, and to raise it within the reach of the man on the platform just as the return roll commenced.[15]

Alf Howard operating the Nansen-Pettersson water bottle

'My memory of operating the Nansen-Pettersson water-sampler was that I'd be there on the platform with the derrick alongside and [Eric] Douglas — my cabin sharer — running the electric motor which controlled the instrument,' recollected Alf:

The instrument has valves at both ends and was lowered on a wire into the sea. Once it reaches the desired depth a brass weight called a 'messenger' is sent down the wire. The impact caused when the messenger reaches the bottle

> tips the reversing mechanism and inverts the bottle, thus closing the valves and trapping the water sample inside. This device would immediately be hauled in for the temperature to be read and the water to be run off into glass bottles. As I had to lean over the wire on the outer edge of the platform and guide the bottle as it was lowered into the sea and also make sure it didn't jolt against anything on the way up I'd be soaking wet and pretty cold throughout the whole operation especially when there was a heavy swell. When my work in the lab was completed I'd go to the fiddley to warm up.

As there was no heating on the *Discovery* the fiddley, with its raised iron grating over the hatches above the engine and boiler rooms through which hot air escaped, was, except for the fumes, a very popular destination. Even the cramped space of the fiddley's trunkway did not detract from its allure. 'We got very cold working in the saloon or the laboratories during the late hours,' noted Moyes, 'and it became customary to spend a few minutes in the compartment over the engine-room. The "Fiddley Club" usually had a few members in attendance after 11 o'clock each night, and the badge of membership could sometimes be noticed — a circle on the seat of the pants, the sign of the ash-bucket.'[16] 'The fiddley certainly had a full house when the shore party returned from the hut on Heard Island,' recalled Alf.

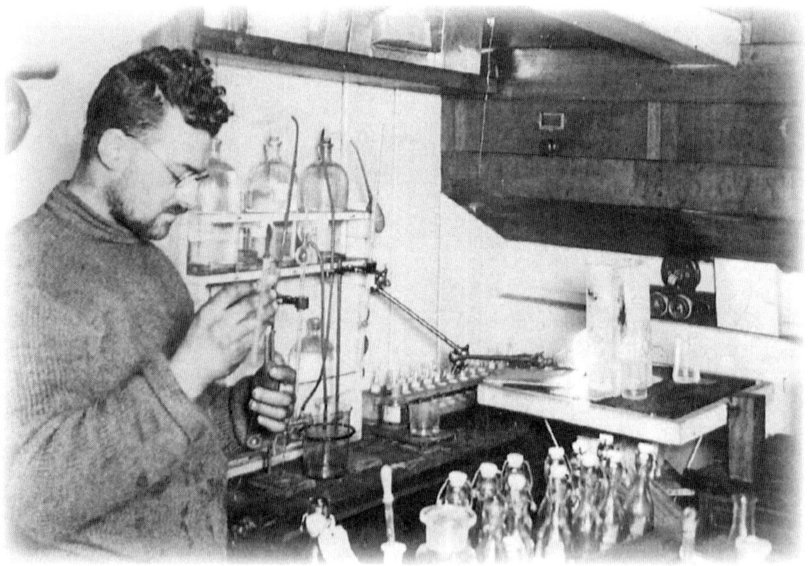

Alf Howard in his laboratory on board the *Discovery* (Photo: Frank Hurley)

Besides the centrally located work bench and a large chart table, the chemical laboratory was fitted out with bins, drawers and cupboards for the storage of glassware and other apparatus. Both the laboratory and Hurley's darkroom within had sinks with access to fresh and salt water. 'The facilities for the chemical work were very good. The biggest snag of course was that you would take your samples, then because most of the nutrients were not stable you had to analyse them straight away and carry out your colorimetric techniques so that within, say, a few hours of having taken your sample you've got all your data,' Alf pointed out. 'Fortunately there were special crates to carry the tagged samples bottles down the fairly steep companionway to my lab which opened off the wardroom.'

> It would take about six to seven hours to do the job so that you would have a pretty heavy day. But if the weather deteriorated at any stage then the ship would soon be rolling, and the *Discovery* was renowned for its ability to roll. This presented problems from the point of view of trying to work with delicate things. The gimbal tables Simmers and myself arranged to be constructed while we were in Cape Town turned out to be a real godsend for our work, as they remained perfectly level no matter how much the old ship rolled.

While most of Alf's salinity determinations were carried out on the *Discovery* soon after water samples were taken, some had to be completed in the laboratory of the University of Melbourne's Chemistry Department; in these cases no more than two months elapsed between the collection and examination of the samples.

Sir Douglas wasted no time in briefing Henderson when the 'programme of complete hydrographic and plankton stations' commenced, mentioning some of Alf's specialised tasks: 'With depth of sea as existing today namely somewhat over 3,000 metres, hydrologist Howard determines temperatures and takes sea-water samples at twenty successive intervals from surface down to bottom. Thus finds that below surface, a belt of some 160 metres thickness consisting of cold water of low salinity originating from melting of floating ice formations, there is a deeper stratum of warmer highly saline water which represents southward flowing tropical waters.'[17]

Alf's work on the determination of phosphates, silicates, nitrites and nitrates in sea water was published in *The Queenslander* and others newspapers between the two voyages. His results indicated that in the region between Queen Mary Land and Enderby Land the Antarctic Ocean from the continent to approximately latitude 45°S was characterised by a high surface content of nutrient salts: 'This abundance is due to the fact that when the plankton in the waters of lower latitudes die they slowly sink and decompose reforming the salts which they originally consumed. Thus a high content of nutrient salts is formed in the depths and when this water flows south and reaches the continental shelf vigorous mixing takes place and a uniform distribution is set up.'[18] In the same article Alf also drew attention to the fact that because little was known about the fluctuations that occurred in physical and chemical properties of the water at any fixed position in Antarctic waters at the time of the BANZAR Expedition, future research in the area would be invaluable to the fishing industry, thus making it possible to predict the movement of feeding areas.[19]

The *Discovery* meets the ice pack

*

The *Discovery* in latitude 60° 17′S met the pack-ice on 8 December after days of navigating through waters strewn with icebergs and floating ice. Mawson mentioned that there were 'many large icebergs in view, most tabular, one with much terrigenous matter. By 1 pm bergs and bergy bits very numerous. One Silver-Grey petrel. … Completed winding winch wire about 9.30 pm with Campbell, donkey-man, self, and Howard, with help from Hurley and Douglas.'[20] The *Discovery* had entered an enchanted yet forbidding world with few birds, but home to an abundance of marine life. Sir Douglas noted a number of 'shelf icebergs of 10 to 30 ft high and 100 to 500 yds long. Larger shelf icebergs to 80 ft scattered occasionally. Also some bluer glacier ice, irregular bergs or capsized bergs.'[21] 'What really struck me were the colours and shapes of the ice,' said Alf. 'As the ship drew closer to the ice shelf groups of Adélie penguins — mostly yearlings — could sometimes be seen at the water's edge checking for predators, and especially leopard seals, before plunging. Quite often we saw Crabeater seals in the pack ice and it surprised me how fast they could move. The Emperor penguins seemed rather solitary creatures and we rarely saw more than four or five at the same time.'

Moving in the pack was difficult, but at the same time rewarding: 'We had to commence the zig-zagging method of advance. … A calm sunny day in the ice pack region cannot be surpassed for beauty,' recorded Moyes. 'The sunlight glistening on the broken ice, the blue sky reflected in the calm water in which the occasional krill darts on important business, the petrels and the penguins, which dive fearfully away or stand firm to give a cry of protest at the invasion of their territory, all make it difficult to turn away from the ship's rail, even when the dinner gong sounds.'[22]

On 'December 11th 1929, Lat 64° 34′S, Long 78° 58′E' Davis wrote: '8 a.m. We have continued to steam Southward through scattered floes this morning. … 1.40 p.m. Ship stopped in open water area between two fields of pack for oceanographical station N° 23.'[23] Now sheltered in the pack from heavy ocean swells, Mawson's full program was at last under way, which meant all hands on deck.

Pitching In

Captain Davis recognised that he could not 'afford to have one dissatisfied man' on board and felt it was a good sign that his crew had 'shaped well during the passage from London to Table Bay ... in view of the stiff work ahead.' The crew had been carefully chosen: 'Hundreds of men and even a few women wanted to come with us. ... Then I sent all the likely applicants down to see the ship in London Docks to gain an idea of the discomfort, to meet the bo'sun, and to learn how unromantic it is all going to be down there in the roaring forties.'[1] As far as the scientific members were concerned they too were made aware before departure that besides their own specialised work they would have to be prepared to help each other and the crew when necessary. 'Most of us had never set foot on a sailing ship, and after having been on two liners to get to Cape Town the *Discovery* seemed very small to me,' reminisced Alf. 'I'm sure I wasn't the only one to have these sentiments. I believe we all felt the same that as the ship had been home to Captain Scott and his party in Antarctica for three years everything would be OK.'

As was the case for Scott's 1901-04 expedition, coal — and everything to do with obtaining, storing and redistributing it — was of paramount importance to the success of BANZARE. 'It would be fair to say that having a satisfactory cargo of coal onboard at all times had priority over any scientific program the Dux had in mind for us,' remarked Alf. 'Without it we really would have been stuck as you can't sail around in the pack ice.' The storage of coal in every recess did at times hold up the scientific work as noted in a message from Mawson to Henderson on 8 December 1929: 'Coal on deck and in winch house has now been consumed allowing letting out and rewinding 3,000 fathoms dredge cable [for] preparatory commencement of full oceanographic programme. Aviators Campbell and Douglas rendering valuable aid to scientific work by taking charge of winding engines and other mechanisms.'[2]

Mawson often made note of regular chores and the more specialised tasks shared by the scientific staff, ship's officers and crew: 'Scientific staff transfer

5 tons coal from sail locker to starboard bunker';[3] 'Completed winding winch wire about 9.30 pm — chiefly Campbell, donkeyman, self, Howard, with help from others such as Hurley, Douglas.'[4] The ambitious oceanographic program, which included the operation of the water bottles for Alf's hydrological work and the plankton nets and dredges required for the biological work of Harvey Johnston, Marr, Fletcher, Falla and medical officer Ingram, who was also assistant biologist, 'called for the participation of the ship's officers on the bridge and the engine-room staff.'[5]

Wherever circumstances permitted, the work program included operating a plankton station. Other hydrological data was obtained at the same time so that correlation of physical, chemical, meteorological and biological factors could be attempted. The plankton was captured in a series of nets varying in diameter and in the degree of fineness of the silk or other material of which its lower end was composed. A plankton station using vertical nets — which were worked from the port side of the vessel and lowered by hand — usually took about three hours to carry out a full series of hauls, and four men to carry out the mechanical and scientific aspects of the operation when the ship was stationary. For oblique hauls the nets were 'towed obliquely for a definite period from the stern of the vessel while travelling at about two knots; and were towed horizontally for considerable periods at some distance from the surface.' The otter trawl, with its three attached small fine-meshed nets, was used to collect the smaller organisms disturbed from the sea floor as the foot rope scraped over it. Largest of the dredges was the Monegasque trawl with its heavy steel rectangular frame, which was used during the two voyages and reserved for use in very deep water. While operations with the otter trawl were usually carried out while the ship was steaming at about two knots, heavy dredges such as the Monegasque trawl 'were dragged while the ship was drifting or was steaming at about one knot.'[6]

In the final BANZARE reports Professor T. Harvey Johnston, who was appointed Chief Biologist of the expedition, acknowledged the teamwork involved for the plankton stations and the dredging and trawling operations, which were always followed up with the preliminary sorting of material: 'To my biological colleagues, to Sir Douglas Mawson and the other members of the scientific staff, and to the ship's officers and crew, I tender my appreciation of their help in making the biological work of the expedition so successful as far as collecting was concerned. ... Every possible assistance was readily granted in the endeavour to handle adequately the mass of material which resulted from our dredgings along the Antarctic continental shelf.'[7] Johnston was particularly fascinated by the long-legged sea spiders usually found in the shallow sea adjacent to the continent, which could vary in length from 40 millimetres to about 50 centimetres. He observed that 'in one of the dredgings from very deep water when miles of wire were laid out, some very large "spiders" were obtained with peculiar stalked barnacles living on their bodies.'[8]

'The wardroom table would come to life again well after the second dinner sitting in the evening when the biologists operated a late trawl,' reminisced Alf:

> You see by mid December we were having nearly 24 hours of daylight, so everyone would lend a hand to sort out an evening catch of marine specimens no matter how late it was. Sometimes there would be a few brightly coloured starfish and little corals in among the sponges and sea worms; quite often there would be a variety of molluscs, and there was one that had a beautiful transparent glassy shell. It was a real smorgasbord of the denizens of the deep but one that certainly never whetted my appetite.

Mawson made reference to these occasions in his diary: 'The 2 metre net run out about 9.30 pm. Down 1500 metres by 10 pm. Trawl for 1 hour, then inboard by 12.10 am. A fine catch, beautiful in glass bowl under electric light. Many species of fish — crustaceans (including a krill), beautiful medusae [jellyfish], giant ostracods ... cuttlefish, nemertians.'[9]

Sir Douglas was the first to lend a hand, but this did not always meet the approval of the Captain: 'He [Davis] sees me doing things about the ship. ... He said yesterday after I had been working long hours on the big winch with a gang of staff "You make yourself into a regular boatswain. Why don't you get somebody else to do that?" My experience is that under these conditions to get a job like that done properly one must take a hand.'[10] Alf clearly recalled his leader's willingness to help out:

> When I was taking samples from the platform Mawson would be working up on the forehead part of the ship and turn on the steam, and I am sure that had I fallen ill for any length of time he would have been the most likely person to step in and carry out the water analysis. I would have discussions with him in connection with the running of the sampling bottles and that sort of thing, but in most cases we knew jolly well what we were supposed to be doing, and once Mawson decided we'd run a station then we'd all go to our various jobs and go through with it. He was a serious and fairly quiet person, but quite sociable and certainly a great leader.

Soon after the full oceanographic program was under way the *Discovery* had to deviate from its course in order to find the safest passage. Entering the pack ice left a lasting impression on Alf:

> We sighted our first iceberg early December and ran our first deep-sea station a few days later. Within a couple of days we entered the pack. This was an indication that it was likely to be a season of heavy sea-ice as we were some 300 miles from the coast, and before mid December the ice became impenetrable to the south, forcing us to turn south west and then west but we were soon stopped by very heavy pack. It was now apparent that we had little chance of reaching Gaussberg and were using up coal needed to reach our main objective — Enderby Land. In fact we were more or less following the track along which the *Challenger* cruised towards Gaussberg in 1874. Our vessel stopped for an oceanographical station surrounded by bergs of all shapes and sizes, and while we were aware that the pack was closing in the sight of so many crabeater seals tobogganing over the ice, whales breaching and Emperor penguins basking on the floes took our minds away from the encroaching hazards.
>
> On a lighter note, Eric Douglas and Doc Ingram celebrated their birthdays on the same day. As far as I remember this was about the time of our first deep-sea station. I shared with Douglas on the first voyage and what a hell of a din the officers and scientists made singing very early that morning outside our cabin. We then joined the happy troubadours to sing Happy Birthday to Ingram.

Harold Fletcher noted that there were more celebrations during the evening of 6 December: 'Before retiring, Hurley and Moyes, with great ceremony, produced two bottles of port and the birthday boys were toasted until the supply gave out. Doc Ingram was again suffering from the pangs of seasickness. … Never losing his sense of humour he simply retired to a quiet spot until he recovered.'[11]

The near-impenetrable heavy pack and temperatures below -10°C, combined with high wind speed, resulted in spray blown off the sea freezing immediately on contact with Scott's old ship. 'De-icing the vessel took some time,' said Alf. 'We were on the floe for the icing ship operations helping the crew—it was jolly cold; it's fair to say that the tools we had for the job were pretty basic, not like the de-icing methods used today. The gangways and railings were covered with ice, which made it very tricky to move around safely and I recall that Davis and his men had difficulty releasing the anchors.' De-icing was important as a build-up of too much ice on deck machinery and rescue equipment such as lifeboats and other installations on board could have caused the *Discovery* to capsize.

Icebound (Photo: Frank Hurley)

*

Mawson sent a wireless message about the ship's potentially dangerous route as she avoided 'belts of drifting grave-yard ice, result of heavy pressure during winter upon floe-ice, crumpling and over-thrusting it, so that surface rafts studded with innumerable vertical slabs not unlike tombstones. Regions subjected to such conditions of intense ice pressure as evidenced here are graveyards of many fine polar vessels.'[12] By noon 13 December both the weather and ice conditions had deteriorated. Later in the day Sir Douglas sent a radio message to the Prime Minister outlining the situation: 'Blizzard commenced this morning and the ice gripped the ship closely, even water between rafts froze. This evening when [it] could no longer be doubted that we are tightly held at pleasure and mercy of the ice, only the most optimistic could remain cheerful. Even those bright souls lost much of their buoyancy when realising that it is both Friday and 13th of month.'[13] News of this difficult period appeared some days later in newspapers across the globe on Boxing Day headed 'THE DISCOVERY. Heavy Pack Ice. Progress Impeded.':

> The day following 'Black Friday,' December 13, heavy snow fell and an attempt was made to escape from the ice embrace, but this proved abortive. On December 15 the weather cleared by the afternoon, when we made a determined and successful effort to escape to lead situated two miles distant. Latitude 65°S was reached, where we met an impenetrable pack. On December 16 we retreated north and west along leads; the brilliant sunshine scintillating from varied surfaces of ice rafts and bergs offered Captain Hurley, our photographer, unexcelled opportunities. We passed tabular bergs four miles long and 90 feet high [14]

Press rights were shared between Australia, the United Kingdom and North America. The Hearst Press offer to Mawson of $US 40,000 for exclusive press rights during the first voyage for the United States of America and Canada was far higher than those of other countries. One condition that Randolph Hearst insisted on, as early as May 1929, was that the 'time of release of news to be co-ordinated as between Australia, America and Great Britain to avoid leakages. Messages to be published exactly as received without additions or omissions.'[15]

In a letter dated 19 September 1929 Casey informed Prime Minister Bruce of the London *Times*' 'Sale of Press Rights': 'I hear by telephone from the *Times* that they have completed the following agreements for Sir Douglas Mawson's press material: 'South America: *La Nacion*, £200; South Africa: The *Argus* group, £150; India: The *Statesman*, £100; Norway: *Aftenposten*, £50; Austria: *Neue Freie Presse*, £25; Spain: *El Sol*, £50; Holland: *Telegraaf*, £50. ... The list is not yet complete, and they expect to be able to place the material at about £50 in several other countries.'[16]

'We never really knew just how much news was being sent, but Sir Douglas was apparently transmitting messages to papers across the world,' pondered Alf. 'As far as the people on board like me were concerned, all we knew was that Mawson was sending information to Australia and that it was going into the Australian Press.' Many parts of the world were following the voyage of the *Discovery*, which had by this time entered uncharted waters.

It was now the moment for Campbell and Douglas to unpack and assemble the De Haviland Gipsy Moth seaplane. 'Today a start was made on unpacking the aeroplane and rapid progress has been made on what the pilots say will be a four-day job,' recorded Simmers; 'She is painted a vivid yellow. Fitted with an 85-100 HP engine, floats, and special skis for landing on ice. She is capable of a speed of 90 mph and on her 19 gallons of petrol has a range of

400 miles.'[17] Because of *Discovery*'s very limited storage space the top portion of the plane had to be housed separately from the undercarriage, necessitating a couple of hours work prior to each flight in order to bolt the under-carriage in position. Well before departure, Sir Douglas had briefed Squadron Leader Drummond about his flying program for the expedition:

> The flying proposed is not in the nature of long-distance stunts as Byrd and Wilkins are committed to, but are to be short reconnaissance flights extending to no great distance from the vessel. For instance, ascents to 10,000 ft from the vessel when in pack ice would yield very valuable information, both regarding the distribution of the pack ice for navigation purposes and from such a height long stretches of coast could be roughly plotted on the map. ... A short flight with the plane, not exceeding 100 miles, from the vessel would be immensely important in roughly charting the coastline of the continent.[18]

Mawson was anxious to see the plane wing its way in search of new lands as he was aware that soon any ice-free strips in the pack would be completely frozen, making it impossible for the Gipsy Moth to taxi. December 19, Sir Douglas noted that 'airmen busy on aeroplane which was set up by late evening, but much to do yet to secure it adequately against blizzards.'[19] Work continued on the Moth. Windy conditions persisted and so any attempt to fly had to be postponed. *Discovery*'s rigging posed a problem as the plane had to be hoisted and suspended from the derrick before lowering it overboard on to an ice-free runway. Campbell or Douglas would be in the pilot's seat during the delicate operation to help manoeuvre the aeroplane, as the slightest impact with any of the ship's rigging or structures could result in very serious damage to the fuselage. Preparing the Moth for a flight required teamwork and much care and time on the part of the aviators, crew and scientists. The pilots had been fully occupied assisting the scientists with their various tasks, but after nearly 10 weeks at sea they were more than ready for take-off. Eric Douglas last piloted a Moth soon after leaving the *Nestor* when he 'went out to the drome, had 35 min in Gipsy Moth over Cape Town', and then had another opportunity to fly just before going south when he 'went out to the aerodrome and had 30 min in Gipsy Moth and flew down over Muizenberg near Simmons Bay.'[20]

On the morning of 22 December 'the water pool in which ship is has closed up much in night, pack everywhere is tighter,' recorded Sir Douglas. Nevertheless there were great expectations on deck that Campbell and Douglas were making final preparations and checks to take the seaplane for its inaugural Antarctic flight. The launch was lowered to be at the ready if required. Mawson's diary jottings testify that the day did not go exactly to plan:

> We are hanging about in water pool waiting for airmen to complete and ascend. The day is magnificent for it — scarcely a cloud in sky and only faint S wind. But the pool is contracting rapidly. The airmen advise that in about two hours they will be ready. Balloon sent up accidentally lost at about 15,000 ft. Showed that up to almost 12,000 ft the air moving to N & W above that, current moving south, probably SE. An Emperor penguin and several Adélies about. 2 pm: By lunch the airmen had not got ready, but promised to be ready immediately after. The pool has grown so small that they may not be able to take off — ice rafts moving N under influence of wind. 4 pm: Capt Davis moved ship about 1 mile south to larger pool which developed. Airmen got ready soon after 2 pm, but could not get engine started. They worked all afternoon till now when they give up till tomorrow. They could not start engine — too cold.[21]

Swinging the Gipsy Moth outboard (Photo: Frank Hurley)

*

Alf remembered the first attempt to have the Gipsy Moth airborne: 'A few of us were in the motor launch with the Dux ready to help protect the seaplane from any damage when it was lowered on to the water. After waiting a couple of hours for its departure Sir Douglas suggested we shoot a few birds for the biologists' collections. We got quite a variety, including an Emperor penguin that was destined to provide fresh meat for Christmas dinner. Later Davis gave the order to hoist the launch on board.' That same evening Mawson observed that the fog was coming from the south with cold air, which he believed was a 'land breeze. Same happened last night,' he wrote. 'There is a regular nightly land breeze — we cannot be far from land.'[22]

Sir Douglas' observations were on track as the following morning Hurley and Davis sighted 'a dome-topped structure' from the crow's nest about 30 miles south-west, which they agreed could be an island. A couple of attempts to get the Moth in the air were unsuccessful and further efforts to get her airborne were put on hold. For Simmers, the increase in wind velocity, the diminishing visibility together with changing cloud formations, all pointed to an oncoming blizzard: 'It has been an interesting time for me watching the complete approach of the blizzard from the first wisps of cirrus cloud to the north about noon through the various phases of cirrus and stratus to the ice crystals which have just ushered in the blizzard proper. ... All morning the ship presented the most beautiful sight imaginable — the rigging all being covered with a ¾ inch coating of rime deposited from the dense fog which we had all night.'[23] The ship's position at noon was 66° 22′S, 73° 01′E, and Davis proposed to take her into pack then go west, but before he could do so the snow thickened and the blizzard was upon them.[24]

Christmas — 66° 28′S, 73° 28′E

The *Discovery* was now slowly steaming in the lee of 'several very long tabular bergs about 40 feet high.'[1] 'The blizzard continued to hamper our progress and we seemed to be going round and round in circles; I don't think any of us really worried about it too much,' reflected Alf. 'There was much activity in the wardroom and as I recall most of Christmas Eve was spent tracking down boxes containing special foods and parcels for the coming festivities.' 'In the evening we crowded into one of the cabins and had a bit of a get together — didn't think so many could ever cram into one cabin,' wrote Simmers, 'but they seemed always to be able to make room for just one more and moderately comfortable in the heat. The singing wasn't very tuneful but it was streets better than if Babe [Marr] hadn't been there. He can play, it seems, any and every conceivable instrument.'[2] Sir Douglas was also looking forward to events the following day: 'Have spent much time today getting out stores for Christmas and making up a menu which Hurley is preparing in good style, by photographic process. After dinner tonight I had the luxury of a wash in tub in engine room.'[3]

Just a few hours into Christmas Day the deck and masts of the *Discovery* were covered with a heavy mantle of snow. For Alf, 'the ship looked rather ghostly, as though Jack Frost had visited her in the early hours. I didn't get much sleep as Campbell roped me into helping him deliver some amusing gifts to the team. With a bit of help from the officers and crew we disguised ourselves as Santa's helpers. Of course I didn't mind, I'd give anything a go. Somehow I don't think the 6 am call was appreciated by everyone but it was good fun.' From Ingram's notes it would seem that Santa himself made his rounds an hour later in order to make sure that everyone was ready for the festive day ahead: 'Awakened at 7 am by Hurley dressed as Father Xmas with a large beard of cotton and wool. From his sack he produced for me a bag of nuts.'[4]

*

The old vessel was a real warhorse and Captain Davis knew her history. The *Discovery* was icebound in McMurdo Sound for the Christmas of 1902 and that of 1903 and was accustomed to being the venue for such celebratory occasions. On 25 December 1902 Scott and his men were on a sledging trip to Cape Crozier; however, in 1903 they just managed to return to the ship on Christmas Eve from a final long sledging journey south. In *The Voyage of the Discovery*, Scott writes: 'Ford had become cook for the few who remained on board, and that, as a result of studying Mrs. Beeton's cookery book, he was achieving dishes of a more savoury nature than we had thought possible with the resources at our command. It was unfortunate that the highest development of the cooking art should have occurred at this season, as it found us too morally weak to resist its allurements, and, as a consequence, we suffered from the most violent indigestion.'[5]

Indigestion was also suffered by some members of the party, according to a communication sent by Sir Douglas to the *Times* and other newspapers:

> Though we are far within icefields never before traversed, and upon the margin of an unknown land, Christmas Day for us lost nothing of its festive character, thanks to our many friends in the world outside. On our breakfast table were bundles of wireless messages of good cheer. Dinner was made cheerful and full of fun by personal presents and table decorations from Australia. On our elaborate menu figured products of famous manufacturing firms of Great Britain and Australia, but the principal item was a strictly local production — namely, an emperor penguin, which was voted by all quite equal to grouse. Indeed, the dinner was so successful that Dr Ingram is now attending several of the ship's company who dined well though not wisely.[6]

Hurley's souvenir menu featured portraits of Sir Douglas and Captain Davis superimposed on a photograph of pack ice, and the Christmas dinner courses listed would have delighted the most discerning epicurean.

'The bird itself weighed almost 30 kilograms,' noted Fletcher and 'more than five kilograms of dark-coloured flesh was later taken from the breast by the ship's cook.'[7] There would have also been generous helpings of dessert as the food inventory lists two dozen cases of Christmas puddings each containing 12 puddings in 4 lb. tins. The Christmas cake that Mawson noted as being 'a very fine one in 2 decks with marzipan between, decorated with boomerangs, emus, kangaroos, holly, etc.,'[8] was made by Ellis Brothers, well-known caterers in Adelaide, and could easily have been baked in *Discovery*'s kitchen as there was a good supply of marzipan and every dried fruit, spice and essence imaginable as well as 49 lbs. of ginger in the larder.[9]

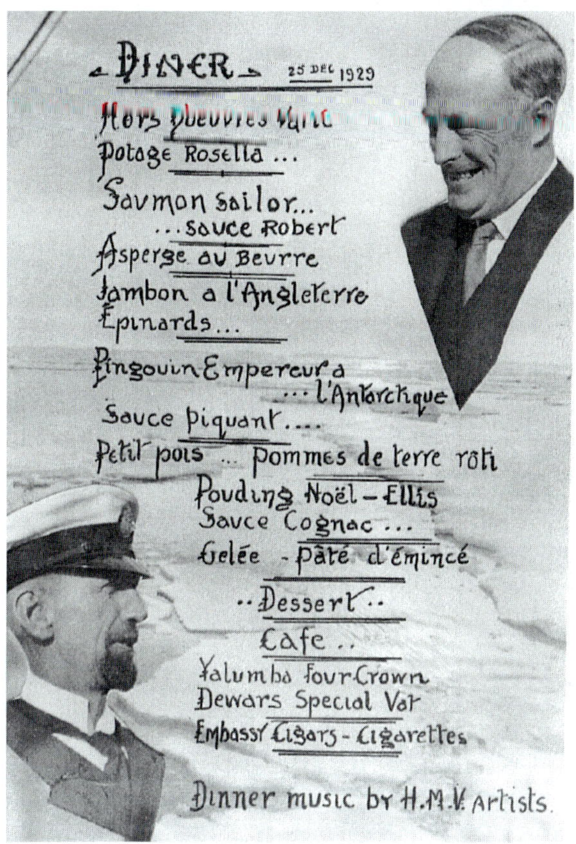

DINER 25 DEC 1929

Hors Oeuvres Varie
Potage Rosella …
Saumon sailor…
… Sauce Robert
Asperge au Beurre
Jambon a l'Angleterre
Epinards…
Pingouin Empereur a
… l'Antarctique
Sauce Piquant….
Petit pois … pommes de terre roti
Pouding Noël – Ellis
Sauce Cognac …
Gelée - pâté d'émincé
.. Dessert ..
Cafe ..
Yalumba four Crown
Dewars Special Vat
Embassy Cigars - Cigarettes

Dinner music by H.M.V. Artists.

Christmas Dinner Menu 1929

All the cooking for the ship's company was done on an open coal range below deck and the cook, before joining the expedition, had been working on a Union Castle liner and so knew 'how to make a cast-off sea boot taste like fried sole.'[10] 'I certainly had no complaints about the food being dished up,' said Alf, 'in fact I was surprised how long the kitchen was able to last out the fresh provisions. Of course today this would not happen, but once we got into the pack ice our menu was supplemented by seal fritters, whale steaks and penguin hash. I must say I have always had a soft spot for penguins and especially the Adélies, but I do recall Christmas on the *Discovery* and have to admit I found the penguin to be very tasty indeed.'

The scientific staff and ship's officers decorated the wardroom with streamers, then a huge Christmas cake was positioned in the middle of the table around which many parcels were placed.[11] Fletcher documented the Yuletide festivities that followed:

> At midday all hands, except those on watch, gathered in the wardroom. The cake was cut by Sir Douglas, glasses charged and toasts drunk to the King, and success of the expedition. Captain Davis was in a very cheery mood and read wireless messages from Lord Passfield, the Antarctic Committee in London, and Mr Scullin, Prime Minister of Australia.
>
> First sitting of Christmas Dinner was at 12.45 pm. A beautifully prepared souvenir menu was presented to each member as he was seated.
>
> Commander Moyes, dressed in full commissionaire's uniform complete with medals — one for each year of undetected crime — assisted with drinks and smokes, and was a tremendous success. He also acted as conductor of the orchestra played on the gramophone. Presents from pupils of the Woodlands Church of England Girls' Grammar School of Adelaide were addressed specifically to expedition members and distributed by Sir Douglas. In no time the wardroom resembled a jumble sale as we rummaged through parcels containing tin whistles, bottles of sweets, books and all types of novelties. It was a wonderful and very much appreciated thought of the pupils.[12]

'I was at the first sitting, but a few of us stayed on for the second and joined in the singing,' reminisced Alf:

> While we were still around the table suddenly smoke started to come out of Hurley's ears; he was a born comedian and was always carrying out some sort of mischievous prank to brighten up the day. Well of course it was all done with tubes hidden in his clothing. A lot of his jokes depended on smoke or flour, or something like that through rubber tubes. Then there was a sort of impromptu stage show and Falla dressed up as a waitress and had us all in stitches as he handed out smokes and drinks. Hurley was busy with his flashlight. By this time I would say we were a little tipsy, and what with the smoke from cigars, cigarettes and the flashlight, the wardroom was beginning to look like a tavern.

By all accounts there were good supplies of tobacco, wine and spirits on board: 21 boxes of cigars, nearly 300 lbs. of tobacco and 45,000 cigarettes, which included Three Castles, Gold Flake, Capstans and Australian brands. While bottles of Yalumba's 4-Crown Port graced the festive table, the ship's supply list also included a small cargo of rum, whisky, brandy and champagne.[13]

Christmas Day 1929 in Antarctica (Photo: Frank Hurley)

Fletcher had just retired to his bunk feeling a little fragile after smoking a second cigar when mid-afternoon Sir Douglas called the biologists and zoologists on deck to carry out the first Monegasque dredge of the voyage. The trawl was taken in 700 fathoms on a 2200-metre line and drew a good catch. Mawson recorded that there was a 'fair abundance of organisms in it but most of them much crushed by stones. Washed out material after tea. Echinoids [sea urchins], brittle stars, pyenogonids [sea spiders], holothurians [sea cucumbers], red prawns, a tiny limpet [sea snail], etc. Stones up to 2 ft diam, manganese stained.'[14]

*

'Sometimes,' recalled Alf, 'I'd go aloft, look out over the frozen sea and then at the activities on deck; there were moments when I felt like pinching myself as it was hard to believe that I was looking down at Scott's ship. More unbelievable for me was that I was on it and was in fact a part of an incredible journey. Mind you, when I was up on the rigging I'd be hanging on for dear life, so much so that it was surprising I didn't bring the mast down':

I think it would be fair to say that for most of us there were times, especially over Christmas, when we yearned to be able to have a chat with family and friends to share our experiences. Mawson rounded up a great team and we all got on with each other very well, and I found Eric Douglas to be a very congenial cabin mate. He often helped me with deck operations connected with the vertical station when working the Nansen-Pettersson bottles. He and Campbell were forever tinkering with the Moth on the upper deck and sometimes I'd give them a hand in the evening when I'd finished in the lab. December's continual adverse flying conditions must have been frustrating for them; there was much excitement on board and mounting anticipation each day that they would soon be airborne.

Boxing Day and the *Discovery* 'was blindly groping about in a maze of ice.' Crew aloft could make out land about 30 miles away, but it was impossible to navigate the vessel through the fast ice. 'It is the most desolate spot I have been in,' remarked Davis. 'Even the seals are not able to live here. ... The land is inaccessible and the pressure evident in all the floes makes this area a good one not to get caught in by the moving pack. I am glad after all our battle with the pack we have got a sight of the land, although it is very disappointing not to be able to get nearer to it. ... Farthest South at 11.15 p.m. Lat 67° 00'S, Long 72° 10'E.'[15]

Despite the almost ice-locked position of the ship the oceanographical program continued with Alf's hydrographical stations as well as a number of soundings and dredges. Mawson recorded in detail an incident that very nearly cost the life of the scientific staff:

> After station dredged 1100 metre wire out — large Monegasque trawl; ... Hurley hauled net in after 20 minutes on bottom, during most of which time anchored. ... In upper part of net a mass of life uncrushed, a truly wonderful haul — long-legged opiuroids [brittle starfish] doing their best to escape as trawl remained in water during time of hitching on to derrick. ... [Haul] so heavy that great trouble lifting on derrick. ... All our men and some of the crew on the hauling rope could scarcely budge it. It was then taken to winch and lifted considerably by it. I marvelled that the rope lifted it at all for it certainly was a great weight, quite 2½-3 tons. I had explained to Davis that as it came out of the water it would be heavier (non-floated) and that the extra weight might be critical. ... I did, however, call out to Johnston to get from under as [it] was dangerous. Then down came the derrick, carried away from the mast. Fortunately nobody was killed, but it lost us almost all the catch.[16]

'Yes, we were all helping on the rope as we usually did with a haul, but this one weighed tons. We were lucky, but as the derrick dropped the boom knocked off Johnston's headgear missing his head by a fraction of an inch — it was such a close shave with death,' recalled Alf. 'Everyone was rather shaken not to mention Johnston. The deck was strewn with octopi, worms and other marine life and we were slipping and sliding all over the place to recuperate what was left of the catch that mostly got away.'

New Year's Eve Mawson sent a message to Henderson informing him that the year had ended on a successful note: 'Campbell and Douglas ascending height 5,000 feet sighted to south at distance about 50 miles what appears to be low hilly ice-covered land.'[17] Years later Eric Douglas recounted this important event:[18]

> Stuart Campbell and I went off for two reasons, one was to test the aeroplane and see how it flew in that type of region, and the other was to make it an ice reconnaissance flight so we could help to guide the ship through. But to our amazement when we climbed up to about five thousand feet there to the south-west we could see jagged black peaks sticking up … no sign of any snow or ice, and standing startling clear from the frozen sea. That was probably the first time that human eyes had seen land in that part. We almost jumped out of the aeroplane. It was absolutely terrific.

*

New Year's Day 1929 the cook prepared a special dinner at the end of which 'Sir Douglas produced a bottle of rum and toasts were drunk to all and sundry.' It was then announced that the Antarctic Circle Concert Party (ACCP) would shortly entertain members of the wardroom with a program of original songs such as "On the *Discovery*", "The Intrepid Antarctic Explorer" and "The Captain's Lament" and two sketches: "Hawaiian Island" and "Shooting a Trawl". A rendition of the "Haka" by the ACCP would be a highlight and performed by Falla, Doc, Fletcher, Eric Douglas and Campbell. The concert was well received and all performers given a standing ovation.[19]

'It was a jolly good show,' recalled Alf. 'There were a number of topical songs, but the one that made an impression of me was "The Captain's Lament" as it sort of summed up life on board our ship in Scott's time and in ours, but in a light-hearted manner':

> Once I went exploring in the old *Discovery*
>
> We had one ruddy scientist and seamen 53

We didn't have an aeroplane or echo sounder then
We didn't have any long-haired sheep in a wooden pen.

Chorus:
The sea we sailed like Captain Cook
Our stars we knew like a ruddy book
We ate salt horse and we liked it very well
In 40 years things have gone to hell.

We didn't have Yalumba or Tomargo squash
We didn't have hot water and we never had a wash
We didn't play with plankton nets or shoot the Otter trawls
We didn't dredge with Monegasques and make an utter balls.

We didn't have an engine to help us on our way
We didn't let the scientist have stations every day
We didn't count the dust motes or let balloons go free
We only sailed like Captain Cook upon the wide blue sea.

But now those days are over and seamen six have we
Thirteen ruddy scientists who do not know the sea
They say all sorts of stupid things which pain me in the head
So now I think I'll leave the bridge and make my way to bed.[20]

The day ended with much cheer when, as Sir Douglas wrote, the 'good health of Mr MacRobertson, to whose munificence the Expedition is chiefly indebted for its existence, [was] drunk in heartiest manner in good Yalumba Port.'[21]

Simmers' final entry for the year seemed to reflect the general mood on board: 'The evening did the day full justice being the most wonderful imaginable. No wind, a glassy sea, a few pieces of loose ice and that calm glittering expanse of fast ice over which a low golden sun faintly shone. Who wouldn't come down here to see such sights as these'![22]

Toasting loved ones back home, 1st January 1930. From left to right (standing):--Johnston, Williams, Steward, Simmers, Child, Fletcher, Hurley; (seated): — Marr, MacKenzie, Howard, Falla, Moyes, Colbeck, Ingram, Douglas Mawson (Photo: Frank Hurley)

MASTER VERSUS COMMANDER

Zigzagging through heavy ice floes in an attempt to find new lands was now having a serious impact on the diminishing fuel supply and was threatening not only Sir Douglas' commission for the Crown, but also causing tension between the ship's master and the commander of the expedition. Mawson was anxious: 'Whilst we waited for something to turn up we burnt 2½ tons of coal per day, and our stay in the Antarctic was measured in terms of coal; whatever we did now must be in concord with our obligations in regard to Enderby Land where we must make our most concerted effort to reach land and raise the flag.'[1]

Early 1 January 1930 the heavy pack ice was closing in once again. Davis was cautious: 'At 1 p.m. we stood to NE in a big pool of open water. Better steam a few miles back than stick in one place for three weeks. ... I have spent a happier New Year's Day than today, which seems to be the culmination of a long series of set backs which I hope are going to end soon,' recorded Davis.[2]

For Mawson, it seemed a good idea to 'spend 1½ hours' with the Captain and try to sort out a few problems. 'Davis is a very old friend, and am loath to break off my patience for am certain he is mentally strained. ... At meal times he rarely says a word throughout a meal [and] it is the rarest thing that he ever says a word to any member of the staff.'[3]

Nevertheless there was a strong bond between them. Davis returned to Commonwealth Bay to bring Mawson home after his harrowing ordeal during his 1911-1914 expedition; he was Sir Douglas' best man, and he also rescued Mawson from a crevasse during Ernest Shackleton's 1907-1909 *Nimrod* expedition. Shackleton recorded the incident:

> The crevasse was bridged with a suitable piece of sawn timber, and Davis, with that spirit of thoroughness which characterises all his work, promptly had himself lowered down the crevasse. On reaching the bottom he transferred the rope by which he had been lowered to Mawson, and with a long pull and a strong pull and a pull altogether, the company of the *Nimrod* soon had Mawson safe on top, none the worse for the accident with the exception that his back was

slightly bruised. As soon as the rope was cast free from Mawson, it was let down again for Davis, and presently he, too, was safely on top.[4]

'None of us was aware at the time that there was so much friction between the captain and our leader until many years after the expedition when their diaries were published,' recollected Alf:

> We all knew Davis was worried about being locked in the ice with not enough coal to get us out, and Mawson was anxious to carry out his oceanographical program and chart new territory. As far as we were concerned we had our work and answered to Sir Douglas, while the officers and crew had their duties and answered to Davis. Yes, I suppose Davis was a bit brusque at times in his relations with other people, but on the whole he kept to himself. I can't recall having any discussions with him. He wasn't going around saying do you want to have a talk. It was strange though because whenever the ship was in dangerous ice conditions his mood would change from being rather morose to almost jovial, and you'd hear him going around in his cabin singing to himself.

Coal was indeed the main bone of contention between them. Mawson had a scientific program to carry out and orders to claim new lands. Any delay obviously frustrated him: 'All day long we have slowly steamed up and down the lake in lee of large shelf icebergs. Davis could save some of this steaming and thus coal.'[5] Davis was aware that coal stocks were gradually being depleted due to the fact that once the *Discovery* was in the vicinity of East Antarctica's Enderby Land she was constantly buffeted by gale-force winds and quite often had to fight her way out of the ice pack. Davis recorded that such conditions challenged him on Christmas Eve when a 'portion of the pack between the bergs broke away and drifted down our pool. It was a difficult job at times in the strong breeze to steer clear of the pieces, but we managed to do so, steaming up and down in the open water.'[6] Days later and the vessel was 'making very little headway against the wind,' noted Davis. 'Our coal is gradually getting used up and very little being done, and for a midsummer blow this one has been a lasting breeze.'[7]

Davis and his crew spent most of New Year's Day trying to steer the ship away from the heavy pack. For Mawson, the day was a mixture of work and celebration:

> We had a fine dinner at midday with Yalumba. The cooks made [a] fine menu, credit to them. Also at tea this evening they produced a splendid 2-tier cake made on board, beautifully iced. ... At afternoon tea we had a fine cake sent to Hurley from Mrs Tom Baker. Marr goes on with the dredge, Hurley helps.

> ... Capt D came out on deck for a time after tea and talked to Moyes and Johnston in a friendly way. Evidently my discussion with him today has done [some] good.[8]

However, tirades between master and commander continued, but for the most part it appears to have been a private war confined to note exchanges or to their respective journals. Davis believed that 'with a scientific man as leader of an expedition, the master of the exploring vessel is constantly pressed to engage in risky adventures, which if successful are hailed as great evidence of the leader's capacity; but if in the end they finish in disaster, then your scientific head disclaims all responsibility.'[9] For Mawson, 'Davis talked a lot of rubbish and blasphemed some. All the time he was in the wrong. I had asked him merely to steam along edge of pack to east to be ready to go south through any avenue presenting as soon as weather improved.'[10] Both came out equal players in their fencing duels on paper.

*

It would be just a matter of time before the *Discovery* and the *Norwegia* crossed paths. Two days before Mawson received a radiogram on 2 January 1930 from Casey that the Norwegians were claiming Antarctic territory it was announced in the London *Times*, via their correspondent in Oslo, that 'a strip of 100 kilometres (62 miles) of new land was discovered between Enderby Land and Kemp Land. ... The wireless message received from Captain Rüser Larsen, dated from the *Norwegia*, December 29, reports that all are well on board.'[11] In the following days more cables arrived with reports that the Norwegian vessel was in the same sector of the Antarctic Continent as Mawson. In one of the telegrams sent to Sir Douglas the wishes of the Department of External Affairs in Canberra were made very clear: 'Government has decided that you should take no cognisance of any acts of *Norwegia* in raising Norwegian flag and should carry out your original instructions concerning raising British flag at every point where it is possible to do so.'[12] Now more than ever it was imperative that the aviators were airborne again.

Early 5 January Alf carried out another successful hydrological station, this time drawing the 'deepest water sample from near bottom at 2000 metres. The vertical nets show that water here very rich in life — krill very abundant, salps rich in surface waters, say down to 150 metres.'[13] Campbell made preparations before breakfast to take the commander for a reconnaissance flight, but drifting ice rafts delayed the trip until after lunch. Sir Douglas noted that he felt cramped as the Moth was heavily laden with wireless gear which did not work, possibly due to a wrong wire connection:

> At 600 ft I got a similar view of the land to south as had from the barrel [crow's nest] last night; ... As we rose, a wider and wider view of the land unfolded. A black, rugged mountain appeared to the east of the rising plateau slopes. Tips of peaks rose from the plateau elsewhere. Rock mountain outcrops appeared at intervals right around to even north of west. A few dimly seen black mountain masses showed up to extreme W.
>
> There is a definite shore, much of it apparently being rocky coast in height of summer but now some miles inland of sea front. ... About SSE some very large barrier bergs were jumbled together and aground off the coast. ... Between the ship and the fast-ice edge, say 15 miles of scattered pack, or pack with slack belts of easy ice through which the ship could certainly proceed. ... We flew about 10 miles over pack towards land. Peak on plateau to S of ship probably 15 miles inland and probably only 500 ft high above... . Height of plateau where rise may be 3000 ft, so total height of peak 3500 ft. The black mountains to east probably from 2000 to 3500 ft high.
>
> In air just over 1 hour; on arrival at ship plane taken on board and left on floats as hoped for another flight further to west tomorrow. Simmers, however, later reported conditions developing — suggestive of a blizzard coming soon. I anticipate sufficient warning if weather changes to get plane off floats.[14]

It had been a good day at the end of which Mawson managed to fit in a plankton station before going west. 'The evening was magnificent,' he noted. 'Placid water, scattered picturesque ice, plentiful Emperor penguins, Adélies, petrels of all sorts, seals (1 Leopard, a number of Crabeaters) on floes. ... We went slowly towards the sun, practically did not hit any ice rafts and went on for miles, making a little S of W.'[15]

'Once we got down among the bergs Hurley was working flat out,' recalled Alf:

> More often than not when I worked late Hurley would be in the darkroom developing rolls of films. Sometimes he'd call me in to have a look and say: 'What do you think of this one, Alfie'? It took me a couple of minutes to get accustomed to the dark; there were trays of various solutions and photographs hanging from lines all over his small area. He certainly went to great lengths to get a good shot. He'd be up in the crow's nest and if he couldn't get the right angle from there he would somehow lift his camera to the very tip of the mast on a pole and with a sort of mechanism would operate it from below. You would see him sitting on the tip of the jib boom precariously hanging over the ice floe

with his camera to get a close-up of a pod of Killer whales, a small colony of Adélies or a Leopard seal. He'd set up his 35 mm hand-crank movie camera on a tripod to capture the take-offs and landings of the Moth from the deck or from the launch. I think it's fair to say that Hurley took risks to take the most spectacular photograph he could. He'd jump from the launch on to the ice with his equipment to record anything that moved on the floe, and also to get shots of the *Discovery* to make her look isolated amid the hazards of the south.

Ice seascape, Crabeater seals and Adélie penguins (Photo: Frank Hurley)

The ship was, for the present, out of the ice pushing north and being constantly manoeuvred to dodge the loose pack drifting down. Gale-force winds, strong swell and poor visibility due to snow and low cloud not only banished any prospects of more flights, but were battering the Gipsy Moth: 'Cannot see far but ocean almost clear of ice,' noted Mawson. 'At 6.30 am ice from rigging commenced to fall down in large pieces and, for safety, men on deck needed iron helmets. A party did [their] best to save aeroplane wings by covering them with bagging, etc — the chart room mat was commandeered for this purpose but blew overboard immediately. Some holes, made in aeroplane wings, need repairing.'[16]

At last on 12 January the *Discovery* was moving along the pack edge. Mawson recorded that 'very large bergs' and a 'school of 50 Killer Whales' had been sighted by the morning watch. Later in the morning 'Mr Child report[ed] great extent [of] land to south' and by 12.30 'splendid land ice slopes to south … a number of rocky peaks seen protruding from the ice slopes to elevations of more than 3000 feet.' Finally the ship was travelling in sight of the coast. Mawson closed his jottings for the day with great anticipation: 'Late in evening Mr Child points out a black island ahead. … Island bearing N 89° W.'[17]

PROCLAIMING NEW LANDS

The *Discovery* forging a passage through loose pack ice to Proclamation Island. East Enderby Land, Antarctica (Photo: Frank Hurley)

Monday, 13 January 1930 was by all accounts a momentous day for Sir Douglas and his party. 'Many more days like today will be the death of me and more than the death of the rest of the shore party. And no wonder — unusual exertion and excitement,' noted Simmers; 'Black bare rock ahead was sighted last night and this morning at four we were standing off, quite close, and it looked the goods all right — one huge bare black rock and several lower and more distant ones that appeared to be part of the land while round about were some magnificent bergs and small ice-capped islets.'[1] Frenzied preparations for a landing were well under way by 5.30 am with Sir Douglas calling instructions for the scientists to have their equipment on deck ready to put in the motorboat. Fletcher noted that he was awakened by Sir Douglas shouting: 'Rise and shine, the shore party leaves in thirty minutes.'[2]

'We were all rather excited at the thought of at last landing on the Antarctic Continent,' recalled Alf, 'but also a little frustrated as there was a mad rush to get ready at the crack of dawn, and then we didn't leave the ship until around mid-morning. Sir Douglas requested that Simmers and I run a full set of magnetic dips and force determinations once on shore.' The landing party consisted of Mawson, Hurley, Johnston, Moyes, Marr, Ingram, Falla, Fletcher, Ritchie Simmers and Alf Howard. Simmers described the landing, noting that Stuart Campbell and Eric Douglas were unable to leave the vessel as they were still repairing the Moth's wings, which had been damaged in a recent storm:

> The motor boat loaded with all the scientific party, … a flag, flagpole and proclamation, copies of God Save the King and three cheers, and a heap of photographic and scientific gear pushed off for what Sir Douglas had decided to name Proclamation Island (65° 21′S, 53° 10′E).' It was an uneventful run — uneventful if one excludes an engine jib necessitating oars which soon brought us to the shore. … Sir Douglas jumped ashore — the first of the BANZARE on the Antarctic terra firma. … While the remainder of the party laboured up to the top of the island to raise the flag, Alf and I remained behind dip circling.[3]

From Mawson's jottings it appears that a variety of marine inhabitants had already proclaimed the rocky outpost and thereabout as their territory:

> About 20 seals seen on the ice in neighbourhood of the island. Also an Emperor Penguin and numbers of Adélies. Silver-grey, Antarctic, Snow, Wilson Petrels and Cape Pigeons playing about. Several skuas also. As [we] neared shore on SW end of island found large areas of lower slopes covered with Adélie Penguins. Landed and whilst main party hastened to summit of island to fly the flag, Simmers and Howard ran a magnetic station. We ascended through the rookery. … Very steep climb to top, but rewarded by magnificent view over grounded bergs — over 100 large ones in sight.[4]

Hurley was last to make it to the rock's summit 850 feet above sea level as he had taken a short cut up one of the steep sides and was found 'in an awkward position, unable to move in any direction' until he was relieved of his cumbersome camera equipment. Everyone then set to work stacking rocks to construct a cairn with the flagpole secured in the middle. A tablet of wood on which Hurley had carved 'The British Flag was hoisted and British Sovereignty asserted on 13th Jan., 1930' was attached to the pole facing south. The Union Jack was raised, and at noon Sir Douglas read the Proclamation, which was followed by three cheers for the King and God Save the King. There was, as Fletcher noted, a slight technical hitch in the ceremonial proceedings when Sir Douglas was about to read the handwritten Proclamation. 'Unfortunately, it had been unthinkingly sealed in a canister, now buried deep in the cairn. However, with recourse to his memory and promptings from Moyes and Hurley, he was almost word perfect as he repeated the Proclamation.'[5]

> In the name of His Majesty King George the Fifth, King of Great Britain, Ireland and the British Dominions beyond the Seas, Emperor of India.
>
> Where I have it in command from His Majesty King George the Fifth to assert the sovereign rights of His Majesty over British land discoveries met with in Antarctica.
>
> Now, therefore, I, Sir Douglas Mawson, do hereby proclaim and declare to all men that, from and after the date of these presents, the full sovereignty of the territory of Enderby Land, Kemp Land, MacRobertson Land together with off-lying Islands as located in our charts constituting a sector of the Antarctic Regions lying between Longitudes 73° East of Greenwich and 47° East of Greenwich and South of Latitude 65° vests in His Majesty King George the Fifth, His Heirs and successors for ever. Given under my hand on board the Exploring vessel *Discovery* now lying off the coast of this annexed land, in Latitude 65° 50′S. Longitude 53° 30′E. The Thirteenth Day of January, 1930.
>
> Witness
>
> [*Signed*]
> J.K. DAVIS
> Master S.Y. *Discovery*
> 13.1.1930
>
> [*Signed*]
> DOUGLAS MAWSON
> Commanding Antarctic Expedition
> 13.1.1930 [6]

After Alf and Simmers had finished their work there was time to become acquainted with the locals: 'There must have been tens of thousands of Adélie penguins in the colony all squawking and waddling up and down the slopes and around the base of the island,' recalled Alf. Our presence didn't seem to bother these comics at all, they simply went about their business building nests with small stones carried in their beaks.' Simmers was also fascinated by the myriads of penguins with their tuxedo shirt fronts and white-ringed eyes: 'Mating was going on in all stages of advancement, from the preliminary overtures of the single males to the couples with chicks some only weeks old. Most of the birds had chicks — fat, dark, ugly, fluffy balls of quarrelsomeness — while some were still sitting. On my approach they rose upright, heads back in rowdy indignation, which increased on closer approach to open warfare. I received many pecks on my thick trousers.'[7]

The landing party gathered a variety of Antarctic rocks, which included some beautiful garnet-studded specimens of various sizes and colours. Fletcher recorded how he and Falla came across a small colony of Antarctic petrels just 30 metres below the summit: 'Nests were situated between rocks on fairly level, narrow ledges on the steeply sloping sides of the island. … The only other records of nesting Antarctic petrels were made during Mawson's 1911-14 expedition when colonies were found at Cape Hunter, Adélie Land and Haswell Island near Queen Mary Land.'[8] Nests of cape pigeons and snow petrels were also seen on the upper ledges. Being a geologist Sir Douglas naturally took great interest in the various rock formations and specimens:

> On way down I collected quantity of rocks, making very heavy load. Had rucksack of rocks, camera case with rocks inside, rocks in pocket and hands, and pick. Had very arduous descent. … All upper slopes strewn with erratics. … On lower slopes rocks discoloured by guano obliterates obviousness of erratics. Also, probably, local ice on lower slopes for a time after recession of continental sheet would sweep erratics off lower slopes. Collected some algae and a few items from bay whilst embarking.[9]

Captain Davis was concerned about the landing party as the icescape was changing: 'They have been away four hours so I hope they will soon be back. They have no food or gear but seem to trust to Providence entirely.'[10] Mawson was also aware that it was time to return to the ship: 'The pack ice had closed around whilst we were ashore so that we [were] gradually becoming isolated from *Discovery*. On this account could no longer remain on island but need to push off and join ship. Launch broke down several times on way to ship.'[11] Davis decided to push the vessel through the pack between the grounded bergs in order to reach open water and then steam along the coast and complete the mapping of Enderby Land. 'The slow forge out through the brash was perhaps the most beautiful part of the whole journey so far and everyone just stood round drinking the exquisite scenery. The ice had taken on a gleaming silvery sheen, the wind had dropped. … The mate from the mast top counted 95 bergs — most of them grounded tabular in all states of weathering.'[12] Sir Douglas' entry at the end of the day was prophetic: 'In departing from here we hope to meet better landings to W, and in any case can fall back on this on return. In meantime it is important to push W to our limit of 40° E without delay, as Norwegians may be busy W of us.'

*

'I thought by this evening that after the last two and a half days we had run through the whole gamut of excitements but eight thirty brought a bombshell — the *Norwegia* has just been sighted by Mr Child,' began Simmers' entry on 14 January.[13] 'We all scrambled on deck and a few of us went aloft to get a better view,' recalled Alf; 'The *Norwegia* had two masts; it was ketch rigged and looked very small. The vessel was stationary with her derricks swung out which looked like she had stopped for a sounding or something like that. In Cape Town we had heard that the Norwegians were already in East Antarctica. Of course the newspapers immediately seized upon this as being a race between Mawson and Larsen to proclaim the same territory.'

There was much excitement on board as the *Discovery* had not been within sight of another ship since the *Kilfinora* in the Kerguelen Islands. MacKenzie wrote an excellent account of the meeting of the two polar ships where everything proceeded according to nautical etiquette:

> The two vessels steamed head on till about a mile separated them when both parted ¼ point, *Norwegia* passing under our lee now at a distance of 3 cables when colours were exchanged. *Discovery* then ran up T.D.L. (Wish you a pleasant voyage) and was answered by X.O.R. (Thank you) during which action both vessels stopped. *Norwegia* coming up under our stern and passing on our weather beam then hailed in the old fashion '*Discovery*, Ahoy. Captain Larsen speaking. I would like very much to speak with Sir Douglas Mawson if I may come aboard?' Capt. Davis megaphoned 'Yes Sir. Sir Douglas would be delighted to meet you aboard.' Whereupon *Norwegia* lowered their lee boat bringing off Capt. Rüser Larsen and Mr Neilsen, mate, in their long boat which was managed in a truly seamanlike manner. Capt. Larsen was received by Capt. Davis and presented to Sir Douglas Mawson then conducted to the Captain's cabin for a conference.[14]

For Davis, 'Capt Rüser Larsen was very friendly and told us what they had been doing, and remained on board for an hour. ... He impressed me very favourably, and one felt that he was trying to meet a rather delicate moment in a very tactful way, and we all felt glad that he had come on board.'[15] Sir Douglas noted that 'Larsen said "There has been much said in the newspapers about our expedition." ... He said that they had been warned from Norway against doing many things which they were told would be resented by Great Britain. I judged from what he said that they had been instructed from Norway not to raise the Norwegian flag on Enderby Land or Kemp Land.' Mawson listened and then told Larsen that he had been 'very sorry to learn in Cape Town that there was the possibility of a Norwegian expedition operating in an area that might overlap ours' and hoped 'that the Norwegian expedition would keep W of 40°E longitude, and that Norway had been informed that we would not go west of that line.' The meeting was cordial and apparently cleared any earlier misunderstandings. 'Rüser Larsen is a very fine fellow,' recorded Mawson at the end of the day: 'I showed him quickly over the vessel during which time the First Mate, who was in charge of the boats alongside, had a conversation with Davis. The Mate had been in the wardroom conversing with expedition members prior to this. When they departed we all gave them 3 cheers for the *Norwegia*.'[16]

The meeting of the two polar ships was well documented. Davis observed that the *Norwegia* was 'loaded very deeply; she has two large aeroplanes on deck and looked very small to us. Rüser Larsen told us that they had coaled from a whaler in the pack, two whales being used as fenders … I should not care to be in her during a gale in her present condition. She looks like a half tide rock.'[17] While Mawson and Davis were with Larsen, *Norwegia*'s Mate, according to Simmers, had an attentive audience in the wardroom hanging on to his every word:

> The Mate, once the Commander was well in with his pouring out of his stiff lunch, came aboard and was trotted round by the whole horde of scientists. He spoke very presentable English and brought us plenty of news which we drank in along with some grand Moyes-cum-Hurley brandy. 'Byrd had flown to the pole before Xmas. Wilkins was still at Deception looking for a suitable place to take off. A Norwegian had been lost in a Moth in the Ross Sea. Yes their vessel could roll. The wings of the planes occasionally dipped into the water. They had a complement of only 18. … She had left the Stromness only 8 days before and was now chock-full of coal.' He was a really decent fellow and we all liked him.[18]

The brief encounter with the *Norwegia* had left a positive impression with all on board. So much so that two expedition members must have listened attentively to the Norwegian accent the day before and so decided to play charades. 'Tonight there has been the most priceless rag since we came aboard. Stew [Campbell] & Cherub [Fletcher] who have both had particularly forest-like beards had a shave which so transformed them that they didn't look a bit like their Cape Town selves and Stew when he put a hat on was quite unrecognisable,' noted Simmers. 'Anyway after making most of us roar at their appearance, they climbed into flying togs and went to the engine room where they were introduced as two Norwegians completely taking the chief in and being shown round the engines like important personages. I'm afraid our laughter rather disturbed the watch below.'[19]

The events of the past days had invigorated the ship's company and Mawson's oceanographical program was again in full swing with Alf back on the plank and in his laboratory, the biologists running marine and plankton stations, Simmers releasing hydrogen filled meteorological balloons, and the aviators keeping the Moth in check for the next take off.

*

A near catastrophe was recorded in Davis' journal on 16 January: 'The ship's cat fell overboard. Martin A.B. went in after it and had a cold time. The cat was hauled on board aft and Martin was hauled on board forward. Fortunately for both of them we were stopped at the time.'[20] Fletcher described the incident in more detail:

> One of the crew happened to see Blackie, the ship's cat, jump from the gunwale into a sloping-out rubbish chute. Frantically clawing at the sides to save herself, she finally shot out into the sea. A cry of 'cat overboard' brought all hands on deck and attempts were made to rescue Blackie as she swam alongside the drifting ship. Frustrated by the ineffectual efforts at rescue, Lofty Martin jumped overboard to save his pet, but the water was so cold he barely had time to tie a rope around his waist before succumbing to the cold. Dragged to the side, he was hauled on board half frozen, but soon recovered after a change of clothes and a good nip of rum provided by Captain Davis. In the meantime, Falla had rescued Blackie by scooping her out of the water with a long-handled landing net.[21]

News of *Discovery*'s mascot falling overboard was relayed by Sir Douglas to Casey in a radiogram at the end of which Mawson added: 'This diversion did not affect Martin but the cat which was waterlogged was revived with difficulty after many hours heating in engine room. Blackie now quite restored will have no wish again essay world beyond ship. Blackie had never yet been ashore, as very small kitten was transferred to *Discovery* at Cape Town Docks direct from research ship *William Scoresby*.'[22]

Alf remembered the cat: 'Yes, the cat was soon given the run of the whole ship. Everyone sort of owned it, but Lofty became particularly attached to it. The cat would dart around the decks and sometimes go aloft. All was well until the time the biologists took in a wounded penguin; when they let it roam the decks the cat eyed it with fear and hid behind barrels or anything it could find.'

'Lofty' Martin with the *Discovery*'s mascot, Blackie

The *Discovery* had now turned about and was coasting west outside the pack somewhere between Australia's Mawson and Russia's Molodezhnaya stations in present-day Antarctica. The weather was clear and fine and 'a number of whales, the high blowing type' were spotted congregating in the area. Sir Douglas wished to carry out aerial surveys in the region, but no sheltered area was found for the Moth to take off. By 20 January, the ship was caught in strong winds and snow squalls that pushed her through turbulent ice-filled waters. *Discovery* was 'hove to and rolling and tumbling about terribly. We had a good deal of difficulty in clearing some bergs yesterday and the vessel appears to be very unwieldy as she gets lighter,' 'Burning coal and getting no further forward very depressing work. ... Two hard gales in January are unusual, even in the Antarctic,' wrote Davis.[23] The master of the *Discovery* felt uneasy as continued bad weather would impact on the ever-dwindling coal reserves and in turn the long voyage to Australia.

North to Kerguelen

Discovery's position at noon 22 January was 66° 38¾'S, 46° 26'E. The wind had died down but there was a heavy swell making it impossible to get the plane airborne. Meantime, Sir Douglas had received a wireless message from Henderson in Canberra reminding him that the 'flag should be hoisted as often as possible on lands seen, that so far we had hoisted it once only and then only on island.'[1] Mawson observed that the recent gale had changed the pack-edge line making it possible 'to steam 6 miles further south than when last here. This enables us to see strip of coastline not seen previously.'[2] 'Little has happened,' wrote Simmers, 'we have made about 5 knots … skirting the pack.' However, life on board was about to liven up: 'Cherub and I fell in this evening a beaut. At ten we were swanking round after having had a bath each when the Dux announced "coaling". Hell.'[3]

Early morning 25 January the ship was out of the pack and in open water making it possible for the airmen to prepare the Moth and make a test flight. Hurley went up with Douglas to take photos and shoot some movie footage of Proclamation Island and its surroundings. Sir Douglas then flew with Campbell:

> After flying over land-ice for a couple miles inland at 3000 ft I passed Campbell the flag attached to mast, and he stalled engine and passed [it] over side. I retained the proclamation, claiming once more all the land discovered, and this time including the newly discovered slice at our farthest west. Campbell spotted the flag lying on the ice surface and drew my attention to it. We then flew back to ship. I advised Captain Davis of the possibility of getting into the water along coast. … Capt. Davis refused to take the ship into this pack to look for slack water off coast, and as from the mast I could not assure him that there still was so large an area of water within, and as the lane had partly closed, I could not take a strong stand in pressing him to push in. … All members [of] staff were broken-hearted that Capt D would not make an attempt to get in and put foot on mainland.[4]

The Gipsy Moth was lowered overboard for short flights the following day. Hurley went up again with Eric Douglas armed with both still and cine photographic equipment. From the plane's maximum altitude of 4200 feet, an ice plateau was seen with peaks rising to approximately 7000 feet. A little later Moyes went up with Campbell to survey the coastline and the inland peaks.[5] 'I shall be glad to see it safely on board again,' wrote Davis. 'Of course if they came down in the pack we should have a nice time trying to find out what had become of them.'[6]

Mawson had been in radio contact with the South African whaling ship *Radioleine* and hoped there may be a possibility to transfer 150 tons of coal from her at sea. Davis was not at all enthusiastic about the idea: 'The difficulty of coaling from the *Radioleine* is that we are gambling on getting fine weather. ... It seems to me that as the ship has now been out more than three months and completed a good season's work ... to embark on another campaign in the ice would not be wise at this time. We have 110 tons which is just sufficient to see us to Australia.'[7]

Coal may have been running low, but not the food provisions. 'Here we are three months out and still eating fresh eggs while up to three or four days ago we still had oranges and nuts,' recorded Simmers. 'I'm still dazed as a result of seeing the wealth of other good things the cook has in stock and he says there are enough tins of Quaker Oats to take everyone to Hell and back.'[8] Davis was also impressed with the longevity of the fresh supplies: 'Our potatoes from Cape Town are still holding out and the quantity, 4 tons, has lasted well.'[9]

January 27, Mawson and his team successfully carried out the 44th marine station. The day was one of varied interests: 'A station was held at 2 pm. I gave Alf Howard a hand on his water bottle tests; the water temperatures are interesting as they show a warm layer of water at 100 fathoms and 800 fathoms,' wrote Douglas. 'Plenty of birds about. Sooty albatross, Antarctic petrels, Snow petrels and the Wilson petrel. ... We had seal meat for dinner today, it is dark in colour but not unlike good beef in taste. Steamed alongside the most spectacular berg we have seen yet — estimated height 250 feet. The sun sets these nights at 9 pm.'[10]

Sir Douglas was crestfallen that weather and ice conditions of the past weeks had upset plans to survey more land from the air: 'I have left the Antarctic coast with great regret — another week here with aeroplane would have completed mapping MacRobertson Land and added detail of Scott Mountains.'[11] Within days of leaving the frozen continent Mawson sent a radiogram to Henderson briefly outlining the comprehensive oceanographic work so far attempted: many hundreds of soundings that revealed the character and limits of the continental shelf fringing Antarctic lands; chemical operations relating to the examination of surface samples taken continuously every 12 hours and serial samples taken from surface to bottom in vertical stations; information relating to life in Antarctic seas traversed was secured by horizontal and vertical nets and bottom trawls; distribution of planktonic life and its special economic aspect defining whale feeding areas; delineation of geographical range of bird varieties and feeding habits; and the poverty of plant life in the regions visited.[12]

*

A full house: Members of the Fiddley Club enjoying a 'smoke,' a chat and some gramophone records. Alf front R. (Photo: Frank Hurley)

'Yes, we were rather disappointed to leave without actually stepping on the Antarctic continent, but cheered up considerably at the prospect of a break in Kerguelen and the possibility of signing up for a second voyage,' admitted Alf:

> In fact we were, I would say, a very compatible group and just took things as they came — even the coaling, which to be perfectly honest was a bit of a bugbear at times. Somehow in between carrying out the oceanographical work, which

could be at any time as there was close to 24 hours of daylight down there, we managed to get together for a smoke in one of the cabins. For a few of us it was pipes, others cigarettes.

We'd chat about anything and everything and just generally relax. Cherub [Fletcher] was good fun to talk to — a very outgoing chap. Birdie [Falla] was very knowledgeable about birds and apparently had been involved in examining various flights of birds that had flown up from the Antarctic and sort of crashed in New Zealand. Prof [Harvey Johnston] would have been in his 40s and had been at the same university in Adelaide as Mawson. He was fairly quiet and more concerned with his specialty, which was parasitology. In the evenings he would spend time with the scientific staff and sometimes join Mawson, Hurley and Moyes. Babe [Marr] was the expert in planktonology and handling of equipment; his specialty was marine worms and if we were doing a dredge you'd almost certainly get some. Simmers was good company and we became cobbers pretty well as soon as we met in London; his degree was physics and mine was chemistry/physics, so we spoke the same language. Stew [Campbell] and Douglas were both easy-going and Douglas an excellent cabin mate.

Alf believed that Ingram, the medical officer, was the person who got the biggest kick out of the expedition:

I remember when we were in the Crozet Islands — we were just walking around — Simmers and I were doing some magnetic work and lo and behold here is Doc coming along with a great big albatross youngster in his arms. He was lugging this thing back to present it to the ornithologists. Doc was interested in everything that was going on and would join us in the evenings. I guess we were a bit of a mixed bunch, but always found each other's company most agreeable for a game of cards, a singsong or an evening of listening to records on the hand-cranked HMV gramophone.

Fletcher also made note of the general *bonhomie* on board: 'The *Discovery* was a happy ship with scientists and crew always on the best of terms. Only on one occasion did I see two of the crew come to blows. It was a short-lived fight. Lofty Martin, with his great height and strength, lifted the two combatants by their collars and held them squirming in the air until they simmered down. Lowered to the deck they shook hands and were good friends again.'[13]

*

At 5.30 pm on 28 January the *Discovery* was 'standing North': 'It will be a relief to get out of the ice again,' penned Davis, 'as the continuous strain and the bad weather are very wearing to the master on a ship like this. I have been fortunate in my officers and crew.'[14] The ship was small and sturdy, but packed to the rafters. Davis lamented: 'It is impossible to get any exercise as she has not a bit of deck space anywhere clear enough to get a walk on. And after three months cooped up, one is not at one's top. However, if we have a bit of luck and are able to get into Kerguelen, we shall get a spell there which will be welcome.'[15] During the days ahead the ship laboured in a north-westerly swell against a force 8-9 gale. 'Vessel rolling heavily and taking water aboard forward,' noted Sir Douglas.[16] Heavy seas, gusty winds accompanied by heavy snow squalls continued for another three days, and then sail was set for the first time in two months.

'We were all called to give a hand hoisting the sails, as Davis only had half-a-dozen seamen, not like when Scott took her south. Of course, Hurley was delighted and couldn't wait to go aloft,' recalled Alf. Simmers jotted down the procedure: 'Attenuated rig of inner and outer jibs, fore top mast staysail, main topmast staysail, topsail and the fore and upper and lower fore topsails. The spanker is badly cut and is a bit big for the gaff which has been strained, so it has been replaced by a miniature topsail.'[17] The last day of January became even more exciting when a huge Blue whale was seen being chased by a pod of Orca Killer whales. 'Twice it leapt clear out of the water in a porpoise-like upward dive, and once it shot up vertically till its snout must have been thirty to forty feet in the air. For quite a while it lashed round on the surface blowing and churning the water into white foam.'[18] Four days earlier Sir Douglas had observed 'a school of 33 Blue Whales … going in W direction' when the ship was in 66° 02′S, 54° 50′E.[19]

February 2 and the *Discovery* was rolling heavily and taking water on board, but making good headway north despite the swell. Mawson recorded sighting 10 bergs: 'One was very unusual—overturned glacier ice half white, half black at distance but close up seen to be transparent green ice loaded and clouded with pebbles and morainic matter.'[20] Davis was beginning to feel more optimistic as the ship was now 'going 6 knots with all sail', thus temporarily alleviating concerns about the diminishing coal stock. 'Everything is in remarkably good order for a wooden ship,' he wrote. 'She is rather wonderful, as so far we have had no trouble with bilges or pumps.'[21] 'Captain Davis had been in a cheerful and more friendly mood since leaving the coast,' noted Fletcher, and 'it was rumoured that he was heard singing sea shanties; one in particular being "Rolling home, rolling home, rolling home".'[22]

Noon position on 6 February was 50° 37′S, 64° 3½′E. 'Two King penguins were seen today more than 100 miles from land,' wrote Sir Douglas. At 9.25 am the next morning 'the high peaks of Kerguelen could be seen. ... Numerous birds about the ship — albatrosses, prions, Cape Hens, etc.' Work for the scientific party had not ceased. There was a sounding with the Kelvin machine 'on a course 072° about 12 miles from coast' and 'a dredge was shot in 82 fathoms — pebbly bottom north of rocks.'[23] Soon after entering Royal Sound signals were exchanged with a French sealer, the SS *Austral*, which was observed at a nearby anchorage. By 11 am on 8 February the *Discovery* was approaching the jetty at Port Jeanne d'Arc: 'We had hardly completed making the vessel fast when the wind came away from SW, blowing in gusts up to force 7,' recorded Davis. 'Had we been an hour later we should have been unable to berth. As it is, we are now firmly alongside the rather crazy old wharf, with all the wires we have got ashore and both anchors down forward. ... It was a great relief to be safely alongside again, with coal and water available.'[24]

Mawson expressed great satisfaction that even the far corners of the world were in radio contact with the *Discovery*: 'Australian stations have been good last several nights, coming in again, but now, after arriving at Kerguelen, are bad. ... In Antarctic, and till now, Admiralty [radio] good, also Marion (Washington) comes through every night. We could hear Admiralty talking to Halifax every night and sometimes the Chinese station talking.'[25] One night, Williams received a message from Russia, and there were also 'messages received from two vessels in distress, one of which was subsequently lost off the Panama coast.'[26]

*

'We couldn't wait to get ashore and Sir Douglas gave us a couple of days off before scheduling any work. Of course the big thing was being able to wash our clothes and ourselves without water restrictions. There was plenty of it for all of us and for filling the water tanks on board,' recalled Alf. 'The old whaling station looked better than on our last visit and we guessed that the crew from the whaler — which coaled us on the way down — must have been busy fixing up some of the houses. I remember there being a stove in one or two of the dwellings. Simmers arrived with a bad chest infection so took up lodgings in one of the houses.'

Simmers noted that Alf was also one of the casualties on arrival at Jeanne d'Arc: 'Monday Feb. 10th Doc's big day for patients: me — doctor's orders 1 week in bed in Manager's House; Captain — injured eye; Alf — poisoned finger; Stoker — burnt.'[27] Nevertheless, 'Doc' Ingram attributed the overall good health of *Discovery*'s men 'to the careful medical examination at the outset, and to the very complete and thorough arrangements made for clothing and feeding the expedition.'[28] Apart from the live sheep and a large consignment of eggs, fresh fruit and vegetables taken on board in Cape Town, there was also 'an iron can for converting the Truemilk powder into the nearest approach to cow's milk … thus retaining a large percentage of its vitamin content.' In addition, a gift of 60 gallons of 'almost pure orange juice with very little preservative' was given by Durban's Tomango orange factory for the first voyage. However, the medical report revealed that there were a few calamities during the first voyage: 'There has been very little sickness, apart from the usual minor ailments met with amongst a healthy ship's crew. Stoppings have come out of teeth; hands have been skinned and lacerated from handling coal briquettes and from nails in wooden cases. The cook and the firemen have suffered from minor burns, and a few sprained joints have resulted from tripping over encumbrances on deck at night.'[29]

Davis was still worried about the *Discovery* as continuing violent gusts up to force 9 could try the moorings despite 'the Starboard anchor and 60 fathoms of chain, and the Port anchor underfoot with 20 fathoms.' As there was now no steam in the ship's main engines and the crew were scaling the boiler, the Captain was relieved when the first 11 tons of coal were on board; by 13 February 77 tons were in the bunkers. Coaling would still take several days as Davis wished to leave Kerguelen with no less than 200 tons.[30]

One day to settle in, 'an issue of Dewar's whisky to everyone's delight,'[31] and Sir Douglas was down to work as usual. The island was greener now, a Samoyed dog had been seen — accidentally introduced by a German expedition some years earlier — and there were rabbits galore, which together with the island's teal ducks, made for a more tempting menu. There were excursions to Swain's harbour where Elephant seals and King penguins were sighted, some dredgings and shore collecting had been done, and blubber collected in Antarctica for the Hudson Bay Company had been rendered down. 'The Club' had now moved ashore to the deserted whaling station's Manager's Office in one of the large red buildings sheltering under the rocky ridges.[32]

Recovering, Simmers made a few notes about life away from the ship:

> In the next room the Club has taken up its abode around the stove and most of the day there has been someone about playing the gramophone or talking. Doc and Cherub and later Alf, who has a poisoned finger, have been sleeping over here too so I haven't been lonely. … The chief activity among the scientific staff has been as far as I can make out clothes washing, which has been going on all week in the next hut. After laboriously boiling and scrubbing for some days they have found that much labour is saved by simply dousing articles in petrol thereby dry cleaning them. Today Alf and I did a dip determination — my first thought of work for a week.[33]

Mawson had hoped to leave Kerguelen by 19 February, but there were unforeseen problems: 'Now engineers say that scraping boilers and adjusting engines will take longer. So coaling is dragged on to coincide with engine repairs. … One of the firemen is still off duty, and so other two have been unduly taxed.' The Spring tide was so low for several hours each day that the ship was well and truly aground; however, as Sir Douglas noted: 'At low tide much shore collecting done. As many as 50 fish got in 1 h; collecting under stones in evening.'[34]

In the days that followed the launch came into its own ferrying Mawson and his party to different bays and islands in the archipelago. Overnight camping at Greenland Harbour, where alkali rocks were discovered and a day trip to Observatory Bay specifically for taking photos. Moyes surveyed the area around Port Jeanne d'Arc, Sir Douglas collected soil samples, Falla and Fletcher were skinning birds ashore and Campbell and Douglas were preparing the Moth to take off on the first calm day. After a test flight early 18 February Hurley went up and took many photos of Mt Ross, the harbours and other outstanding geographical sites such as the many deep fjords that cut into Kerguelen's coastline.[35] Early next morning he had another chance to take more aerial shots, returning in time to join the rest of the party for a trip planned by Sir Douglas: 'I have arranged with entire scientific staff to go to Observatory Bay and camp 2 nights, then ship will come to pick us up as coaling will be done then. In the meantime we are to explore several little-known channels leading off from Royal Sound.'[36]

The camping party boarded the *Discovery* in rough seas and gale-force winds when she anchored in Observatory Bay just after lunch on 21 February. Successful soundings and hauls with the dredge and trawl were made the following day, but then the weather changed and for a week there were snowfalls and strong wind gusts every day, making it impossible to carry out the planned marine program 'so time spent ashore on Murray and other islands and on mainland, awaiting better conditions.'[37] March 1, and despite the continuing strong westerly wind, snow and rain, the scientific party continued their treks to collect rocks, fossils, plants, etc. Fletcher recounted one trip to Cat's Ears Peak near the entrance to Royal Sound, which could have resulted in the disappearance of both Falla and Alf:

> We arrived at the base of the peak without mishap and set out to return to the boat. ... On the walk back we descended almost to shore level where we were faced with almost continuous marshy flats. Falla, while trailing behind, stepped into a sea elephant wallow and was up to his waist before catching hold of strong undergrowth near the edge. His repeated calls for assistance could not be heard above the noise of the wind. By the time I realised he was not following, he had laboriously dragged himself out on to solid ground. Later, when we were describing the incident, we learnt that Alf Howard had stumbled into two wallows during the day.[38]

Mawson had proposed that the *Discovery* leave the archipelago and return to Australia via Heard Island in order to complete the mapping of its coastline, which had been started on the way down. 'Even this proposal was eventually prohibited for a succession of gales swept over Kerguelen Island and it appeared that winter conditions had set in by the end of February. Accordingly, on March 2nd, the weather having improved somewhat, a course was set for the south-western extremity of Australia.'[39]

SS *Cathay*'s Surprise Barrel Drop

March 21, the ship was 'off Albany at noon. … It has been a long voyage since we left the Cape five months ago, and I feel they all have done well and will be pleased to know that we are homeward bound,'[1] wrote Davis. Station 76 — the last oceanographic operation for the first voyage — ran for about three hours. A bucket dredge pulled up coralline sand, a trawl dragged up a few fish, 'lots of nice invertebrate life; one very large sponge.' Mawson was disappointed: 'After the station, for which we did not get in more than one otter trawling and tow-netting, night came on and we were not in suitable water. I was so fed up I said, "We are done, now straight for Adelaide". I still pressed upon JK that the course should be about Lat 35°, north of steamer track to get in valuable line of soundings.'[2]

Slow progress across the Great Australian Bight afforded ample time for the sailors and scientific staff to work together on painting and cleaning the ship. Much wire was let out and greased if necessary before being wound in. All the oceanographic gear was overhauled and reconditioned with the help of the crew so that it could be used on the planned second voyage before being stowed away. Fletcher wrote that the 'natural history specimens, estimated at between 18 and 20 tonnes, had been packed ready for transfer to the University of Adelaide.' There was more activity inside the vessel: 'The wardroom table was covered with reports in various stages of completion by Howard and Simmers. Commander Moyes was busily engaged in completing charts of lands visited in Antarctica. At the same time he was compiling a line of soundings as we crossed the Great Australian Bight.'[3] For Sir Douglas it was important that the 'Ship should present a yacht-like appearance on arrival.'[4]

The monotony of the long, slow route to Adelaide was broken by the antics of a captive albatross onboard awaiting release once Falla checked it for parasites. 'They sit about the decks in more or less friendly and interested fashion, occasionally snapping with their great beaks at passers-by,' observed Sir Douglas. 'On one such occasion Howard, our chemist hydrologist, was relieved of considerable part of most necessary garment.' Hurley caught the moment on his cinecamera as the bird pecked a sizeable piece of material from the seat of Alf's trousers — an incident he included in his film *The Siege of the South*.[5]

Fletcher (left) and Falla (right) preparing bird specimens for museum distribution in the 'bird cage' aboard the *Discovery* (Photo: Frank Hurley)

Crossing the Bight the *Discovery* was up against fresh north/north-easterly winds and heavy swells. She was now in the shipping lanes of vessels plying to and from Australian ports and had passed the coastal steamer *West Australia* to the loud cheers of all on board.[6] For two days the ship covered less than 70 miles. 'What I do remember about the last leg,' recounted Alf, 'was that although we were all very occupied getting everything in order, the ship wasn't making much headway and Adelaide still seemed far off. Mind you we all bucked up when passengers on a passing liner cheered us on and threw a barrel of goodies overboard for us.' Davis' journal entry of 27 March noted the happy event: 'At noon today the P&O liner *Cathay* passed us close. When just ahead she stopped and dropped over a barrel which we managed to get hold of without difficulty. It contained some papers, chickens, apples, salads, etc., which were most welcome and have given us our first touch of home coming. It was a very kindly action … and deeply appreciated by us all.'[7]

*

Late Monday afternoon, 31 March 1930, Davis sent a radio message to Port Adelaide's Deputy Director of Navigation, Captain Gransbury, informing him that the *Discovery* would arrive at the Semaphore anchorage at 8 pm. The port immediately became a scene of great activity sending and receiving telephone and telegraph messages. The Adelaide *Advertiser* reported that 'long before the vessel came into view nine miles of seafront literally bristled with watchers armed with field glasses, telescopes and other long-range optical instruments. Shortly after 4.30 pm a cry of "Here she comes" spread with remarkable rapidity along the coastline.' Just after 7 pm Gransbury left by special launch 'with four well-filled large mailbags, a number of bulky parcels, a satchel topped up with later telegrams and letters, and a supply of fresh meat and other foodstuffs for the party's breakfast.'[8] Welcoming procedures were already being put in place: Two big Union Jacks would be hoisted near the wharf and barricades erected around the area where the *Discovery* would be moored. Police as well as mounted police would be in attendance as large crowds were expected. 'A long voyage over at last,' wrote Davis. 'We are to go up the river tomorrow. The Committee will come aboard at the Outer Harbour, as a SW wind has sprung up.'[9]

Tuesday morning, 1 April, the ship lay in the midst of a wind-lashed sea. Proceedings commenced with an early visit on board by the Quarantine and Customs officers. The *Discovery* slowly steamed up the Port River to her berth at McLaren Wharf. There were jubilant greetings on the way from fishing parties and passing vessels dipped their flags. 'Three planes of the South Australian section of the Australian Aero Club met the vessel in the river and, flying in formation, escorted her part of the way to Port Adelaide, circling the vessel and dipping gracefully in salutation as they returned to the aerodrome.'[10] 'Three cheers were given when the figure of Sir Douglas Mawson was seen on the deck as the *Discovery* was made fast.' The crowd started to sway to and fro when some people in the rear ranks of the crowd tried to force their way to the front, resulting in a man falling off the wharf. 'Fortunately he could swim and clambered on to the anchor, which was hanging down within a foot or so of the water.'[11]

In the evening the Antarctic Research Expedition Committee invited members of the expedition to a dinner given in their honour at the Town Hall. Sir Douglas gave a brief account of the expedition's work, emphasising that its success 'was due to the team work of the party and thanked every member for the loyal assistance given throughout. ... The work of the expedition had given them good knowledge of the conditions in the various basins in the Indian and Southern oceans. There was not much left to complete the job, and he urged Australia to do it.'[12] Among those present were the Governor-General — Lord Stonehaven, and the Governor of South Australia — Sir Alexander Hore-Ruthven.

Wednesday's civic reception in the Adelaide Town Hall was given full coverage in the media:

> The main hall was crowded to the doors long before the time fixed for the arrival of the explorers and the vice-regal representatives. Outside the building another large crowd gathered in the hope of catching a fleeting glimpse of the members of the expedition as they entered the hall. The party proceeded along King William Street between beflagged buildings, and the services of mounted constables were necessary to enable the explorers to enter the Town Hall unhindered by the enthusiastic attentions of the crowd. The entry of the members of the expedition, headed by the tall figure of the leader, Sir Douglas Mawson, was the signal for prolonged applause.

There was more applause a few minutes later when the Governor-General, the Governor and others, which included Sir David Orme Masson and Sir Edgeworth David, mounted the stage. Many speeches of welcome followed and congratulatory messages read out from across Australia, New Zealand and the United Kingdom, one of which was a cable message received by the Governor-General from His Majesty, King George V: 'Please deliver the following to Sir Douglas Mawson — On your safe return from the Antarctic. I warmly congratulate you and your companions upon the success achieved in the face of formidable hardships.'[13]

Alf was well-prepared for any formal gathering as a week earlier when crossing the Bight he sent a brief radiogram to his father at the Customs House in Melbourne: 'POST DINNER SUIT AND ACCESSORIES *DISCOVERY* ADELAIDE. REGARDS ALL. ALF.' 'The red-carpet treatment given to us by the people of Adelaide was quite overwhelming,' said Alf:

> Many welcoming functions and outings were arranged for our short stopover and we all had a good laugh seeing how well we managed to scrub up for the formal occasions. The one at the Town Hall was a particularly grand event. The Lord Mayor of Adelaide and the Governor-General officially welcomed us. Everyone from the ship was there on the dais. The place was packed. Another

day a few of us went over to the Barossa Valley at the invitation of Yalumba, who had donated a generous number of cases for the expedition. We were taken over the whole show — the vineyards, the winemaking process and then they put on lunch for us. It was good to be on land for a couple of days and get some mail off. Davis wanted to get the ship to Melbourne so we all gave a hand to unload the cases of scientific specimens destined for the Adelaide University.

Official reception at the Adelaide Town Hall to mark the return of the first BANZARE voyage in April 1930. Alf left-hand side of Lady Mawson and her two daughters, front row, far right.

After berthing at Port Adelaide for 48 hours, the *Discovery* was ready for the final leg. The now reduced scientific party gave the crew a hand to weigh anchor. 'At 5 pm the bow and stern lines were let go, then the bow was swung out and around and once more we made seawards,' noted Eric Douglas. 'The Doc., Capt. Hurley and Com. Moyes left for Sydney on Wednesday night, Sir Douglas is coming across to Melbourne by train, Prof. Johnston lives in Adelaide and Simmers left tonight by train for Melbourne as he has some work to do at the Melbourne University before he leaves for New Zealand. Aboard we have Campbell, Falla, Fletcher, Marr, Howard and I left out of the scientific staff.' The Outer Harbour was passed at 6.30 pm, the pilot dropped, and the *Discovery* was on her way. 'We should have a nice quiet cruise to Melbourne,' continued Douglas, 'fine evening, light head wind, gentle swell and we are making good speed. There was plenty of fresh food aboard and a big box of grapes and peaches. We are setting to pass between Kangaroo Is and the mainland — back stair passage.'[14]

*

Tuesday morning, 8 April 1930, three aircraft from the Royal Air Force circled above the *Discovery* as she crossed 'The Rip' and made her way leisurely up Port Phillip Bay, thus ending her long voyage of Antarctic exploration. The Customs launch, with Captain Bolger, the Deputy Director of Navigation, met the ship in the bay. On board with Bolger was Customs officer Alfred Samuel Howard, who was eager to greet his son. 'It was a total surprise to see my father again in the middle of the Bay. The point was that he worked at the Customs Office and I can only assume he would have made some arrangement so that he could be on duty to board the vessel,' recalled Alf. 'A number of dignitaries came up the gangway on arrival and there was a big crowd on the wharf, which was unexpected as Sir Douglas and some of the party didn't arrive until later in the day.' There was another agreeable surprise: 'One of the first visitors who boarded the *Discovery* when she berthed at Port Melbourne at 4 pm to-day was Mr. Clarence H. Hare, who sailed in the vessel on her first voyage of exploration in 1901-1904 as Captain Scott's cabin boy.'[15]

Wednesday morning the expedition's scientific staff and officers of the *Discovery* were given a civic reception at the Town Hall by the Lord Mayor and on the Friday evening were the guests of honour at a function hosted by the Victoria League at the Hotel Windsor. Mawson responded to the welcoming speeches given by Sir David Orme Masson and Professor Sir Edgeworth David at the Windsor then summarised the work carried out by the BANZARE. He also drew attention to the fact that the expedition — in the course of its scientific work and the work of charting the Antarctic coastline — discovered a whaling area worth millions of pounds, which was immediately communicated to South African and British whalers in the region. He emphasised that a second voyage in the *Discovery* would enable the work of charting the coastline to be completed, and this together with more scientific investigations would be necessary before the whaling and sealing areas could be developed.[16]

Now in Melbourne Alf returned to the family home in Camberwell. There was time to catch up with his old scouting companions and to accept an invitation to revisit University High School; time also to do some ice-skating at the Glaciarium near Flinders Street Station: 'I took my ice skates down to Antarctica just in case I could give it a go there, but as soon as I saw how uneven and jagged most of the ice was I gave up on the idea. Of course I never told the others that I'd packed them.' Within a couple of days of leaving the *Discovery* Alf was back at the University of Melbourne's Chemistry

Department analysing salinity determinations from the first voyage. 'I believe we did wonder if in fact there would be a second voyage because of the Depression; the ship was a few days out from Cape Town when we first heard about the Wall Street crash,' recalled Alf. 'Once the ship was in dock the team disbanded; Hurley returned to Sydney to work on the expedition film, others went interstate, and of course Simmers and Falla returned to New Zealand. At the time there was no indication as to whether or not we would be going south again with Sir Douglas.'

On The Road With Hurley

Early May 1930 Alf was working in his old laboratory at the University of Melbourne. He contacted the Council for Scientific and Industrial Research (CSIR) to find out about work prospects, then wrote to Sir Douglas in May informing him of his present activities and enclosing an account of his 'expenses up to date', which included 'small claims for repairs to apparatus' from the first voyage: 'So far I have heard nothing from the CSIR beyond the fact that my application has been received. Until I hear further from them I intend to put in the greater part of my time at the university testing some analytic methods that I hope to incorporate in next season's programme.'[1]

News that the *Discovery* expedition would continue Antarctic exploration from November 1930 to March 1931 and that Sir Douglas Mawson would again take command was announced by the Prime Minister, Mr J.H. Scullin, in Canberra on 22 May. The vessel had been made available for the second voyage by the British Government without charge until 14 July 1931. Furthermore, Mr Mac Robertson, who had given £10,000 towards the first voyage, informed the Expedition Committee that he was prepared to contribute up to £6000 towards the second season's operations.[2]

The *Discovery* entered the Alfred Graving Dock at Williamstown on 10 May 1930 and was now perched high above the concrete floor of the dry dock ready for her first overhaul since leaving London's East India Dock in August 1929. Sailors had scraped off the barnacles and were ready to paint and tar the hull as soon as it was thoroughly dry; 'Twenty seamen, floating in long red punts slung from the vessel's side, had scrubbed the famous oaken hull when all the water had been pumped out. Captain J.K. Davis, who has sailed the *Discovery* safely through many icefields, stood on the floor of the dock today, eyeing the ship affectionately.'[3] A comprehensive report of work carried out on the vessel over three weeks included: repairs to the forward end of the keel, which was dented and fractured in three places; repairs to the butts of the hull's rib planking found to be weeping in 21 places; and repairs to the rudder and propeller shaft. Once afloat and after an inspection of the bilges was made, the vessel was given a clean bill of health.[4]

The ship remained in Williamstown but was soon in the news again. Hobart's *Mercury* reported that on 22 June a worker from Williamstown and a member of *Discovery*'s crew had been to a party on board and helped themselves to a case containing tins of salmon, some preserved fruit, seven tins of herrings, four tins of Rex-Pye, three tins of sheep tongues and other items. 'Both the men charged had taken a lot of drink on the vessel on 22 June, and it would be interesting to know just what was the condition of the nightwatchman, who was responsible for the safe custody of the expedition's property,'[5] said a local Justice of the Peace in Court.

*

The BANZARE Committee sent letters to all scientific staff of the 1929-1930 voyage inviting them to accompany the 1930-1931 expedition on the same terms as last time. 'Of course I officially signed up for the second voyage without any hesitation,' confirmed Alf. 'Australia had been hit by the Depression like everywhere else and I considered myself quite fortunate as uni offered me the use of their lab, so all I really had to think about was how I would fill in a few months before going south again. It's fair to say that Sir Douglas solved that one for me':

Adelaide. 9th July, 1930.

Dear Howard,

Hurley has now prepared the picture story of the last cruise, and will be showing it to a leading picture house in Melbourne, Sydney and Adelaide during August, September and October. We find that there have to be four sessions a day, and Hurley finds it impossible to talk to more than two of these. Consequently, he has asked us to find somebody to appear with the film at two of the sessions each day. I write to ask whether you would care to do this. We would pay you your Expedition salary plus living and travelling expenses.

The film and the lecture are completed. If you are going to undertake the work it will be necessary to go to Sydney in about a week or ten days' time, in order to take part in the rehearsals that will precede the opening exhibition on the 1st August.

Let me know by wire whether you are available, so that I can advise Hurley. He has, I believe, someone up his sleeve who has lectured to such films on previous occasions, but I think it would be better for a member of the Expedition to appear with the film.

Yours sincerely,

[Douglas Mawson][6]

Alf accepted immediately and received a further letter from Mawson dated 15 July: 'Dear Howard, A letter from Hurley indicates that you would be able to lecture with him satisfactorily, and he is agreeable for you to go up to Sydney in a few days' time to take part in rehearsals, though the first showing will not take place until the 16th August, when the film will open in the Lyceum Theatre, Sydney.'[7]

Alf Howard's new appointment as Frank Hurley's assistant was formalised in a letter from Mawson to Mr F. Strahan at the Prime Minister's Department in Canberra[8] 'Under arrangements made at the last Antarctic Committee meeting, Mr A. Howard, a member of the scientific staff of the Expedition, will be helping Hurley in the exhibition of the film. In the picture houses there will be three or four sessions a day, and Howard is to lecture to two of these.' Alf's salary for the first voyage had ceased at the end of April, but would commence again as soon as he started his new work in Sydney. In the same letter Sir Douglas requested that Alf 'receive travelling expenses, board and lodging in Sydney, and a salary of £25/-/- a month' and that he (Mawson) would 'be writing to the Prime Minister's Department requesting that a sum of £25/-/- be immediately sent to [Alf], which will pay for his fare from Melbourne and other costs.'[9]

*

Frank Hurley was now in Sydney developing and printing more than 1000 still studies and 15,000 feet of cinema film taken aboard the *Discovery*, on shore and from the seaplane. While he was busy selecting stills for press releases and making enlargements for cinema foyers, his main concern was preparing his feature film of the first BANZARE voyage: *Southward-Ho! with Mawson*. Hurley alone worked on every aspect of his film — writing an accompanying script, working out the sound effects and choosing appropriate music.

On his arrival in Sydney Alf was invited to stay at Hurley's home until he found lodgings. '*Southward-Ho!* was in fact a silent picture with some still camera studies introduced from time to time,' explained Alf:

> Hurley accompanied the footage with the sailors singing sea shanties, which were taped onboard the *Discovery*. He had an assortment of odds and ends for various sound effects as well as recordings of the sounds of birds, penguins and seals; this together with his amusing commentary made the final result pretty realistic. Hurley ran me through the procedure a few times before I did my

first stand-in session for him. It was really all a matter of timing. Once I had introduced myself on stage and apologised for Hurley's absence — as it was stated in all the entertainment advertisements that he would speak at all sessions — I would give his lecture from the projection box. An image of Sir Douglas was shown on the screen together with a recorded message from him. After a showing of coloured stills to music it was my cue to talk along with the film. Of course I had Hurley's script and there was an assistant who looked after the sound effects and the music accompaniment.

Poster for Hurley's film: *Southward Ho! With Mawson*

Large newspaper advertisements — some with illustrations of the *Discovery* in full sail — signalled that Captain Frank Hurley's film had been 'MADE BY THE AUSTRALIAN GOVERNMENT FOR THE AUSTRALIAN PEOPLE AS A PROUD RECORD OF NATIONAL ACHIEVEMENT' and quoted a testimonial from 'One eminent educationalist' who stated 'My boys SIMPLY CANNOT AFFORD to miss it. Attendance to see and hear these new wonders is more than equal to attendance at school.' Prices of day sessions were listed as 1/- to 2/- shillings, evening sessions 2/- to 4/- shillings, with a slight increase on Saturdays and 'Special concessions to school parties.' Every line in the promotion urged the public to 'See and Hear the sights and sounds, the majesty and wonder, the undreamed-of beauty, in a land that has been sleeping since the dawn of creation' especially 'as Captain Hurley leaves shortly on the return voyage.'[10]

Southward Ho! With Mawson had its premiere in Sydney's Lyceum Theatre on 9 August 1930, a week earlier than first anticipated. 'An interesting film record of the expedition led by Sir Douglas Mawson,' wrote the *Sydney Morning Herald*. 'The sea-lions on Crozet Island for instance, utter curious shrill roars. The hull of the ship sends out a sustained hiss as it cleaves the ice. The sailors sing shanties while they work. All this increases the realism of the story, while at the same time it has not been made obtrusive enough to drown Captain Hurley's voice as he speaks through a microphone and gives a stream of comments on the various incidents.' The reviewer drew attention to the fact that some scenes were 'photographed from a seaplane' and that it was 'an entirely novel sensation to look upon Antarctica from above, spread out in all its lace-like magnificence.'[11]

The film had a good run at the Lyceum before being released interstate by Union Theatres Ltd. Early September 1930 it opened at Melbourne's Majestic Theatre as the main feature after the intermission, which was preceded by two news segments, two short 'all-talking comedies' and a Mickey Mouse sound cartoon; by mid-October interest in the film was such that extra sessions had to be put on. It was a similar scenario in Brisbane where Hurley's picture had a successful season at the Wintergarden Theatre. Surprisingly, *Southward-Ho! with Mawson* did not reach Sir Douglas' home town until 18 October, where it was initially screened at West's Theatre for a week. 'I helped out with the sessions in Sydney, Melbourne and Adelaide and Hurley covered all the showings in Brisbane by himself,' recounted Alf. 'The picture had a long run in Sydney, which for me was a bit of a holiday as I had only been there once before for a scout assembly, so it gave me a chance to look around.'

September 16, Alf was still on the road with Hurley, but had some preparatory work to do before the second voyage: 'Dear Sir Douglas, Could you give me some idea of the date of the *Discovery*'s departure and how long it is likely to be at Hobart. I am asking as I want to know how much time

I will have for making up standard solutions, etc. after the film is finished.'[12] Mawson replied immediately: 'I am now proposing that the *Discovery* shall leave Melbourne at the end of October and depart from Hobart in the middle of November. … Marr has been ill in England and a cable advises that he cannot come South with us again.'[13]

'Marr was a good companion to all of us and I was sorry to hear he would not be joining us,' reflected Alf. 'Hurley was certainly keen to give it another go once he heard that MacKenzie was the new skipper. I knew Simmers had signed up as we had kept in touch. Fletcher and I met up a couple of times during my stint in Sydney, so I was aware that he would also be onboard, but as for the rest it was really a matter of wait and see.' Mid-October and *Discovery*'s crew for the next expedition were being signed on as the ship was preparing to leave Williamstown for Hobart on 1 November 1930. 'A chief officer, a chief steward, two cooks, three stewards, and 10 seamen were engaged and picked from hundreds of applicants.'[14]

'I managed to scrounge tickets for the last performance of *Southward Ho! With Mawson*,' noted Simmers who had arrived in Melbourne from New Zealand on the 15th. 'Capt. Hurley was suffering from throat trouble so we heard Alf give the lecture. The public seemed to like it. Being in the film and interested in it, it is hard to judge how good it is. Tomorrow Alf is going on to Adelaide so I have charged him with several commissions to Mawson.'[15] When Alf returned to Melbourne after working with *Southward Ho!* at Adelaide's West's Theatre for a week he had less than 24 hours to organise his equipment and personal luggage and be on the ship before she sailed. Alf reflected: 'There was a lot of hustle and bustle on board when I returned to port the day before departure. It was all a bit of a rush. Simmers and I went into town and managed to buy a couple of items we needed at Scout Headquarters and I made a hurried visit to the Chemistry Department where I had material and papers to pick up and planned to dash home early the next morning.'

'Now the real rush began,' recorded Simmers on Saturday, 1 November 1930. 'Not much time was left now before the noon sailing but there was plenty of worry as Alf's luggage hadn't arrived. We heard by phone that the ferry across the Yarra had broken down and many people were held up. Alf got his luggage out by custom's launch but he didn't see his people to say good-bye.'[16]

*

An 'Impressive Farewell' was given to the *Discovery* as she left Williamstown: 'Her departure was marked by the cheers of several hundred people gathered on the wharf, or the jests of the crew and their friends. Other shipping in port acknowledged the event with blasts of sirens and the dipping of ensigns. The tug *James Paterson* took the *Discovery* in tow, and at midday she passed through the Heads under sail and steam on her way to Hobart.'[17] Of historical interest was the fact that 'the pilot who boarded the *Discovery* to take her down the channel to the Heads was Captain G. Doorly, who under Admiral E.R.G.R. Evans sailed to Antarctica in 1902 on the *Morning* to the relief of Captain Scott, whose ship was the *Discovery*.'[18] Among those to bid farewell to those on board were Sir David Orme Masson, Mr Macpherson Robertson and Captain J.K. Davis. Still to join the expedition in Hobart were Sir Douglas, Hurley, Johnston, Ingram, Fletcher and Alexander Lorimer Kennedy — the cartographer replacing Moyes.

There was another important member of the ship's company yet to come on board. 'Blackie' — *Discovery*'s intrepid mascot — was missing. Simmers recorded the potentially dramatic event:

> When we were leaving Williamstown Martin couldn't find his pet anywhere and told Mr Mac Robertson. However, when we were out on the Bay the cat turned up and Martin forgot to tell Mr Mac, who interested in the cat, offered a £5 reward for its return. For days he was inundated with boys carrying cats which he tried to identify by means of a small snapshot and naturally did not succeed in his search. Williamstown cat owners had a good moan as most of them had their cats pinched by £5 hungry boys.[19]

Of the scientific staff only Alf, Simmers, Douglas, Campbell, Falla and Oom were aboard. 'We're all feeling fine,' wrote Simmers, 'and have had a good time aloft where we now all feel very much at home — more so than some of the seamen who have never been on a square rig before and naturally feel rather at a loss on a yard. The newcomers to the crew appear a good crowd, though one or two are very sick despite the easy motion of the vessel.'[20] Three-quarters of a century later, Alf would meet a distant relative of one of the crew members taken on in Williamstown — Murdo Morrison from Ness, Isle of Lewis.

Wednesday, 5 November 1930, the *Discovery*, which had made her way down the East Coast of Tasmania under sail and steam, was sighted at 3.45 pm off Cape Raoul at the entrance to Storm Bay. 'She entered the river Derwent at 9 pm and without the services of a pilot, and under her own power, was expected to anchor in midstream off Hobart at 11 pm and go alongside Queen's Pier at 7 am the next morning.'[21] The first stage of the second voyage of the British, Australian and New Zealand Antarctic Research Expedition was complete.

2ND BANZARE Voyage

from Hobart, 22 November 1930 to Hobart, 19 March 1931

South to Macquarie Island

With the *Discovery* berthed at Queen's Pier the first job was to unload all her cargo into the wharf shed for Sir Douglas to make a final decision as to what should be left behind, as coal would again be the most important commodity on board, even at the cost of sacrificing some foods and non-essential equipment. In addition, there were cases labelled for the expedition that had arrived from Sydney and Brisbane that had to be sorted out. It was now Friday, 7 November 1930, and every man on the vessel was involved from early morning until late evening with preparations for her departure south.

'We scientists, in our usual untidy rig are doing all the wharf and store work before the gaze of many of Hobart's curious citizens, who seem quite able to contentedly watch us for hours doing the same thing,' noted Simmers.[1] 'We were all very aware that many of the bystanders watching us move one crate of food after another on to the dockside were possibly unemployed,' recounted Alf. 'The Depression hit hard everywhere. Some of the reserve cases initially loaded in Cape Town came back to Australia untouched. We heard later that unopened boxes of food and warm clothing after the second voyage would either be given to charity or returned to manufacturers.'

The method of classification for sorting the stores and equipment was one used by Sir Douglas when he departed from Hobart on the *Aurora* in 1911:

> To identify the cases immediately, many of them have distinguishing marks in the form of various coloured bands painted on them. Scientific equipment was placed in a section by itself, and all medical goods, marked with red crosses, were put together. The various sections are named with chalk letters on the floor of the shed. Here lie cases of Bisto, next to soups, with pickles in the next section. Elsewhere there were cases of sausages, fish packed in Norway, condensed milk and malted milk, biscuits, flour, cornflour, candles, yeast, tongues, custard powder, Quaker oats, butter, cheese, a special pile of Mac. Robertson's sweets, spirits and 'steak and kidney,' as one section was marked, and a host of other provisions.[2]

All supplies from the *Discovery*'s decks and holds were in the wharf shed by noon. 'During the morning it was decided to put a large rope between the ship and the wharf so we all lined the edge of the wharf and pushed her bodily clear; the ease with which she moved being a pleasant surprise,' wrote Simmers. 'The afternoon has been noisy, the vessel being open to the public. They haven't seen much as all below decks has been closed and there have been practically none of the staff about and those who were have been carefully disguising their identity.'[3]

Alf was overwhelmed by the Tasmanian capital's warm reception: 'Even before Sir Douglas' arrival the people of Hobart made sure we visited in and around the city. The first weekend in port we were taken out for the day in small groups.' 'It was my first visit to the city and it soon became apparent that much of the life centred around the harbour. The locals took great interest in the activities on board and on the wharf, and we were prepared to answer all sorts of questions and especially those from inquisitive schoolchildren whenever we went down the gangway.'

The two weeks of final preparations for the expedition were punctuated with the intermittent arrival of Sir Douglas and members of the scientific staff. Sir Douglas, Lady Mawson and Professor Harvey Johnston arrived in Hobart from Adelaide on Tuesday, 11 November, followed by Kennedy from Melbourne on the Thursday and then by Hurley, Ingram and Fletcher — the remaining three members of the scientific staff — who arrived by the *Zealandia* from Sydney on Monday, 17 November.[4]

'It was good to see the rest of the team again and to catch up with Hurley's latest news about *Southward Ho!* Doing some of the sessions of his film was an interesting experience and I considered myself most fortunate to have been offered the chance by Sir Douglas,' ruminated Alf. 'While we were in Hobart the film was still being screened in Sydney and had apparently met with appreciative audiences in Brisbane. Before leaving the mainland Hurley had recorded a voiceover for the movie. Hobart's daily paper was advertising the film while we were there, but apparently it didn't hit Tasmania's cinemas until we were well south.'

Hurley was excited at the prospect of making a sound-picture record of the second phase of the expedition: 'The introduction of sound to motion pictures is a tremendous advantage to Antarctic photography,' said the photographer. 'When the public sees a ship nosing its way through ice it is but a picture, but when they can hear it, it lives. What a difference when the ship is seen leaving the pier and the commands on board are heard above the strains of an emotional air played by a band, from the time when such a scene could only be conveyed in silence.' Any profits from Hurley's motion sound picture would, like *Southward Ho! With Mawson*, be devoted to the funds of the BANZAR Expedition.[5]

The *Discovery* leaving Queen's Pier, Hobart, 22 November 1930 on her second BANZARE voyage

There were a number of special functions hosted by the Mayor and various clubs and institutions during the *Discovery*'s two weeks in port. The day after Mawson's arrival the University Council staged a ceremony at the Masonic Hall, Chancellor Elliott Lewis presiding, where the Honorary Degree of Doctor of Science of the Tasmanian University was conferred upon Sir Douglas. At Hobart's Town Hall on 13 November, Sir Douglas, Lady Mawson and the officers and scientific staff of the *Discovery* were the guests of honour at a reception and morning tea given by the Mayor, Mr. J. Soundy. In between supervising the *Discovery*'s re-stowing operation, Sir Douglas accepted an invitation to the weekly luncheon of the Hobart Rotary Club, and on 19 November met with members of the city's Remembrance Club. Falla gave an illustrated lecture at the Museum to the Field Naturalists' Club on Thursday, 20 November, and the same evening Lady Mawson hosted a dinner at Hadleys Hotel for the officers and scientific staff. The Hobart Marine Board also tendered a reception for Sir Douglas and Lady Mawson and to the staff and officers.[6]

On the eve of departure Sir Douglas received many messages of goodwill from New Zealand, Great Britain and from across the nation, which included one from the chairman of the Antarctic Committee — the Acting Attorney-General, Senator Daly: 'The B.A.N.Z.A.R.E. Committee wish you, Captain MacKenzie, and all members of the expedition every success. We feel confident that you and your companions will on the forthcoming cruise materially add to the achievements of last year. Australians will follow your progress with the utmost interest, and will look forward to your safe return from the Antarctic.'[7]

*

At 2.30 pm on Saturday, 22 November 1930, hundreds of spectators — including Lady Mawson — crowded the Queen's Pier to bid 'God speed' as the *Discovery* weighed anchor after 16 days in Hobart preparing for her next exploratory adventure in Antarctica:

> Motion picture and other photographers were busy. Many of the personnel collected on the foredeck of the *Discovery* looking very happy. On the after-deck Captain Frank Hurley was making a motion picture of the crowds. On the wharf, cheers answered cheers, and the cooees of some Australian members who had climbed the rigging brought an immediate response from those on the wharf. As the vessel cleared the wharf, Sir Douglas Mawson appeared in the bows in a sports coat and cap, and with one foot on the bowsprit called upon his men to give a final cheer for the people of Hobart. The *Discovery*, carrying much deck cargo, was well down in the water. She turned slowly amidst the graceful manoeuvres of many yachts and immediately proceeded down the river against a head wind which dropped towards evening. She was off Yellow Bluff at sunset.[8]

At the striking of five bells Hurley was filled with a deep sense of nostalgia: 'It was a heartening farewell worthy of the cause and the city. As we drew away, there came to my mind a similar departure in 1911, when under similar circumstances I left with Sir Douglas Mawson and his colleagues aboard the *Aurora*. Well do I remember the overloaded decks, the leaky vessel and the thrill of anticipation which greeted my first adventure.'[9]

Scott's old vessel left with 450 tons of coal, more than on any of her previous expeditions. Perishable goods taken on board just prior to sailing included 650 dozen eggs and 20 sheep, which were penned on the roof of the winch house. Another last-minute arrival was Williams, the wireless operator, who hobbled up the companionway on crutches as he had an accident while riding a motorcycle in the Huon district and was in a private hospital for several days.[10] As the *Discovery* left Queen's Pier Captain MacKenzie had the crew check the ship inside and out for stowaways, but not one was found. 'During the evening, however, one of the seamen coming off watch was turning into his bunk when his feet touched something. He leapt to the deck crying "Stowaways". An investigation revealed that they were tucked away warmly in Seaman Ayres' blankets. Blackie, the expedition's famous cat, is now the proud and petted mother of five.'[11]

Deeply laden, the *Discovery* cleared the Tasmanian coast the next morning. 'A heavy swell was encountered and the heave and flounder of the deeply laden vessel evoked mixed emotion in most members. These were swallowed with splendid stoicism when it was announced that a marine station would be worked during the afternoon,' noted Sir Douglas. 'When working today's station owing to excessive rolling of ship, extreme caution was essential to avoid loss or damage to gear. Several members operating on small platforms extending from ship's side were constantly submerged to neck when ship rolled deeply in beam swells.'[12] For Mawson, the working of marine stations from the Australian continental shelf to Antarctic coastal waters was one of the most important branches of the expedition's research activities.

The first days out from Hobart remained etched in Alf's memory:

> Well the ship was up to her old tricks and rolling like blazes in a heavy swell as soon as we left the coastline; on more than one occasion I saw the indicator on the wall hit 45 degrees. Water was swirling all over the deck and the masts were swaying so much they looked like they'd snap in two at any moment. I managed to make it to the cabin and lie down a bit. Then the Dux called a station. To this day I don't know how I managed to keep my footing on the outboard platform. I was drenched from head to toe for hours and felt poorly for a couple of days. We were in the roaring forties and the *Discovery* was being tossed around like a cork. I would say that most of us experienced being thrown out of our bunks more than once. Meal times were a challenge — I mean sometimes you'd be lucky to have a couple of mouthfuls before your serving took off and landed on someone else's plate or in the middle of the wardroom dining table, and of course the condiments ended up all over the place.

November 27, and the *Discovery* was still heaving in stormy seas. Mawson again communicated with Strahan in Canberra: 'A tempest is booming from the north, goading our leisurely paced vessel southward through turbulent waters at reasonable speed. Though our progress is gratifying ship's motion is downright aggravating. Lurching and lunging, throwing and bucking, we have become exasperated participants in a seagoing rodeo.'[13] The rough passage and sudden drop in temperature was according to Ingram's 'Medical Log' responsible for a number of casualties: '23.xi.30: Sir Douglas Mawson has severe cold … He feels the motion of the boat. Confined to bed and treated; Mr Kennedy, Mr Fletcher, Mr Colbeck also complain of mild sore throats. All treated; 25.xi.30: Sir Douglas a little better. Everyone feeling the motion of the boat. Hurley — slight abrasion of head treated; 26.xi.30: Sail maker — left forefinger injury due to penetrating wound from wire rope.' On the positive side it was recorded that Williams was recovering from his motorcycle accident: 'foot improving — swelling much less.'[14]

Captain MacKenzie's log includes a number of bird species observed in the first 48 hours of the voyage: an Antarctic skua, a Cape hen and a few Sooty albatrosses. From then on there were increasing numbers of prions and Molly Mawks. A Wandering albatross and a Snowy albatross were also spotted, as well as a number of Black-bellied storm petrels which followed the ship for some time. Just before sunset one evening three large flocks of Tasmanian mutton birds were seen flying north. He also noted that on 30 November 'the first icebergs were seen at 19.30 in 53° 29′S 156° 06′E.'[15]

*

Macquarie Island became barely visible through a curtain of rain and fog soon after midday on 1 December. The first recorded landfall on the island was made by the sealing Captain Frederick Hasselborough on 11 July 1810, who named it in honour of the then Governor of New South Wales — Lachlan Macquarie. Thirty-four kilometres long and in places up to five kilometres wide, apart from the island's astonishing abundance of bird and animal life it is unique in that 'the rocks that form Macquarie are being forced up from the bed of the ocean by the collision of two oceanic plates. It is the only place on Earth where mid-oceanic crustal rocks, all formed on or below the sea-bed, are exposed on the surface.'[16]

On the approach from the west soundings were taken that indicated a decrease from 1520 to 102 fathoms in less than three miles. When closer to the coast two dredgings were operated, but only gave a haul of shells and crabs. By late afternoon a westerly gale was blowing as the ship came to rest in Buckles Bay. From the decks could be seen hundreds of young sea elephants lining the shore, and even though the *Discovery* was anchored a mile away their loud roars traversed the breakwater of giant kelp. The next morning after an early breakfast Sir Douglas' program was immediately put into action. Two trips in the dingy from the ship and Mawson and his team were ashore with food and equipment. The weather was bad so the tents were immediately erected above the beach and all gear put inside. 'Dr Ingram and Fletcher with net and gun were to visit the lakes on the summit of the island in order to secure life from the fresh waters. Falla and Howard were to visit the Nuggets rookery in quest of bird information,' wrote Sir Douglas. 'Hurley, Campbell and Douglas were to photograph, first visiting the Nuggets rookery. Kennedy and Oom were to do magnetics and astronomics on the spit, occupying the old magnetic station. … Prof Johnston was to collect biologically in the neighbourhood of the spit. Simmers and self were to visit old hut and wireless station.'[17]

Alf described his first visit to the Nuggets as an extraordinary experience:

> Falla and I had company all the way to the rookery. There were sea elephant pups everywhere on shore. While crossing the tussock-covered slopes we could hear grunting and snorting and nearly tripped over massive bulls wallowing, half buried in the mud. On rounding the point to Nuggets Beach we were faced with thousands upon thousands of Royals jostling one another and making one hell of a din. Their numbers covered every inch of the beachfront and the slopes above and beyond. It was like two lanes of traffic going both ways. Some were trying to make a path to the sea while others were coming out of the sea and making for the hills. The penguin traffic was dense so we moved very slowly and were careful where we put our feet as there were quite a few nesting on mounds of pebbles. Royals are about the height of two rulers with bright orange beaks and with white feathers on their face and throat. The few Kings we saw on landing seemed to me rather regal and aloof compared to their whimsical-looking neighbours.

Alf was amazed that there was such a large rookery as for many years the species was killed and boiled down for oil by the early sealers and whalers. During their brief stay the landing party sighted a number of rusting digesters on the beaches — grim reminders of a deplorable chapter in Macquarie's history. Mawson found the old expedition hut — built during his 1911 visit — in a poor state and the masts on top of Wireless Hill snapped off at ground level, but was heartened by the fact that the wild-life once slaughtered for oil was slowly recovering.

"SOUTHWARD HO! WITH MAWSON."
Top: Fight between two sea elephants. Below: Captain Frank Hurley, Australian cameraman, with a penguin audience.

Frank Hurley capturing the denizens of Macquarie Island with his camera
(Cartoon: Harry Julius)

As Simmers records, everyone returned to the tents just before dark loaded with rocks and other specimens to find that 'Hurley had got a large stove roaring in the boiling-down shack where a hot supper was waiting. … During the night a westerly gale sprang up and Kennedy, Johnston and the Dux who were lying in the magnetic tent had the doubtful pleasure of their tent collapsing on them. They slept but little, while we down in the shingle hut had an uninterrupted night except for the intrusion of sea elephant pups.[18]

Wednesday, 3 December, MacKenzie noted that the usual routine work was carried out on board and that 'the landing party returned to the ship at 1800 very wet and laden with specimens.' The following morning the ship weighed anchor at 05.30 and proceeded to Lusitania Bay where anchor was dropped four hours later. 'From the landing everyone set out for Lusitania to photograph the King Penguins,' noted Sir Douglas: 'Falla and Howard first visited a Royal Penguin rookery ½ mile to north of landing, then later went to Lusitania. … Johnston and I went before lunch to Lusitania and found several areas of nesting Kings. Young in various stages of losing chick down. The Kings have rather a habit of walking single file. It is very notable how a mob walks oriented in one direction — at one time all backs showing at another all fronts.'[19]

On the slopes behind the bay were many sea elephant wallows, some 20 paces in diameter and filled with thick, peaty mud. 'I was very vigilant on Macquarie after having stumbled into a couple of wallows on Kerguelen during the first trip,' recalled Alf. Mawson made mention of the great numbers of rabbits on the grassy slopes above the shore: 'They are very tame and can be seen scampering up the hills at the back to heights of 400ft at least. … At the boat landing Ingram and Fletcher had skinned some young Elephants [seals] for testing commercial value of skins. I collected a great lot of rocks, especially agglomerate and tachylyte loose boulders. We all got back safely to the *Discovery* about 6 pm.'[20]

Rendezvous with the *Sir James Clark Ross*

Icebergs were met soon after leaving Macquarie Island and before reaching the pack ice the ship encountered bad weather with very strong winds. The rolling was violent, resulting in a certain amount of straining which caused deck seams to leak. The cabins and the wardroom were soaked and there were 'various wreckages,' recorded Simmers: 'Alf lost a gimbal table of glass ware and Prof had a tin of kerosene burst in the lab.'[1] 'The ship indulged in every gyration, throw, pitch and toss conceivable and many other motions. Big seas kept leaping aboard to flood the deck,' wrote Hurley.[2] 'I spent the morning photographing the ship in the throes of the storm from various vantage points and narrowly escaped several duckings. So fierce were the seas that it was necessary to alter course and run before the storm. All will be mightily glad to enter the pack ice.' On a more positive note there was a double issue of chocolate and port to mark the birthdays of Douglas and Ingram on 6 December and 'Doc produced some fine shortbread made by an old Scotch cook of his'; three days later it was Harvey Johnston's and 'several bottles of *Discovery* port were put on the table and the Professor brought forth a very welcome cake.'[3]

Contact was at last made with the floating whale factory *Sir James Clark Ross* on 10 December. The whaler — which had steamed south from New Zealand — had 100 tons of coal on board for the *Discovery*. 'To our great mortification she is not in the vicinity of the Balleny Islands where we had expected to meet her,' wrote Sir Douglas, 'but is four days steam further east which is quite exasperating when our objective lies to the west.'[4] The detour to take extra coal took the vessel 500-600 miles off course and cost the expedition a valuable 10 days and 60 tons of coal. Mawson made the most of the circumstances by carrying out oceanographic operations further east than originally planned. No time was wasted. 'Everyone was busy,' noted Simmers: 'Hurley developing his Macquarie shots; Alf testing the zero points of thermometers; Stew [Campbell] trying to solve the mysteries of a Compur shutter his having rusted up after its ducking; Falla still hard at work on birds; and I lab tidying and making a rack for the theodolite.'[5]

Ingram was also busy: Sir Douglas felt his wrist 'snap' when lifting heavy loads of rocks resulting in a very swollen hand; Carpenter Williams suffering from depression attacks: stuttering, sleep deprivation, fear of heights on rigging; Eric Douglas: acute sore throat; Kennedy: lumbago; Stanton (Chief Officer): fluid swelling over joint after lifting very heavy weights, and Child (3rd Officer): lacerated nose from hit in face with block and tackle. Hurley had a bad cold due to the sudden change in temperature from 65° in the darkroom to only 34° in the wardroom and was 'prescribed a hot lemon drink copiously flavoured with whisky.'[6] The various treatments offered by Ingram cured most of his patients within a few days, however, Carpenter Williams remained under treatment and was later transferred to the *Sir James Ross Clark*, which planned to return to New Zealand early in February. Sir Douglas left enough money with the captain to pay Williams' fare from New Zealand home to Adelaide and £10 for pocket money.[7]

Decks were cleared in preparation for the approaching 100-ton coal transfer and drastic measures had to be taken to make every possible space available, which included clearing the sheep pen: 'The sheep have all been killed the past few days and now are hanging frozen forward of the bridge,' wrote Simmers. 'Coal chutes have reappeared so progress in the wardroom is hindered.'[8] 'We were all busy writing letters to our families and loved ones the evening before our meeting with the *Clark Ross*,' recollected Alf, 'the point was that any ship we came across could take our mail. By the second voyage we had a special expedition stamp mark, which was an added incentive.'

After days of steaming through scattered pack ice the *Clark Ross* was located on 15 December in Lat. 65° 41S, Long. 178° 29½E. As soon as Captain MacKenzie brought the *Discovery* alongside, with whales in between the ships as buffers, coaling operations commenced. After the scientific staff and crew had helped with the transfer of coal they were invited by Captain Nilsen to watch operations on board. Alf summarised the visit:

> The whales weighing anything from say 65 to 100 tons are brought alongside by the chasers and hauled aboard through a skidway in the stern of the ship to a massive flensing deck where they rip the skin off and cut the blubber out, and eventually everything is passed into the digesters on the factory deck below. There were many men doing this gory work and we were told that they can

treat as many as 20 a day and that the ship had the capacity to carry more than 20,000 tons of whale oil. Throughout the operation the entire deck is running with blood and guts, which they empty into the sea from the back of the ship, and you can see it floating around the ship for half a mile or so. Of course the stench is unbearable, but the sea birds all have a hell of a good time.

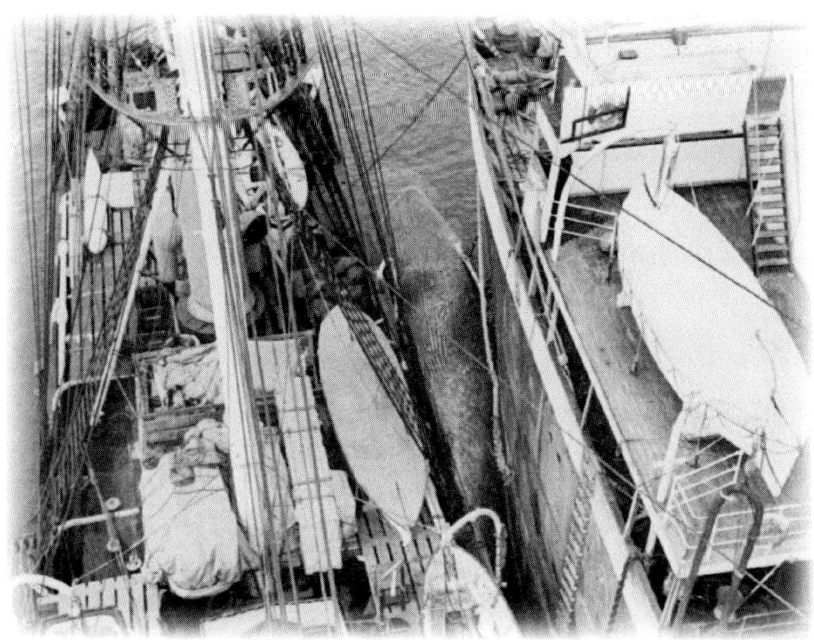

The *Discovery* coaling from the whaling factory ship *Sir James Clark Ross* (Photo: Frank Hurley)

An extra load of coal in the bunkers was vital and Mawson had only praise for Captain Nilsen and his men: 'With their assistance the transfer of 100 tons of coal and 25 tons of fresh water occupied only five working hours.'[9] Filling the bunkers was one thing, but as Simmers noted, getting aboard the *Discovery* was another: 'It was a precarious job as the ships were too far apart for safety and all we could do was to catch on to the braces as she rolled towards the *Ross* and be swung away from them and caught by chaps standing on the rail.'[10] The *Discovery* was then cast off and oceanographic investigations made in 2400 fathoms while waiting for Hurley, who was on one of the chasers photographing the harpooning of whales.[11] He returned to the ship the following evening and recounted his most memorable experience on board the *Star X*:

> The seamen work four hours on, four hours off. Two hours of this time being spent at the wheel and two hours aloft in the crow's nest while the Captain and his mate maintain a tireless vigil over the sea. Then all awake from heavy drowsy staring. The man in the crow's nest hollers down. Norwegian exclamations! They are replied to — the ship swerves from her course and the chase begins. As we draw closer, however, Larsen informs me that it is only a sperm whale and as it is very little they will run the *Star X* close to let me film it. I hasten down to the gun platform with my hand Kineomatograph. The whale is idly lolling to and fro, probably enjoying the sunshine as much as we are. He comes within range of my camera; I press the trigger instead of a harpoon. I shoot him at the rate of 24 pictures a second. Evidently the monster is unaware of our approach. Heedlessly, he continues basking. The ship draws closer and I get no end of a thrill at being able to photograph a whale in close aperture. The ship is almost on top of him and then 'Old Man Sperm' awakens as our prow all but runs him down. This is the closest I have been to a whale.[12]

*

The *Discovery* was once again on course for Adélie Land steaming along the northern edge of the heavy pack. Over the next days oceanographic procedures were resumed by the scientific staff, even though many of them felt off colour. 'Since Dux brought a very heavy one on board at Hobart,' wrote Simmers, 'colds have been with us going almost the entire rounds of the company. Alf has had a recurrence of his last year's complaint — nose bleeding — and is off all hard work or lifting. Still he works his usual exceptionally long hours in his lab.'[13] By Saturday, 20 December the sun was out, the sea was free of pack ice and Captain MacKenzie recorded the sighting of a pod of Killer whales, several Molly Mawks, a mottled petrel and six Humpbacks.[14]

The vessel's coaling detour had taken her through never-ending icescapes of extraordinary colours and formations—images that lingered with Alf long after the BANZARE:

> I have always been fascinated by the beauty of icebergs and the various effects of the sun on the ice, but when our vessel met up with the *Clark Ross* on the second voyage we were off course and as a result of the deviation we found ourselves in an area of fantastic ice formations mirrored in calm waters for days on end. You could get a good view from the deck, but from the crow's nest the panorama was unbelievably beautiful as the sun's rays transformed everything into glittering crystals. The glacier bergs in particular were in every conceivable shape and size. Some resembled majestic cathedral towers, others were cavernous with curtains of icicles hanging over grotto-like entrances; I recall being amazed how

the ice could pick up so many shades of blue, green and pink from the sunlight and give such marvellous effects. It would be fair to say that you could look at these ice sculptures and imagine anything you wished to.

'For days past the *Discovery* has headed west through pack-strewn seas. ... Never before have I seen such assemblage of fantastic shapes,' wrote Sir Douglas in a radio dispatch to Canberra on 22 December. The ship — at 63° 46.5′S 159° 15′E — was soon pushing her way through thick mist, falling snow and gale winds. Mawson was nervous: 'Last night we had an anxious reminder of what may have been the fate of the *Copenhagen*, when a towering berg some ½ mile in length was perceived through the mist square across our course leaving barely time to swing ship and avoid a collision.'[15]

The program now was to sail west to Commonwealth Bay; the landing there would be an important one and Hurley was already busy preparing a proclamation and special brass-tube holder. As the *Discovery* pushed closer to her destination more and more krill appeared in the biologists' nets, indicating the presence of whales in the area; pods of Finner and Blue whales as well as a few Adélie penguins, Sooty albatrosses, Wilson's storm-petrels and silver-grey fulmars were sighted. The ship was now progressing very slowly — averaging between 1 and 1½ knots — on account of head seas and headwinds.[16]

There was much activity on board from early morning on Christmas Eve. Hurley was decorating his souvenir menus, Sir Douglas and Ingram were in the kitchen with the chief steward selecting gourmet dishes for the next day's festive dinner, while other members were busy making a sledging harness in the hope of using it upon arrival in Adélie Land.

'Father Christmas visited the ship during the night, depositing in each member's cabin sundry useless oddments with humorous messages attached to them,' noted Hurley. 'I subsequently ascertained that this dear old chap was none other than the second engineer Mr Welch — assisted by Alf Howard.' Johnston and other members of the scientific staff were awakened soon after 7 am by 'a fine selection of Xmas carols' being played on the gramophone by Hurley.[17] After breakfast Williams handed out messages, which included greetings from the Prime Minister and from Sir Edgeworth David. The wardroom was then decorated and the table filled with packages and cards from the Royal Geographical Society of South Australia, Lady Mawson, the boys of the Church Grammar School, Mowbray Heights, Launceston and from 'Woodlands' Church of England Girls Grammar School in Glenelg.

Under an overcast sky with frequent falls of snow the *Discovery* continued to push her way along the edge of the heavy pack ice. Inside, as Simmers recorded, the wardroom was now centre stage for all festivities:

> A short service was held and the entire company was present, except for those on watch. It looked a trifle incongruous with our orchestra — flute, piccolo, four violins, guitar — crammed in the lab while the congregation lounged in cabin doors or sat round the table on which a flag and Bible shared room with cakes and presents, while on the sideboard was a goodly array of bottles. The service was Bob's idea and with the skipper officiating was a most appropriate ceremony. Afterwards we shared the cake and wine and had our presents distributed. Dinner was a good show as we all sat down together, the usual second sitting occupying improvised tables at the after-end of the wardroom. Quite the best things of the meal were the beautiful menus and the refreshments, of which we had an unprecedented amount. We all slept in the afternoon and had little appetite for the big tea and supper provided.[18]

The Chief Steward's menu decorated with mini portraits of the officers and scientific staff offered entrées of salted olives, cured sprats and soup, followed by leg of ham, mushrooms, green vegetables and potatoes, with Christmas pudding and cognac sauce for dessert. Coffee, cigars and cigarettes also appeared on the menu and the various courses were accompanied by champagne, Yalumba port and Swedish punch.

'Everyone was in holiday mood,' noted Johnston, 'all of us in special caps — DM as Mephistopheles; MacKenzie's cap had tartan; mine was a very long dunce's cap — everyone in fine humour. ... Several of the members had brought masks with them and added to the amusement.'[19] 'I have not enjoyed any Christmas among men better,' wrote Hurley. 'So the day passed happily and if we did overeat and imbibe a glass or so of champagne, it had the exemplary result of bringing all hands together, and knitting that understanding amongst all scientists and sailors that we are a team bound together by common interests and objectives.'[20]

Boxing Day was not a holiday on board the *Discovery*. It was a beautiful day so nets were put out in the morning. The sea was calm and the passage through scattered pack ice was soon congested by the heavier pack. Noon position: 65° 16.5′S 147° 32′E. In the afternoon the ship stopped in a pool in pack ice to run a full station — tow nets, vertical nets and reversing water bottles; the latter down to 3000 metres. Adélie penguins were in great numbers on the surrounding floes and some of the more curious ones dived into the pool to investigate the vessel. Crabeater seals on floes beside the ship stayed put during the four-hour operation. The next morning the pack was so heavy that the ship had to turn back, and found itself more or less in the same position as the previous day. A few Emperor penguins and Adélies as well as large flocks of silver-grey and Antarctic petrels were observed by Johnston.[21]

Simmers and Howard about to release a weather balloon; whale factory ship in background

Three whale chasers were sighted soon after 2 am on 29 December and at 8 am the parent ship *Kosmos* came into sight. A wireless message was received almost immediately from Captain Andersen offering Mawson 50 tons of coal.[22] 'By 4 pm we had our yards cock-billed and the *Discovery* otherwise ready to take coal on board. Then Captain MacKenzie ranged her alongside and we were finally secured to the *Kosmos*,' noted Sir Douglas. Whales were again used as fenders and both ships went ahead at slow speed in order to remain head-on to a moderate swell from the NN-E.

'The *Kosmos* was even bigger than the *Clark Ross* — it was gigantic,' recalled Alf: 'By the time the coaling started we were all pretty well done for as we had spent hours re-stowing the coal on board to make room for the extra load. It took time setting up the cargo rollers along the deck, and then while Simmers and I were in the sail locker unearthing the ice carrying boxes, coal was already hurtling down the chute.' The coal transfer from the *Kosmos* was not, according to Simmers, without potential hazards:

> From 5 to 8 pm and in particular from 5 to 6 pm shovelling went ahead at fever heat; some bagging direct from the forward deck and others filling the

> ice boxes and running them aft. Stew, Alf, Cherub, Doc, Grandpa [Oom] and Griggs carried out this end of the work under the rather dangerous mouth of the chute, from which at times huge lumps pelted out and which itself was heaving and swaying enough to be a menace.[23]

In less than three hours coal and fresh water were taken on board and then Sir Douglas and Captain MacKenzie were invited to dinner on the *Kosmos* by Captain Andersen and the officers.[24] 'They are fine people these Norwegians,' wrote Simmers, 'and have given us quite exceptional treatment. They are supposed to be our rivals, yet they offer coal — they don't even know if they are going to charge for it. They gave us information on ice conditions, they gave us meat (a lot of whale and a leg of beef for New Year). As a gesture Dux sent aboard a case of brandy.'[25]

From conversations with some of the whalers it was ascertained that both the *Norwegia* and Commander Byrd's vessel the *City of New York* had recently coaled from the *Kosmos*, which at the time — with a tonnage of 22,000 tons and a capacity to carry 180,000 barrels of oil — was the world's largest whaling factory. 'Today has been as busy as a harbour,' wrote Simmers, 'with the *Kosmos*, the *Discovery*, 4 or 5 chasers in sight and the arrival of the big motor tanker *G.C. Brøvig*.'[26]

*

The barometer started to fall just after midnight. The ship was very slowly wending a passage through the pack ice awaiting conditions to improve. By 3 am a light breeze sprang up from the east and increased to gale force by midday. A sounding taken during the night of just 120 fathoms indicated that the *Discovery* was now on the continental shelf. Numerous Crabeater seals were observed, but the birds had all but vanished from the scene. The ship's log records that in the afternoon of 30 December light snow flurries were soon followed by heavy, driving snow and the wind increased to force 10. The vessel was put into the heavy pack for shelter and the engines manoeuvred so as to keep the rudder clear. Visibility was now reduced to near zero and gale-force winds carried away the main wireless aerials. All hands were having great difficultly to prevent the *Discovery* drifting into a number of very large grounded bergs.[27]

'Last day of year — a day of anxiety,' wrote Johnston; 'blizzard increased during night and has been shrieking all day averaging about 50 miles per hour, with gusts about 75 miles per hour carrying hard snow which hurts the eyes.'[28] Alf remembered New Year's Eve 1930:

> We encountered blizzards on more than one occasion during the two voyages, but the one on our way to Commonwealth Bay sent chills down our spines though at the time I believe we exchanged few words about the dire situation at hand. The *Discovery* was surrounded by storm-tossed ice floes; some of them taller than our masts and very deep. The point was that this mass of ice driven by gale-force winds started to close in on us despite all efforts to keep the vessel clear. The blizzard went on for days and one night there was a hell of a bang as a massive ice floe hit the ship. The outcome of all this was a crack in the bulkhead and water leaked through into some of the cabins—my bunk was soaked.

In a radio communication to Canberra, Mawson reported that it was a miracle that the ship managed to escape crashing into a gigantic tabular berg which suddenly loomed up just a boat's length ahead. 'The brave ship tumbled and staggered in the unequal onslaught, but steadily drove back to leeward onto the most gigantic mill ever conceived — the fury-driven, heaving, frenzied, grinding ice masses of this vicious pack edge.'[29]

Midnight, 31 December, and the blizzard was still raging. 'Have been bumping in heavy, dangerous pack all day and hoping that the ship will stand it,' noted Johnston. 'Dux told us to be dressed ready for eventualities and has been very anxious all day.'[30]

Bound for Commonwealth Bay

The *Discovery* sailing through ice
(Photo: Frank Hurley)

Throughout the early hours of 1 January 1931 the wind continued to howl through the rigging reaching force 11. It was the fourth day of the blizzard. Captain MacKenzie went below for a short break, having been continuously on the bridge for more than 36 hours. The *Discovery* was for the moment in a clear pool of water, but still hemmed in by icebergs and floes. Alf mentioned how everyone pitched in: 'For a couple of days during the blizzard we each took turns on watch at the lee wheel — hourly shifts to assist the steersman.'

> All hands were called to clear coal away from the steering gear so that there was easy access in case of an emergency. We assisted the crew with the sails; being aloft and furling the sail in a raging hurricane was both exciting and terrifying. We steamed up and down hoping to break through and at the same time trying to avoid the heaving and grinding ice surrounding us. The vessel was rolling heavily as the winds transformed the pool into a rough sea. One thing I do remember was that there was no drink to welcome the New Year in — a bar of chocolate was the go I believe.

On the evening of 4 January, the *Discovery* — after weathering a five-day blizzard — rounded Cape Denison and limped into Commonwealth Bay with its huge U-shaped basin, 20 miles wide at the entrance. The vessel eventually dropped anchor in 20 fathoms within a few hundred metres of huge ice cliffs. The sea was too rough so a landing was postponed indefinitely. 'All day the gusts rose to demonical shrieking in the rigging, but in the evening it abated slightly. Truly this has been well called the "Home of the Blizzard",' recorded Campbell.[1]

Mawson's 1911-14 Australasian Antarctic Expedition hut at Commonwealth Bay revisited in January 1931

Hurley was on deck with his binoculars pointing towards his old winter quarters of the 1911-1914 Australian Antarctic Expedition: 'Through the glasses I could make out the outline of a cross on a salient ridge, which was erected to commemorate the supreme sacrifice made by Dr Xavier Mertz and Lieutenant B.E.S. Ninnis,' wrote Hurley. 'Then came into view the lower section of the wireless mast, and various small huts created for various instruments. The main hut was also partly visible, being mostly covered with snow.'[2]

After an early breakfast the motorboat was loaded with gear, which included reindeer sleeping bags. Mawson and his party headed across the bay to a shallow inlet and landed without difficulty. 'I stepped ashore and filmed the disembarkation much to the perplexity of a bevy of penguins which had waddled over to investigate at close range,' noted Hurley. It was sunny and the wind had dropped. Close to the main hut and half buried in the snow — where it had been abandoned after the engine was removed — was the rusty fuselage of the first aeroplane in Antarctica brought there by Mawson when he led the AAE.[3]

'Sir Douglas, Hurley and Kennedy couldn't wait to view their old living quarters, which they hadn't seen for 17 years. Boots and shattered fragments of wireless masts were scattered outside the hut and the only way to enter was from the roof,' recounted Alf. 'Simmers and I lowered ourselves carefully through a skylight and landed on a carpet of solid ice. We were conscious that Hurley wanted to photograph inside so were careful not to touch anything':

> The old hut was festooned with bulbous, crystal-like stalagmites and stalactites of ice. We came across a cubicle tightly filled with snow and hard ice, which turned out to be Sir Douglas's; only the bunk was ice-free. We could just make out some of Hurley's old photographic equipment in the darkroom. I recall that it was relatively easy to move around the main living area, though the main entrance was choked with snow and ice. It was silent and eerie inside — signs of the 1911-14 expedition were everywhere. I remember there were tinned foods, slabs of chocolate and a couple of bottles of Russian stout, which were brought back to the ship and later consumed with relish in the wardroom.

The hut needed to be reinforced, but as the *Discovery* lacked spare materials for the task, the Commonwealth Bay visit became a relaxing stopover. Once MacKenzie came ashore everyone gathered on the ridge behind the hut. 'After the reading of the Proclamation, three cheers were given boisterously for the King and then the National Anthem was sung.' Sir Douglas read the Proclamation officially asserting British Sovereignty of King George V Land and its extension under the name of Oates Land, which had been proclaimed in 1911, but was not officially recognised. Following the procedure for the

Proclamation Island ceremony on the first voyage, the flag was raised and the deed placed in a sealed canister and deposited at the base of the flag-pole. According to Hurley everyone then went down to the hut where the primus stoves were ready to heat 'a hearty meal of Rex Pye canned tongue and tea made with purest water from the glacial ice' with bread and jam for dessert.[4]

The Proclamation of King George V Land, 5 January 1931. Alf with back to camera (Photo: Frank Hurley)

'It was unusually warm and we soon began to doff much of our heavy clobber. Some of us were badly sunburnt,' recalled Alf:

> Much time was spent watching a large population of Weddell seals on the surrounding ice flats and observing the antics of a large colony of Adélies with their young chicks. Eric Douglas brought a gramophone over from the ship and a cut-out of Mickey Mouse, which intrigued some of the penguins, while others pecked at the strange intruders in their rookery. Hurley wasted no time setting up his equipment and capturing the comic scene for his film. I can recall sort of

going a few hundred yards up a slope and then sliding down on my hands and coming a cropper.

Eric Douglas introducing the Adélies to some non-polar music (Photo: Frank Hurley)

Apart from the Proclamation ceremony much was accomplished during the short visit: Alf and Simmers kept up hourly sea-current measurements; Johnston collected all biological specimens that were in the vicinity of the hut; Ingram and Fletcher brought back samples of life from the bottom of a nearby shallow freshwater lake; Oom charted the bay and the Mackellar Islets; Kennedy took hourly magnetic observations throughout the stopover; Falla visited all the land rookeries as well as one on the Islets; and Hurley recorded the whole visit with his photographic equipment.[5]

The *Discovery* weighed anchor on the evening of 6 January and steamed out of Commonwealth Bay passing Cape Hunter and then turned north to deeper waters just outside a massive iceberg-grounded area to operate a full oceanographic station.[6] As the warm days and clear skies continued Campbell and Douglas assembled the undercarriage of the Moth, rigged it into position, and were soon taxiing on a 'glassy surface into a slight southerly breeze and then climbed to 3000 feet to see if there was any open water on the other side of the ice-pack.' From above it became obvious that the vessel had to retrace its tracks as the pack was solid and studded with grounded icebergs stretching far out to the horizon.[7]

In between duties everyone on board made the most of the good weather. Footage in Hurley's *Siege of the South* shows members of the scientific staff and crew relaxing on deck like passengers on a cruise ship. For Simmers, 'welcome additions to the deck life during this sunny spell have been Blackie and her five kittens, which are old enough now to be energetically playful. All the family are well and are a constant source of entertainment.' He also noted that 'many penguins were seen; one in particular being especially amusing as it frenziedly tobogganed over a floe in a frantic endeavour to escape from the moving shadows thrown by the sails.'[8]

Sir Douglas and his team on the upper deck of the *Discovery*. Alf, back row, 3rd left.

Alf was busy in his laboratory off the wardroom experimenting with Kelvin tubes used in association with the electrically driven Kelvin sounding machine fitted on the stern. Usually the Kelvin tube registers only as deep as 100 fathoms, but according to Simmers' diary, Alf devised a way that it could register soundings as deep as 1000 fathoms. He 'is very bucked as a test he carried out last night on a new deep-sea Kelvin sounding tube of his own design has proved eminently satisfactory.' 'On the end of a Kelvin tube Alf has sealed a wide tube of exactly nine times the volume, thereby giving the instrument 10 times the range. Fitted with cords into a metal cover it can be fastened to the big winch wire and will give directly the depth for deep-sea tow nettings which up til now have merely been estimated.'[9]

*

The weather deteriorated and the main concern now was to break through the pack and go around the ice barrier to the coast. The ship was in a precarious situation and had to maintain her position during a hurricane, which did not abate until mid-January. 'I think we all wondered at some time or other if the *Discovery* could take much more. The captain and crew worked tirelessly to push her safely through a never-ending gigantic ice maze for days on end,' explained Alf:

> The point was that we were also battling gale-force winds laden with ice and snow, which were coming across from the great inland plateau; we'd advance a little in the pack then be driven off course again. The upshot of this situation was that Campbell or Douglas did some reconnaissance flights in the Moth with Sir Douglas or Oom our cartographer; the take-offs and landings could be risky. On one occasion Mawson and Douglas took off when things weren't too bad, but by the time they got back there was a heavy sea running and the ship had to steam flat out. The plane came alongside to be hooked, but before we could haul it on board there was a heavy swell that smashed the connecting lines and broke one of the wings.

'The plane was thus held up by three hooks and in this unstable position turned completely upside down,' recorded Hurley, who was up in the crow's nest to film the flight and witnessed the unfolding drama. 'Those ready to assist aboard were helpless. Sir Douglas was precipitated to the under side of the machine where he held on half submerged in the icy water. Douglas climbed from the cockpit ready to leap. For a moment it looked as though the machine, which was swinging pendulum wise from the lifting derrick, would crash down onto the Leader.'[10]

The motorboat was put over and Mawson and Douglas were picked up. The plane was salvaged, but as Hurley remarked 'looked as though it would be beyond repair.'[11] Alf helped the aviators repair the wing tip. 'The petrol tank had been completely smashed and Hurley went down into the engine room, found some copper sheeting and made a completely new one. So after we all worked on the plane they tried it out and as far as the aviators were concerned it was flying as good as ever.'

In a radio communication to Canberra on 28 January Mawson described the perilous landing of the seaplane after having sighted new territory between Adélie Land and Queen Mary Land from a height of 5700 feet. In the same message he drew attention to sailor Matheson who, at the same time as the seaplane drama, was rescuing lifebuoys and gear that had floated from the Moth when he became the 'object of interest to several whales which snorted and sported around his boat in a most disturbing manner … and he was obviously glad when the *Discovery* steamed alongside his cockleshell.'[12]

*

Sunday, 8 February, the *Discovery* found herself in a shipping lane as busy as the Straits of Dover. From 4.45 am until 10 pm there was a constant dipping of flags and messages sent between the *Discovery* and heavy whaling traffic. Already before breakfast whale chasers had been sighted by the first mate: the *Koeberg* from Cape Town, the *Southern Floe* and two factory ships. The *Discovery*'s ensign was hoisted as she passed the SS *Tafelberg* of Cape Town about two miles away. A little later the *Discovery* dipped to the chaser *Thorgaut* as she came alongside, while in the distance the factory ship *Southern Empress* could be seen. 'About 11.30 am another chaser, the *Thorbyn*, circled around us and when we stopped the Captain, Mikkelson, came on board and had a yarn with Sir Douglas about the condition of the ice further south,' recorded Campbell. 'He told us how to find open water and also raised our hopes by saying that Rüser Larsen, the Norwegian, was not in the area.'[13] The chaser *Hauken 2* from Norway hoisted their ensign as they passed just after 6 pm, soon followed by the factory ship *Thorshammer* — a converted tanker of 15,000 tons with high-built sides and a maze of derricks. Four more chasers brought to a close the day's whaling flotilla parade. During the next days more reconnaissance flights were made and a few more chasers and factory ships steamed by at close quarters, which included the *New Sevilla*, whose captain welcomed Sir Douglas on board, giving him 'gauge glasses and collars for the boilers.'[14]

Survey work, soundings and frequent stations were carried out as the *Discovery* proceeded cautiously along the barrier face owing to the presence of numerous snow-capped islets and submerged reefs. Late in the afternoon of 11 February the ship found shelter in the lee of an enormous iceberg in 'ice-encircled waters.' The aeroplane took off, geographical observations were made and a marine station was run. The ship was in an extensive region of 'shallow sea ranging from 100 to 250 fathoms deep,' wrote Mawson. 'Here the water is uniformly cold. Howard found bottom water coldest yet recorded by this expedition namely 28.3 Fahrenheit. Large numbers of small fish floated past the ship apparently frozen. Hurley sculled the pram into some remarkable grotto formations sculptured in grounded bergs and obtained a striking photographic record.'[15]

Early next morning the *Discovery* was steaming west along the ice cliffs of MacRobertson Land in order to resume detailed charting. At this point the ship's position was Lat 67 47′S, Long 66 56′E. Mawson observed thousands of Antarctic petrels nesting on the rocky shore, Adélie penguins 'scrambling' up the steep, icy slopes and Weddell seals along the 'boulder-strewn water-front.'[16] New names were added to the charts, which included Campbell Head, Cape Fletcher, Colbeck Archipelago, Douglas Bay, Howard Bay, MacKenzie Sea, Masson Range, Scullin Monolith and Strahan Glacier, honouring the expedition's major sponsors, Heads of State, the BANZARE Committee Members and last but not least the company of good men on board the *Discovery*. 'Sir Douglas was ready to raise the flag wherever he could,' noted Alf:

> We sailed out of MacKenzie Sea and were able to skirt the sheer cliffs of MacRobertson Land where no landing was possible. On the 13th we continued along the ice cliffs and reached a remarkable rock, the Murray Monolith. A landing was attempted, but it was possible only to throw a flag ashore. Further on was another rock outcrop, the Scullin Monolith, and a successful landing was made by a few of the party and another proclamation made covering the territory from Adélie Land to MacRobertson Land. Continuing along the ice cliffs we passed over numerous submerged reefs and between islets. At this stage when about 25 miles off the coast we could see the mountain ranges that had been sighted on the first trip. A little further west we were able to move in towards a rocky outcrop and ultimately found an ideal landing spot at Cape Bruce where we again raised the flag. Collecting was carried out and I, with Hurley and Simmers, climbed up a gentle slope from where it was possible to see the coast — east and west — and the peaks and ranges inland. On our return to the ship no time was lost in getting under way and starting our return to Australia.[17]

Last chance of obtaining more coal and more time in Antarctic waters was dashed when a radio message received from the *Tafelberg* confirmed she was now steaming in the opposite direction.[18] While this meant a considerable amount of reorganising stores and machinery for the return voyage there were some light moments: 'We had a midnight supper in Doc's cabin to celebrate Colbeck's birthday,' recorded Campbell on 21 February. 'A bit late, but nonetheless the celebration was good. Ate a lot and drank beer, Sparkling Hock and brandy and feel none the better for it now.' He also noted that the following evening there was 'a really good gramophone concert in our cabin' and 'at night' on the 24th 'Doc. Doug, Alf and I had our last game of rummy that'll ever be played on this cruise.'[19]

Homeward bound from polar seas
(Photo: Frank Hurley)

'The return was relatively uneventful other than the usual deep-sea sampling, some of which involved working as much in the water as out,' recalled Alf:

> Inevitably, the moment we left the pack the ship rolled like mad. There were a couple of nights on the way back when it was jolly difficult not to tumble out of one's bunk. We were in the middle of a gale and there was the constant clatter of cutlery and crockery and the sound of the sea crashing over the decks. Sometimes it felt like the ship was hovering on the crest of a gigantic wave and then suddenly lurching to one side — it was impossible to sleep.

Once again the *Discovery*, as Captain Scott had noted, 'rose like a cork to the mountainous seas that followed in her wake. The peculiar rounded shape of the stern ... gave additional buoyancy to the after-end, causing the ship to rise more quickly to the seas.'[20] Some days later Alf and his companions witnessed the first of a number of auroral displays: 'It was a brilliant show — curtains of vibrant yellows and greens twisting and spiralling across the sky. We were treated to repeat performances for about three consecutive nights, sometimes with variations; one evening the sky was illuminated by long beams of variegated green light edged with a sort of deep red.'

*

Tuesday, 17 March, the *Discovery* was on course for Hobart in a big westerly swell. 'All sails were handed and made fast.' During the morning Sir Douglas ran a vertical station, commenced a diagonal trawl and in the afternoon 'ran out the big dredge wire to 3600 metres with the net on it.' 'Cats wandering about ship, mother watches them. Decide to call kittens Blackie 1, 2, 3, etc.'[21]

Land was sighted just after 5 am on the 18th and shortly after HMAS *Anzac* came into view — the destroyer being in Tasmanian waters on annual exercises with the rest of the Royal Australian Squadron. One more day to go and Mawson intended to work until the last minute and have everything in order before disembarking. Everyone had their own quarters as well as an assigned area to look after: 'Alf and I have been busy cleaning the lab — first washing all the walls and woodwork with caustic soda and water and then scrubbing the deck after which we oiled all the teak shelving,' noted Simmers.[22] Early afternoon Station N° 112 was commenced. An extra ration of water was issued 'in preparation for arrival in civilization,' as Sir Douglas put it. 'At 9 pm the order was issued to dump three hundred bags of ashes from the main bunker.' Everyone was busy on deck and 'warmed to the job under a plentiful supply of port and whisky.'[23]

Mawson had only praise for the efforts of his team and felt that the information acquired from the extensive oceanographical program during the two voyages would, when published, be of value in connection with the development of fisheries: 'Everyone of the special Scientific Staff, appointed to deal with specific sections of the observational programme, worked selflessly in the interests of the undertaking. Apart from their own special work, all found time to assist, as occasion demanded, with general matters such as coaling, stowing cinders (as ballast) hauling on the ropes, etc., thus helping the sailors or other departments of work.'[24] He had words of appreciation for each member of his staff. Regarding Alf, Sir Douglas wrote: 'Howard's meticulous care in the conduct of the hydrological programme, entailing constant station work and careful chemicals analyses under difficult conditions, deserves the highest praise.'[25]

Alf penned a brief summary of the expedition's main achievements:

> By the end of the 1929-1931 BANZARE voyages most of the coast line between 45′E and 180′E longitude had been charted. Tasks carried out included: Deep-sea sampling for chemical constituents and plankton levels; Trawls and dredgings; Four-hourly meteorological observations and periodic balloon flights; Magnetic dip measurements and reoccupation of the Commonwealth Bay magnetometer station; Geological and biological specimens. The magnitude of the geological and biological collection was impressive.[26]

One hundred and seventeen days had passed since the *Discovery* left Hobart and now she was passing densely wooded slopes on her passage through the D'Entrecasteaux Channel and about to enter the Derwent River after months spent in exploration and research work in the frozen south. It was 1 pm on Thursday, 19 March 1931. The gallant ship had suffered a battering on the return voyage and would have her engines overhauled on arrival before taking on coal and fuel supplies.[27] At 3 pm 'the throng awaiting her sighted the now familiar hull, with its superstructure for sail and steam, nosing through the mist and slowly creeping towards her haven':

> Rousing cheers rose from the decks of HMAS *Canberra*. Those from HMAS *Australia* mingled with the musical greeting of the flagship's band, which crashed into the appropriate strains of "See the Conquering Hero Come". Simultaneously ensigns were dipped in salutation. ... The appearance of Sir Douglas Mawson and other members of the scientific staff was the signal for another outburst of applause. Mawson, clad in oilskins and wearing a fur cap beamed his appreciation of the enthusiastic welcome and as the *Discovery* came alongside called for 'Three cheers for Hobart' and the cheers by his ship's company were lustily given. ... Seven bells struck, and were echoed back clearly from the *Australia* as she made fast.[28]

The Officers of the Guard radioed the *Discovery* once she had weighed anchor and offered everyone the use of all amenities onboard the *Australia* and the *Canberra*. Alf took up the invitation: 'A few of us went over to the *Canberra* for a bath, and what a treat it was after so many months on strict water rations. We only had a couple of days in port and my immediate concern was to contact my father and Clarence to give them some idea as to when to expect me in Melbourne.'

That night the scientific staff gave Sir Douglas a farewell dinner at Hadleys Hotel: 'Everyone agreed that it was one of the best they had ever attended and our rendering of sea shanties was heartily appreciated by the whole hotel,' noted Campbell. 'Some of us left at 8.30 pm the rest arrived back on the ship during the morning hours.' The next day the captain and officers of the *Australia* invited all members of the expedition for lunch. Mawson's close-knit team started to disband when on Sunday 21st, Hurley and Falla embarked on the *Zealandia* for Sydney, and later on the same day 'Kennedy left by train' — all were given a rousing farewell by their companions.[29] On the eve of departure for Melbourne a dinner reception was given for Sir Douglas, the scientific staff and the officers by the Royal Society of Tasmania. 'There was little time in Hobart to reflect on how privileged we had been to go south with Mawson,' recounted Alf:

> Everyone was aware of what Sir Douglas expected from them. There was the mammoth task of writing reports of our respective findings during the two voyages, which would eventually be published in several volumes. I would say that most of us were worried about the Depression and the effect it might have on finding a job. Prior to leaving on the second voyage I had sent a letter inquiring about the possibility of work with the CSIR.[30]

Hobart — the official final destination of the British, Australian and New Zealand Antarctic Research Expedition — had given the Steam Yacht *Discovery* and all on board a very warm welcome home.

Part III
Post BANZARE

Melbourne 1931

Alfred Samuel Howard and his son Clarence were in good company when they greeted the *Discovery* as she berthed at Williamstown on Saturday, 28 March 1931. Also waiting on the wharf were Lady Mawson, Sir David Orme Masson, Lady Masson, Dr Rivett, Mr Mac Robertson and a few dock men. Sir Douglas was on the bridge with Captain MacKenzie and the remaining members of the scientific staff. First to step across the gangway was Lady Mawson, who was presented with one of the kittens by 'Lofty' Martin and the sailors in appreciation for the 'dainties' she had sent to the *Discovery* to brighten their Christmas. Sadly, it was reported that 'Blackie was lost at sea between Hobart and Melbourne.' Lofty, who took special care of her, believed that the cat 'feeling the warmth as the ship came into warmer latitudes, had gone for a sleep well up on the forecastle head and had not been seen since.' [1]

'It was good to see my father and brother on the wharf,' recalled Alf. 'We had a pretty rough crossing and of course the main concern was getting the *Discovery* safely to dock for a major overhaul before she sailed back to London. There had been many celebrations in Hobart and the Committee put on a do for us in Melbourne; I think we were all just looking forward to getting on with things once we left the vessel.'

The 'do' was a dinner at the Hotel Windsor hosted by the BANZARE Committee for Mawson and members of his party during which — after prolonged applause — Sir Douglas made special mention of Mr MacPherson Robertson for his generous financial assistance and underlined that 'the success of the expedition was also due largely to the co-operation of every member of the staff.'[2] The following evening Mawson was invited by Melbourne's Radio 3UZ to speak about the expedition before returning to Adelaide via Sydney where he had arranged to meet Hurley.[3]

The *Discovery*, having been overhauled and coaled, left for England via Cape Horn on Tuesday, 14 April. Alf went down to Williamstown a couple of times while the ship was still berthed:

> The scientific equipment and specimens had been stowed all over the ship making it impossible to retrieve on arrival, so I went over to the docks at weekends to collect my gear, but also because one felt an attachment to the old ship; it had been our home for two Antarctic summers and we all took away lasting memories. Captain Davis was on the dockside the day of her departure and we had a chat. The point was that I wished to farewell Simmers as we had become the best of friends; he went on to New Zealand with the *Discovery* and carried on with his meteorological work before the ship continued across the Pacific. My work for the expedition kept me going and then a couple of months later I was able to secure a Commonwealth research grant from Melbourne University, so all considered I was in a fairly good position.

On his return Alf was 'working at the university standardising reagents and also writing up the General Scientific Log', which he completed mid-May. The scientists' final reports would take some time to complete and Mawson offered support during the long process. By May 1931 there was significant international interest in the oceanographical work achieved by the expedition, and especially regarding 'information on the deep water and bottom water of the southern Indian Ocean.' Sir Douglas wrote to Alf suggesting he 'write up a short statement as an advance summary about water temperatures and the like for publication in *Nature*.'[4] While letters continued to go back and forth about matters concerning the hydrological report, later in the year Mawson sent Alf an update on movements of the BANZARE team: 'Moyes is now on a voyage on board the HMAS *Australia* around the North of Australia and arrives in Adelaide and Melbourne late in October. Hurley has now altered the title of the Antarctic picture to *Siege of the South* and it opens in Brisbane on the 12th of this month.'[5] Hurley wrote to Eric Douglas from Brisbane on the opening day of his film and sent his 'kindest wishes' to 'Our Alfie.'[6]

*

'I am intending to apply for a position as chemist offered by the CSIR and would be grateful if you would favour me with a testimonial,' wrote Alf in his letter of 15 October 1931 to Sir Douglas:

> There was an advertisement for a chemist to join CSIR and I can remember ringing up from home. I think I was told within a couple of days that I'd got the job. I suppose the fact that I'd been down with Mawson must have helped. Then of course there was Rivett, who had been a member of the BANZARE Committee; he was professor in the Chemistry Department when I was doing my Masters before he left to take charge of the CSIR. When Rivett left there was

> no supervision for people doing physical chemistry so we all had to go over and work in the organic chemistry department. Actually I did my Masters in organic chemistry, but by desire I would have wanted it to be in physical chemistry. So I was keen to take up the position at Griffith where I could hone my main interests, which were to do with anything, or relating to, rates of reactions of chemicals — salts of some sort, almost certainly, and things like potassium nitrate.

In the early stages of the first voyage Sir Douglas made special mention of Alf in a radiogram to Dr Henderson, Head of the External Affairs Branch in Canberra: 'Please advise Masson [and] Rivett that Howard great success. [Signed] Mawson.'[7] It was Masson who first approached Alf to join the expedition and it was Rivett who facilitated the process for Alf's passport and other papers despite his initial concern about 'the young chemist … fitting in well under the somewhat trying conditions on board ship.'

Mawson's reference for Alf was as if he had looked into a crystal ball and seen Howard's future impact on scientific research:

> *Mr. Alfred Howard, as a member of the scientific staff of the recent B.A.N.Z. Antarctic Research Expedition, carried out an exhaustive hydrological programme extending over both Antarctic cruises of the* Discovery. *In the execution of this work, he was at all times most methodical and painstaking.*
>
> *Mr. Howard is well imbued with the true spirit of scientific research. In his work he always aims at the attainment of the highest degree of accuracy.*
>
> *On the practical side, he is skilful in manipulation, thus facilitating investigations in new avenues of research.*
>
> *Mr. Howard is favoured with a good personality and a robust constitution. Throughout the whole period of the Expedition he was unaffected by the very trying conditions which were experienced from time to time.*
>
> *In conclusion, the inclusion of Howard in the staff of the Expedition was in every respect an acquisition to the undertaking. As a consequence, I have much pleasure in recommending him for further important appointments in chemical and hydrological science.*
>
> *Yours faithfully,*
>
> *[Douglas Mawson]*
>
> *Commanding Expedition*
>
> *20/10/31.*[8]

With his studies and postgraduate research work at Melbourne University, hydrological training in the UK and the vast experience acquired during the two voyages, Alf Howard was well qualified to join the relatively newly formed CSIR.

CSIR Griffith

Alf Howard's career with the CSIR started at the Commonwealth Research Station at Griffith and was recorded in the organisation's Sixth Annual Report: 'Temporary Chemist — A. Howard, M.Sc. (from 18th December, 1931).' The Station was first established in 1924 with an area of 90 acres. Initially some of the area was planted with oranges, a few acres were sown to irrigated pastures and an area was laid down for permanent irrigation investigations.[1]

Alf first joined a team researching the effect on soil and citrus trees of various methods of green manuring. Earlier experiments in the Murrumbidgee Irrigation Area had shown that citrus yields could be profitably increased by the growth of a winter legume as a green manure. Investigations also proved that 'during the growth of the legume, soil nitrates are depressed', resulting in a positive effect on the growth of both trees and cereals.[2]

Although still working as a 'temporary chemist' in 1933, Alf's analytical work was already being noticed: 'Laboratory work on soils of the area has been carried out by Mr. A. Howard, who has concentrated his attention on certain aspects of the study of the heavy rice soils and on the rate of nitrification in the permanent citrus orchard of the Griffith Research Station devoted to the investigation of effects of green manuring.'[3] Findings of the Station's green manure experiment, which had started in 1924, resulted in the 45-page report, 'Some Effects of Green Manuring on Citrus Trees and on the Soil' written by West and Howard which was published in 1938. The paper reported the results that were 'obtained concerning the effect of various treatments on the growth and yields of the trees and on the fertility, structure and water-holding capacity, the moisture content, and irrigation requirements of the soil.'[4]

Irrigation practices and in particular the hydraulic principles of spray or sprinkler irrigation was another program that Alf was assigned to. His work on this project with E.S. West was published in a joint article, 'The Design of Overhead Irrigation Systems', in 1934. The paper underlined that although the cost involved in setting up an overhead spray irrigation system was higher than that for surface methods, the chief advantage lay 'in the greater control which could be exercised with the former over the quantity and distribution of the water applied.'[5] By now Alf had been given permanent status by the CSIR.

It was during the years at Griffith that Alf first became interested in statistics: 'The Officer-in-Charge got hold of this new book about analysing data in a particular way. His maths were good, but he realised that mine were a hell of a lot better than his so he just said "You're to take this book and see what you can do with it".' The book in question was *The Design of Experiments* written in 1935 by Ronald Aylmer Fisher — the father of modern statistics and experimental design. 'The author was an Englishman from Rothamsted, which is one of the oldest agricultural research stations in the world, where he was working on a way of analysing production data. My job was to analyse the results of the yields of crops, so statistics proved to be a good tool.'

Alf's fascination with statistics was soon put to the test when it was decided that a comprehensive survey be carried out to determine the extent of damage caused to the horticultural farms of the Murrumbidgee Irrigation Areas by abnormal rains in the autumn and winter of 1939. The detailed objectives of the survey were threefold: to obtain accurate information on plantings, irrigation structures and cultural methods for each farm; to compile statistics on crops, extent of flooding and the amount of flood and wet winter damage; and to establish associations between environmental conditions, cultural treatment and the health and spread of trees. The survey took Alf and fellow scientist G.A. McIntyre four years to complete and their work was published in CSIR's Bulletin No. 168: 'A Survey, Census, and Statistical Study of the Horticultural Plantings on the Murrumbidgee Irrigation Areas, New South Wales.'[6]

*

Correspondence concerning Alf's hydrological observations for the final BANZARE report or tracking down material relating to readings of surface-water samples continued between Alf and Sir Douglas. Mawson kept in touch with every member of his team and in turn let the others know of any news. In one letter he assured Alf that 'the whole of the money derived from the showing of the Expedition picture story by Hurley ... will be quite adequate to pay for the printing of the reports.'[7] A closing paragraph at the end of another was to keep Alf informed about the movements of the scientific team: 'Campbell has been over here stopping with us for several weeks past. He is en route to England',[8] and Marr was in Fremantle on board the *Discovery* II as second in charge of the scientific work; the ship was to call at Hobart or Melbourne in the next two weeks. 'Sir Douglas sort of kept us all in touch with one another through his snippets of news,' recounted Alf. '*Discovery* II did call at Williamstown and I was able to get down and say hello to Marr — it was good to see him again.'

'About a year after joining the CSIR Sir Douglas passed on the news that as a result of the two BANZARE voyages Australia would now officially be guardian of a sizeable chunk of Antarctica,' said Alf. A British Order in Council on 7 February 1933 affirmed that King George V had sovereign rights over a large area of Antarctica and stated: 'That part of His Majesty's Dominions in the Antarctic Sea which comprise all the islands and territories — other than Adélie Land — which are situated south of the 60th degree of south latitude and lying between the 45th degree of east longitude and 160th degree of east longitude is hereby placed under the authority of the Commonwealth of Australia.'[9] The Acceptance Bill was passed by the Commonwealth Government and proclaimed in August, 1936.

Alf was still in Griffith when the *Canberra Times* of 1 May 1934 listed 'MEDAL AWARDS: For Antarctic Research Expedition': 'His Excellency the Governor-General has received advice that His Majesty the King has been graciously pleased to approve the grant of Polar Medals in bronze with appropriate clasps to Members of the British, Australian and New Zealand Antarctic Research Expedition, 1929-31.' The Polar Medals were granted to Sir Douglas Mawson, Captain John King Davis, Captain Kenneth Norman MacKenzie, Navigating Officers and crew of the SY *Discovery* and to the scientific and technical staff. Every member of Mawson's 1929-1931 expedition on board the *Discovery* was listed individually, which included 'Alf Howard, M.Sc., chemist, both cruises.'[10]

*

The appointment of 'Miss E. Beck (from 21st March, 1932)' was noted in the Council's 1932 Annual Report and it was not long before Alf met the new staff member, 'Bett was from Sydney and came to the Research Station just a few months after I started. I would say things might have come to a head within the first 12 months. I can't quite remember when I first plucked up courage to ask her out, but I suspect we went to the movies. She was good looking and of course she was a natural blonde, and luckily we were about the same height.'

Alf, 2nd from left, best man at the wedding of his brother Clarence and Hazel Hart in October 1934. (Photo: C. Stuart Tompkins)

Alf made a special trip to Melbourne in October 1933 to be best man at Clarence's wedding on the 19th. Just a year later Alf explained in a letter to Mawson the delay in completing his hydrographical report: 'Dear Sir Douglas … I have been very busy for the past twelve months as there is really more work at Griffith than one chemist can cope with. Also to make matters worse I am getting married in December and ever since the middle of the year all my spare time has been spent in making arrangements for a house I am building in Griffith.'[11]:

> Well I knew Bett for at least 12 months before I proposed. We married in Griffith and after the wedding we drove down to Sydney and then down to Melbourne to see my family. My mother had died while I was still at Melbourne University and my father had married again. After a couple of days in Sydney we drove up to the Blue Mountains for a few days. During our time in Griffith we did quite a bit of touring around in the car, especially in the Murrumbidgee area.

Alf was now 'safely married and enjoying a holiday in Sydney' as he put it to Mawson in a letter written on Boxing Day 1934.[12] 'Bett didn't wish to continue working at the Research Station after we got married so she arranged for a friend of hers to come up from Sydney and take over her job,' said Alf. 'She had her own library for a while and later a friend of hers joined her. It operated full time for a couple of years, but I don't think it was really a financial success.'

*

Alf Howard's work in Griffith was well recognised and the 'marriage was a happy one', but signs of his lifelong attachment to Antarctica were already clear in a letter to Eric Douglas — his cabin sharer on board the *Discovery*:

Research Station

Griffith

9.12.35

Dear Doug,

Congratulations, old man, on getting another trip amongst the Adélie flappers. I don't know what arrangements are being made with regard to the personnel of the land parties but if there is anywhere where I can be fitted in I am very, very keen to go down there again and if possible do some sledging (I might even be of some use in my old job of aeroplane rigger's assistant).

I have written a more or less formal offer of my services to Captain Davis and suggested that the Council for Scientific and Industrial Research might second me for the trip. I would be pleased if you would point out what a fine fellah I am and generally help my application along.

Yours truly,

Alf Howard[13]

Alf was not on board the RRS *Discovery II* when she left Melbourne on 24 December 1935 — with two planes: a Wapiti and a Gipsy Moth — bound for Dunedin then on to the Bay of Whales in the Ross Sea where Lincoln Ellsworth and Hollick Kenyon were reported missing in their plane, the *Polar Star*. From the ship, in January 1936, Eric Douglas led an RAAF search party in a Gypsy Moth for the two adventurers who were spotted and soon met by a land party from *Discovery II* — the *Polar Star* had run out of fuel.

*

In the Council's Annual Report for 1939-40 the letters AACI appeared for the first time after Alf's name; he was now an Associate of the Australian

Chemical Institute. Alf had been with working in Griffith for nearly eight years when war was declared:

> Bett was secretary of the local Red Cross and of course this was when the war was well and truly on. She was involved with the contingent that was more or less disseminated in Singapore — mainly people from the Riverina. You see the troops that went to Singapore were largely from that area and had a bad time. I remember having to go along to some sort of committee that decided whether people should or should not be enlisted. They just said right, OK, you're needed for scientific work so you won't be enlisted.

By June 1943 Alf had been seconded from the Irrigation Research Station at Griffith to work for the CSIR's Division of Food Preservation and Transport at the State Abattoir, Homebush Bay, Sydney.

CSIR Sydney

When the Australian food industry was called upon to feed the Australian and United States armed forces in the tropics from 1942 on, the problem was solved largely by the expansion of the canning industry and the development of dehydration plants. Soon canned and dried food would constitute the major portion of a soldier's rations for months on end. In order to provide much needed technical assistance to the industry the CSIR's Division of Food Preservation (DFP) and Transport at Homebush Bay was also expanded, partly with new recruits and partly by officers seconded from other divisions. Alf, seconded from the Irrigation Research Station at Griffith, was assigned to the new Dried Foods Section.

Work in the new section was partly experimental — devising and improving processes — but mainly in the field assisting in design, setting up and establishing quality control in a number of new factories. Previously there had been virtually no production of the dried foods now needed because there had been no consumer demand. At the time only limited advances in dehydration technology had been made. Those in the section were new to food research and like Alf several had been seconded from other CSIR divisions. The Dried Foods Section during the period 1942-1945 provided technical direction for the setting up of some 32 plants across the nation. 'Individual officers spent weeks at a time in factories, particularly when new equipment was being installed or a new factory was starting production. At such time they might work for 12 or 14 hours at a stretch as they followed a product through all the unit processes.'[1] Alf was involved in the dried vegetables program, but particularly with dried mutton, first at the Homebush laboratory, then later at the nearby Auburn premises.

By dehydrating meat the need for cold storage was avoided. Also, the cost of packaging materials for dried meat proved to be far less than for canned meat. Alf explained the actual drying process and why it was important to be able to transport dried meat to the armed forces and keep them well fed in one of the most undernourished parts of the world:

> Well, they had to have some way to transport meat to the tropics; to take meat as raw meat up to New Guinea by plane under war conditions would have been almost impossible. Frozen meat wasn't an option because you had the problem of transporting frozen equipment and keeping it frozen, so drying was the answer. Of course the big problem was once you dried it would it be any damn good? The meat was minced then dried in hot air with very careful control of temperature. It came out in granulated form — in pieces about the size of peppercorns — and with about two parts of water to one of meat, dehydrated mutton proved to be popular with the troops, especially when used to make dishes like stews or rissoles.

While dehydrated mutton was mainly intended for the troops and for export to Great Britain the possibility of selling it for local consumption was being investigated. It would cost the public about two shillings and sixpence a pound, which would be equivalent to seven pounds of fresh meat. Dehydrated mutton could be packed in cartons for up to six months and in tins for two years. Mr Scully, then Minister for Commerce, believed that 'by the end of June 1943 more than 20 mutton drying plants were expected to be working at full pressure. The building of the plants would cost the Federal Government about £200,000.'[2]

Alf pointed out that the drying of food in tunnels was happening in various other places all over Australia and many companies found this was a good way to get buildings constructed. 'About half-a-dozen of us did practically all our investigations in other peoples' factories out of town and sometimes interstate. We would go along and make sure that the tunnels were functioning correctly, as it was assumed that this was a reasonable method for drying food.' During Alf's years in the Division of Food Preservation, inspections of new installations often took him away from Sydney for long periods: 'When I was moved to Sydney Bett of course came with me; we found a place to live on the North Shore and within weeks she was working with the Red Cross.'

As far as fruit was concerned, in most cases a large amount of it was dried in the sun although some of it went through the tunnel dryer. 'The point about the sun is that because you're getting a sterilising effect with the ultraviolet light you could dry fruit in the sun at no cost,' explained Alf:

> We also did a little bit of work on eggs for those going on the Kokoda Trail, which included experiments to determine the storage life of different samples of dried egg under various conditions, and especially those in the tropics. Much of our investigations concentrated on vegetables. As a matter of fact it was

more vegetables than meat. The vegetables were put through tunnels in drying cabinets. I was second in charge of the scientific side of it and worked with people from the Department of Supply, who were more or less responsible for setting the whole thing up. A certain amount of dry food processing is still done today and popular with the backpackers in much the same way as when I worked on it.

Alf Howard (far right) with members of the Dehydration Section testing reconstituted dried potatoes mid-1940s

By June 1945 Alf, no longer on secondment from Griffith, was listed as a permanent Research Officer of the DFP and within two years he was promoted to Senior Research Officer. Quality assessment on dried foods involved tasting tests by panels of trained and untrained tasters, and Alf became very interested in the design and interpretation of these tests to ensure that they were statistically reliable. It was out of these activities that arose his interest in human behaviour and psychology that he later extended into academic studies. Jack Kefford was at Homebush Bay the same time as Alf: 'I had joined the Division in 1938 and worked in the Canned Foods Section where we were equally committed to war work, so Alf and I never actually worked together. Our war work completely displaced our normal research programs and it was not the sort of work that resulted in published papers. In any case we were all too busy to write papers.'[3]

*

At the beginning of World War II — on the other side of the world in London — Alf's old ship the *Discovery* had her engines and boilers removed for scrap to help with the war effort.

CSIRO Brisbane

Alf Howard moved to Brisbane in October 1949 to take up his appointment as Officer-in-Charge of CSIRO's Meat Research Laboratory in Cannon Hill. Prior to leaving Sydney Alf was working on the production of a superior type of dried mutton for the Australian Army when he was prompted by J.R. Vickery, Chief of the Food Preservation Division, to lead the Organisation's meat investigations in Queensland.

Alf and his team first worked together on co-operative frozen-beef studies aimed at finding out how animals should be treated before slaughtering, and how the meat should be handled and stored before being shipped overseas; it was due to his organisation of land storage trials that by June 1950 the first two experimental shipments of frozen beef had been sent from the CSIRO to the Low Temperature Research Station in Cambridge for detailed examination. Also, at about the same time, he was working on improving the export of chilled meat in a carbon-dioxide atmosphere to the UK. This led to the current, very important method, of vacuum packaging.

Alf's long-term concern about the visual impact of meat for the consumer was already evident in his 1950 co-authored article with Vickery: 'The most important defect in frozen beef is the appearance of the thawed material when it reaches the consumer. Freezing of beef muscle causes a breakdown which results in the fluid known as "drip".'[1] Within the year he had also selected and trained a tasting panel of nine members of the staff to evaluate the eating qualities of beef when cooked, and set up a taste panel to judge subjectively the differences in quality between chilled and frozen beef: 'We were concerned with both the treatment of the live animal and the treatment of the flesh after the animal is killed and about which treatments would work to give the best eating quality. I would say that the visual presentation of meat for the consumer was an important part of the show; probably almost the whole show.'

Co-operative investigations continued between the Brisbane Laboratory, the British Ministry of Food and the Low Temperature Research Station in

Cambridge, and in 1952 'the exchange of information was facilitated by the visit of a senior officer [Howard] of the Brisbane Laboratory to England':[2]

> Our house had just been built in St Lucia when I was sent abroad for a few weeks. Most of my time was spent in Cambridge where I first met Ralston Lawrie, who was later seconded to our Cannon Hill laboratory. I had a couple of days in London before flying home and was curious to see the *Discovery* again. I had first seen her in the East India Docks before Davis took her down to begin the expedition from Cape Town. The old vessel was moored in the Thames along the Victoria Embankment not far from St Paul's Cathedral as I recall; sea scouts were using her as a training ship and looking after her well enough to keep her afloat. There was a small museum on board and although she was missing a few bits and pieces there was plenty to remind me of the voyages south. Mawson kept in touch with us not only about matters relating to the final reports, but also to pass on good or sad news. It was through Sir Douglas that we learnt of the passing of Prof. Johnston and of MacKenzie, who had been our captain on the second voyage.

Within three years Alf's old ship would have a new 'crew' as on 20 July 1955 after repairs and a few changes she was commissioned as HMS *Discovery*, flying the flag of the Admiral Commanding Reserves until 1976; during this period the *Discovery* was a drill ship for the Royal Naval Volunteer Reserve with continued facilities for the Sea Scouts — weekend training and the mooring of their boats.

*

From 1953-56, experiments to reduce the amount of 'drip' started to be recognised by scientific institutes at home and abroad. 'From our viewpoint, the most interesting work of this period was a long series of investigations on the effects of pre-mortem treatment of beef cattle, carried out jointly by A. Howard and R.A. Lawrie of the Low Temperature Research Station.'[3] Professor Ralston Lawrie arrived in Brisbane early January 1953: 'Over a period of three years I came to know Alf quite well':

> His organisation of the various ancillary requirements arising from the investigation was excellent. For example, for the measurement of *rigor mortis* a specially modified kymograph was necessary.[4] I was only able to bring one of these with me from Cambridge but Alf most expeditiously had an exact copy constructed so that measurement could be made of the two different muscles simultaneously. It was also essential that the kymographs were kept at constant humidity and temperature. Alf speedily arranged for a suitable cabinet to be

constructed. During the period 1954-1955 whilst I was back in the UK, Alf had two further kymographs constructed so that on my return it was possible to measure *rigor mortis* on four specific muscles simultaneously.

Apart from being with Alf daily in the laboratory, he and his wife Betty showed my wife and me generous hospitality at their home in St Lucia, and in their bungalow by the beach at Surfers Paradise. Alf and I made several visits to cattle rearing country in south-west Queensland — at Cunnamulla, Thargomindah and Yaraka, where the country was a vast, dry plain and so free of traffic or any surface obstacles that Alf nobly taught me to drive a 15 cwt truck! Later we also had a look at cattle properties on the wet regions of north-east Queensland's coastal belt. I recall taking a photograph of Alf with a Zebu bull at Balmoral Station.[5]

Alf, above right, preparing an animal for pre-slaughter at the Meat Research Laboratory, Cannon Hill, Brisbane in the 1950s

The results of Howard's and Lawrie's co-operative research into methods of preventing nutritious qualities dripping away from frozen beef carcasses after thawing were published in a series of papers between 1956 and 1959 by the CSIRO entitled 'Studies in Beef Quality, I-VIII,' under their joint authorship. However, the close integration of fundamental and applied work envisaged by Howard and Lawrie 10 years earlier did not achieve reality until Scott, Newbold, Lee and Shorthose moved to the new Brisbane laboratories in 1967.[6]

By 1957, Alf had been Officer-in-Charge at Cannon Hill for eight years and together with his team had successfully followed through a number of investigations on frozen as well as chilled beef, the results of which were published in various papers written by him or co-authored with members of his scientific group; topics covered such as 'The Preservation of Beef by Freezing' (1950); 'Chilling of Beef for Export' (1953); 'Experimental Shipment of Chilled Beef per S.S. *Jason*' (1953); 'Preparation of Frozen Packaged Meat' (1955); 'Implications and Conclusions from Investigations on Quality of Frozen Beef' (1956); 'Studies on Beef Quality: The Effect of Blast-Freezing Hot Beef Quarters' (1956); 'The Measurement of Drip from Frozen Meat' (1956); and 'The Cooling, Freezing, Storage and Transport of Frozen Meat' (1957) – give some insight as to the diversity of research then being carried out.

*

During the period Alf was stationed in Griffith and Sydney he made a point of going to the annual reunion dinner of the Antarctic Club of Australia, which coincided with that held each year in London. On more than one occasion the reunion took place at the Royal Sydney Yacht Squadron and each man present had at one time or another been either a member of Shackleton's 1914-17 *Endurance* expedition, Mawson's 1911-14 Australian Antarctic Expedition or Mawson's 1929-31 BANZAR Expedition. 'It was a good chance to catch up with everyone and also meet members of earlier expeditions. Simmers came over from New Zealand a couple of times and of course the rest of us were scattered all over Australia. I remember seeing Mawson, Hurley, Davis, Ingram, Fletcher and Douglas at some of these gatherings, and also Johnston at one of the earlier get-togethers.'

Although Alf's contribution to the final BANZARE reports was printed in 1940 correspondence with Sir Douglas continued. Responding to a letter he received in November 1957 from his former commander, Alf wrote:

26th November, 1957.

Dear Sir Douglas,

Your letter reached me quite safely as I am still with C.S.I.R.O. here in Brisbane and in fact I rather visualise that I am likely to be here for the rest of my days. Unfortunately, my rather infrequent and irregular trips to the southern capitals which only happen 2 or 3 times a year never seem to coincide with the Antarctic Club activities so that, apart from spasmodic correspondence with Fletcher, I am getting out of touch with things. I hope however, to be in Adelaide for A.N.Z.A.A.S. next August if not before.

Please forward any B.A.N.Z.A.R.E. publications to me at the above address.

With kind regards, and compliments of the Season,

Yours sincerely,

[signed: A. Howard]

'I did meet up with Sir Douglas at the ANZAAS [Australian and New Zealand Association for the Advancement of Science] Conference in Adelaide; it was the last time I saw him as within a couple of months he had passed away. At the time of his passing I recall there being an exchange of letters between the remaining members of our old team, which renewed old friendships.'

*

Tim Cassidy, who in 1970 spent a year at Australia's Mawson Station in east Antarctica, was a part-time student in veterinary microbiology at the University of Queensland when he worked at Cannon Hill in 1959. During his year at the CSIRO he was Alf's personal assistant on a visit to the Swifts meatworks in Gladstone to inspect a chilled-beef shipment:

> I drove Alf up to Gladstone and back in a Commonwealth car and we had long chats. He told me a lot about Mawson and the BANZAR Expedition and he also told me a lot of his views, which I found quite radical; he praised Greek café owners because they were an inestimable help to people who wanted to travel around Australia as they were the only ones who ever kept cafés open.
>
> Preparation for the chilled-beef shipment required a lot more delicate handling than for frozen beef and a lot more delicate temperature control as it is cooled down to just above freezing. Alf and I spent four hours on and four hours off for a week in the cold rooms at Swifts. He was extremely athletic and showed his athleticism in moving between floors in a huge freezer chamber, a blast channel with cold air, and climbed up the ice-covered walls using a chimney — quite a specialised mountaineering technique. Years later when I came back from Antarctica I went over to see him with a map showing Howard Bay, which I was able to visit because of its proximity to the base at Mawson.[7]

Alf's background in chemistry, physics and hydrology, his many years at the Griffith and Homebush research stations together with his high capacity to absorb and apply new concepts made him one of Vickery's most important collaborators. For 17 years Alf worked closely with Vickery 'on a number of new programs in meat research, and when more money became available, on further expansion of activities and on building new laboratories.' Alf's scientific intellect enabled him to soon acquire a sound knowledge of the physiology, biochemistry and microbiology of meat so that 'he was able to apply the physical and engineering principles that he had used in work on food dehydration to the design and operation of freezing equipment. As a result of his responsibility for developing accurate methods of taste-testing, he acquired an interest in statistics and psychology.'[8]

In 1956, Alf enrolled as a part-time student at the University of Queensland (UQ) in Arts, majoring in psychology, as an aid to the study of consumer reaction to food stuffs. He studied psychology for three years and was granted credit for pure maths I and II as well as for chemistry I and II towards his Bachelor of Arts on the basis of his postgraduate awards at the University of Melbourne. In 1959 his Arts degree was put on hold so that he could be admitted as a part time candidate for the Degree of Doctor of Philosophy.

Despite the heavy workload and study commitments Alf found time to enjoy and explore his new surroundings:

> Brisbane seemed like a big country town when we arrived in the late 1940s and I recall being fascinated by the silver trams. We had a car, but sometimes on a Saturday morning would walk from St Lucia to Toowong, take a tram to the markets in Roma Street then return home the same way. The house was on a fair size plot of land so I planted a few things, but never acquired the gardening skills of my grandfather, who was a horticulturist and lived with us in Stanhope Grove. Within a year or two we bought a small seaside bungalow at Surfers Paradise and later built a fibro dwelling up in the hills at the back of Tugun. We used to drive to the beach house quite a bit and on long week-ends down into New South Wales around Ballina and along the coast there.
>
> The work at Cannon Hill was very interesting, but also very demanding, and often required my travelling to regional centres in Queensland and interstate as well as visiting meat institutions abroad and sometimes presenting conference papers.

Alf represented the CSIRO at the 10th Pan-Pacific Science Congress at Honolulu in August-September 1961 where he delivered a paper on the 'Preservation of Meat Products in the Tropics without Refrigeration.' In 1962 he was overseas for nearly two months to attend the Seventh Meeting of European Meat Research Workers in Warsaw and then visited meat-research institutes in England, France, Germany, Denmark, Sweden, Finland, Russia, USA, Canada and New Zealand. He was made a Fellow of the Royal Australian Chemical Institute (RACI) in 1964 and in the same year attended the ANZAAS Conference in New Zealand.

Members of Alf's team drawing on his energy and drive included food scientists, microbiologists, biochemists and a group of 10 technical and office staff. Colleagues who worked with him during the 1950s and 1960s remembered him as a serious man with strong leadership qualities who cared about the welfare of each person in his team.

Alf and Bett in the garden of their St Lucia home 1960

Les Brownlie first worked in the microbiology section at Cannon Hill in 1960 and recalled that soon after he started, the English research officer he was assigned to work with had drowned while on holiday near Noosa:

> Naturally it was a terrible shock for his wife and children. Alf realised they were far from home without financial support and would need accommodation so immediately proceeded to build a flat for them under his house in St Lucia. It took six months of labour; in fact a number of us from Alf's section volunteered to do the exercise at weekends. Alf's wife made sure we were well fed and always well looked after — she was a real character and had a heart of gold. When I first took a subscription for concerts I would meet Alf in town on a Saturday, go to the concert, then go home with him and sleep in a spare room

> upstairs and we would work on the building the next morning. The family stayed in the flat for about two years and then returned to England.
>
> Alf was a very conscientious man and I recall on one occasion working on a program that involved applying complicated parametric statistics. Without hesitation Alf just read up a few books so he could analyse my work — he was always very helpful.[9]

Fred Grau was a senior research scientist at Cannon Hill when he left in the late 1990s, but had first met Alf in 1950: 'It was actually my first interview for a job so I wasn't too comfortable. I'd done high school in a Catholic seminary so I did all sorts of odd things like ancient Greek and Latin and I thought this is going to kill me for a job in a science institution,' recollected Grau. 'Anyway Alf quite put me at ease because he was interested that I had done some studies in ancient Greek. I got the job of technician, went to university part-time, stayed at Cannon Hill for five years, then studied in the United States, returning to the CSIRO in 1961 with a MSc and a PhD':

> I was married about two or three weeks by the time we came back from the US and Alf and his wife took us under their wing for a year or so. We went with them to concerts at the City Hall and Alf would sometimes take us on a Sunday to a big old Queenslander house with attractive gardens in Bowen Hills where artists such as Margaret Olley and the potter Milton Moon had preview showings. It was all a new experience for me. They were very kind to us and would come all the way from St Lucia to Cannon Hill to pick us up and take us to various concerts and exhibitions because we didn't have a car for quite some time. I always found Alf easy to talk to and easy to get along with. He was certainly fit and hearty and was well liked and respected.[10]

A senior meat scientist at CSIRO until 2000, Robin Shorthose first met Alf in 1963 at Brisbane's old metropolitan abattoir: 'There were about 15 people and Alf was not only the Officer-in-Charge, but he was the Group Leader as well.' Working conditions in the old laboratory were really terrible and apparently just as cramped as those at Homebush:

> Alf was developing his work on the psychology of taste panels and combining these evaluations with objective measurements of meat tenderness. At the same time he was working with Ed Bouton on the natural ageing of meat, but then moved on to more powerful enzymes similar to papain, which dissolved the meat fibres so that you could get a very rapid ageing. Papain and similar enzymes weaken the muscle fibres and make the meat tenderer. Some of the enzymes that are used are actually activated by cooking, so you can in fact tenderise the meat while it cooks.

> During his time as Office-in-Charge Alf encouraged a lot of the staff who had started work as technicians in the laboratory to do a university degree and then come back as scientists. Although he was incredibly helpful, he was also very demanding of his staff. He judged people by himself and he reasoned he wasn't that different from anyone else, and if people are only the same as him they were by definition not that good. I mean he harshly judged himself. In a subsequent CSIRO-wide evaluation of standards most of our technicians went up two grades because Alf had probably been a bit too strict about qualifications necessary to achieve promotion.[11]

At the time of the move into the new building in 1967 there was an influx of staff from Sydney and the new laboratory grew quite dramatically. Alf was no longer Officer-in-Charge but the Principal Research Scientist, having been replaced by a microbiologist from Homebush.

Tom Larsen was transferred to work with Alf as his personal technician in the new laboratory from 1967 after having joined the CSIRO three years earlier. Much of his work was connected with Alf's research for his PhD, which involved preparing different concentrations of products like Vegemite and giving them to panellists to see if they could identify any variations: 'I believe that Alf felt he deserved to be in charge of the new lab as he'd been a loyal Head of Laboratory in the old one for nearly 20 years. There was no obvious public display of disappointment, but I think deep down it was there.'[12]

Brownlie, Grau, Larsen and Shorthose were all aware of Alf's involvement with the planning and design of the new laboratories and remember Alf walking around with plans and asking everyone for their input as to what they would like. They also recalled his role in overseeing the actual construction of the building during both Stage 1 and later Stage 2, and felt he had also put a lot personal effort into designing the gardens.

Alf's long-term association with the project was recorded in CSIRO's 1979 publication — *50 Years of Food Research*: 'The official opening of stage 1 of the new Meat Research Laboratory at Cannon Hill on 31 May 1967 marked the culmination of eight years of planning and concentrated effort by Vickery and Howard. The process began in 1959 and … during the next three years Vickery and Howard drew up proposals, project lists, estimates, and revised plans for expanding meat research and providing research facilities.'[13] In April 1962, The Australian Cattle and Beef Research Committee (ACBRC) agreed in principle to contribute finance for the new laboratory in April 1962, at which point Alf and his staff began work on detailed plans for the building.

In early 1967, besides his involvement with the final stages of the new laboratories, Alf was also working on the final drafts of his doctorate thesis. The aim of his 'research project was to select and validate a technique for measuring attributes of eating quality of foods (particularly meat) and also for measuring differences in these attributes as a means of studying their dimensionality.'[14] Alf was awarded the Degree of Doctor of Philosophy in Psychology by the University of Queensland in April 1968.

'I believe many of us felt Alf was exploited,' remarked Shorthose. 'He virtually designed the laboratory and did all sorts of work to make sure it was built and at that stage he had other issues to attend to.' About the time of the opening of the new building Alf's wife suffered a heart attack. 'It happened out of the blue. Bett knew it was a heart attack because you see her mother ran a private hospital and so she had some knowledge of the condition. She was in and out of hospital for a while and lasted a little bit over three years after the attack. I lost her in 1972, just months after I retired.'

For Larsen, 'Alf was just such a congenial sort of bloke, an absolute gentleman. I never heard him get angry or cross. I can't even recall him swearing. What I really liked about him was he never talked down to anybody, you always felt that he was treating you like an equal':

> He encouraged me in my studies and also he was the first person who gave me co-authorship on a paper, which was something special for me. He wrote the paper, designed the experiment and I just did the technical hackwork. He drove me up to uni once when I started a part-time degree course out there. I'd been told about his driving. It was terrifying. He had a two-tone green Austin; he drove quite fast and didn't slack off at corners. It was interesting — let's put it that way. You could tell he was miffed because he went out and landscaped the grounds on his own. We would watch this little fellow in his shorts out in the yard moving these huge boulders around. His strength and energy were just incredible.[15]

Always keen to share any knowledge he acquired along the way, be it connected with his research or his interest in statistics and computers, Alf encouraged staff to present papers about meat science at Cannon Hill and invited student employees from meat exporters such as Borthwicks to attend. He also ran voluntary computer lunch-time classes: 'I think the language was called FORTRAN in those days,' reflected Larsen. 'He used to punch cards and put them into a big machine, which would print out huge lengths of paper.

Well he'd lose us all with the technology and terminology of the day, however, we all thought it was great at the time.'[16]

*

Alf Howard retired on 29 April 1971, the day before his 65th birthday, after 40 years with the organisation. 'There was a do and a presentation for him,' recalled Larsen. 'The usual farewell party — it wasn't formal, just a staff gathering in the afternoon — finger food and all that.' After 'retirement' Alf did not cease either work or study; with his unremitting passion and commitment to science, as well as his perdurable scholarship, he continued to publish long and detailed papers on sensory analysis and mentored at the University of Queensland on aspects of computer programming while still following further undergraduate courses.

The University of Queensland Years

In the winter of 1973, amid publishing scientific papers, Alf booked a passage with Burns Philip to the Solomon Islands and Papua New Guinea. 'It was a freighter that took about a dozen passengers so we all dined with the captain,' recalled Alf. 'I would say we had three or four days in Honiara while they unloaded cargo and took on more goods. A couple of days after arriving in Port Moresby I flew in a DC3 to the Mount Hagen Show; it was very colourful — traditional dances in spectacular costumes and headdresses decorated with bird of paradise feathers. There weren't many tourists in those days. It was an enjoyable break and gave me time to think about what I might do next.'

During the candidature for his doctorate degree at the University of Queensland regulations required that Alf put his Arts course on hold; however, as he had already gained more than two-thirds of the credit points, in 1975 he re-enrolled in a number of linguistic subjects as well as courses reflecting his ongoing interest in computers (Fortran language) and philosophy. In September of the following year he was awarded a Bachelor or Arts. Now with the necessary prerequisites Alf enrolled part-time in the honours program in linguistics. The schedule was a gruelling one with 14 courses as well as presenting a dissertation. 'Alf and I were the honours class — no-one else. It was just us,' recollected Lesley Chase. 'We had the most demanding course, many topics as well as the dissertation and one had to get 19 out of 20 for everything. Sometimes we would get together, no elevated discussions, and commiserate with one another like two students who felt they were having a tough deal.' Alf was curious to know how language operates and was particularly interested in the speech signal and what happens inside the mouth to sound changes. His thirst for knowledge led him to enrol in an engineering course so he could design a device and then present it to his dentist to create an apparatus that he could attach to his teeth to record sounds and sound changes.[1]

Alf's 55-page handwritten dissertation: 'A multidimensional scaling study of the perceptual space of vowels,' included numerous tables and 30 pages of hand-drawn diagrams and charts on grid paper for presenting the statistical data. Alf liked working in a team as he had on the BANZARE voyages and during his time at the CSIRO, and soon found he had a group of volunteers 'under inducement of added points' to participate in his various trials. He acknowledged that 'the project would not have been possible without the cooperation of the first and second-year linguistic students who, though perhaps captive subjects, persisted in their cooperation even when some appeared sceptical of the relevance of the project.'[2] Alf was awarded a Bachelor of Arts with Honours in Linguistics in April 1980 — a week before his 74th birthday.

Over the period 1975-80 Alf was a part-time research fellow and temporary lecturer in psycholinguistics in the Department of Psychology; his studies in the psychology of verbal communication led him to approach Barry Wilson, a biomechanist in the Department of Human Movement Studies (HMS), for the use of the Department's electromyographic (EMG) equipment to study the involvement of facial muscles. Wilson told Alf he could use the EMG, but that there was no computer program for it. Alf replied, 'That doesn't matter, I write my own computer programs.' 'The outcome was that he began using our equipment and we gained a computer and statistics "whiz-kid" (albeit one in his 70s!),' said Honorary Associate-Professor Ian Jobling, long-time friend and colleague of Alf's who recalled his move to HMS:

> Alf came over to our building one day and said that the Psychology computer — only had one in those days — was broken down. 'I need to help this graduate student in psychology, could we use your computer?' We were happy to oblige. I told him we had plenty of research students and that we were very much like the Department of Psychology. About six months later he came over and said, 'It's a bit more intimate over here, I'd like to come over and help you.' As there were limited employment opportunities available for young students we weren't allowed to pay Alf, so I asked him what he would like. 'Well, a red parking sticker and a library card,' he replied. At the end of 1983 Alf told us he was ready to come over. We were allowed to call him an honorary research fellow, but to say thank you we used to send him to the ANZAAS Conference every two years. He wouldn't give a paper, he'd just go there and enjoy himself. So we'd cover his airfare, accommodation and registration.[3]

About this time Alf, together with Barry Wilson and Margaret Steinberg, received a grant to do research relating to the stimulus function in children with minimal neurological problems: 'It was the stage of early computing and Alf started writing a program using Fortran so that a statistical analysis could be made of our work,' recalled Professor Steinberg who was doing her PhD at the time. 'I was particularly interested in the righting reactions, which are a kind of reflex reactions children have with or without vision. Alf really got involved and was actually developing programs that were able to identify coordinates so that you could measure where a child's head was in space. It was really early biomechanical work I suppose.'[4]

Many postgraduate students and academics benefited from Alf's mentoring, but what was extraordinary was his flexibility in being able to help them analyse what their experiments meant, no matter whether they were related to biomechanics, functional anatomy, physiology or educational sociology. Professor Doune Macdonald, now Head of the School of Human Movement Studies, needed Alf's expertise when she was an Honours student in 1985 doing some work on teachers and their verbal interactions with students in mixed-sex and single-sex classes:

> I had masses of data and unbeknown to me I actually had a very complex research design that was way beyond my capabilities in terms of statistical analysis of the data sets. I would book a time and go and meet with Alf in the lab where he was always surrounded by reams and reams of continuous paper printout; he would very calmly and systematically try to explain my data and do quite a lot of the data analysis and talk me through it. I think besides his invaluable support in research design statistics he was a wonderful model in a school where people were chronologically very young, so it was important for us to see somebody in their 80s who was able to come to work and have a very active life and a sharp mind. A number of the people Alf helped now have significant positions in academia and beyond, and although he's famous for his Antarctic work he's certainly a notable figure in the university and Human Movement Studies.[5]

Today a lecturer in Human Movement Studies, Dr Craig Engstrom was a fourth-year undergraduate in the mid-1980s working on a small research project looking at biomechanics when it was suggested that he see Alf Howard, the resident statistician: 'Alf sat me down on the old computer, which at that stage was an old mainframe and said: "Craig, first we actually plot up your data. We don't need any fancy stuff." In a nutshell we did the analysis and it showed up some nice changes between the fresh and the fatigued state, so I went away happily and started writing up the results,' recollected Engstrom:

The next year I enrolled to do my Honours and having had that great experience with Alf first up at the beginning of my Honours I asked him if he could help me again. He was quite excited about the topic as I was actually looking at using MRI (Magnetic Resonance Imaging), which was a very new imaging technique at the time, to measure the internal cross-sectional area of the Achilles tendon in long-distance runners versus non-runners. So Alf and I sat down and spoke about the project, what sort of things I'd been looking at and what I was hoping to find. We did the research and measured the strength of the calf muscles and people's heights and weights and how much running they did. Alf set me on the straight and narrow in terms of what analysis we could look at, how to present the data and things like that and the analysis turned out very nicely and I was fortunate enough to go down to Canberra and present my research at a national sports medicine conference. In fact, in no small part thanks to Alf's analysis and his encouragement I actually won an award for the young investigators that year, and again I was greatly indebted to Alf for all his contributions. I did my Masters in Canada and when I returned sure enough Alf was still coming in and working as hard as anybody else in the School. Although I'd learnt a bit more and done some stats courses while overseas, when I started my PhD looking at stress fractures in the lumbar spine of cricket's fast bowlers, I still loved to go down and catch up with Alf and show him what sort of analysis I'd done and discuss it with him.[6]

Clearly Alf's move to HMS was a happy one for him and for the Department. He had no health problems, possessed extraordinary lucidity, and had the energy of a man decades younger than himself. 'The idea of stopping work abruptly never appealed to me,' said Alf. 'The point is the brain doesn't just switch off on a particular date.'

April 30, 1986, 'turned out to be quite an occasion,' wrote Alf in a letter to his niece:

Dear Shirley,

... The Human Movement Department staff stage a party on the basis of any excuse at all. So of course they reckoned my 80th birthday was seen to be the occasion for a real bingo. One of the younger staff invited me to come with him and have a birthday lunch at the Staff Club and then it turned out the whole of the staff and senior students were there with anyone else they could rope in including the Pro-Vice Chancellor. A good time was had by all. However the repercussions then started. The University's publicity department heard about it and wrote it up in the University News *and then as a good public relations exercise for the University they circulated it to all the various news media with the result that I was interviewed and photographed by several of the newspapers and copies*

of various newspaper articles have been pouring into the Human Movement Department — hence the enclosures.

I am still as busy as ever and usually spend a fair part of my week-end at the Uni, though I find I cannot do as much as I used to. ...

I hope you are keeping well and enjoying yourself.

Look after yourself

With all the best

Alf[7]

Later in the year Alf had more news to share: 'I am going with a group from the Human Movement Department to visit Greece for about three weeks to look at archaeological evidence of sport in early Greece, and of course to have a good time generally,' he told his niece. 'I will tour Greece and Crete until Dec 21st when we fly back to Amsterdam and hope to spend 10 days to a fortnight in Italy probably visiting Rome, Florence and Venice.'[8] Alf was referring to a study tour being organised and led by Ian Jobling, Director of the Centre for Olympic Studies, in association with the Department's course HM300: 'Sport and Ancient Physical Activity in Ancient Greece and Rome.' Being a King's Scout Alf was prepared and had already enrolled in the course part-time. 'Alf was my oldest student,' said Jobling, 'we took him to Greece and he studied like any other student and got a high distinction as one would expect.'[9] The study group first flew to Singapore where they were invited to go to the Singapore Sports Council before continuing to Athens for a two-day stopover, during which time some of the students ran the marathon, that is from marathon to the 1896 Olympic Stadium in Athens. After an overnight stop in Delphi they visited Olympia, Nemea and Isthmia — the other three sites of the ancient Panhellenic Games. 'In Olympia the students had five days at the International Olympic Academy where they did further studies and presented their papers,' recalled Jobling. 'I roomed with Alf all the way and we had a wonderful time. We went down to Epidaurus then over to Crete and back to Athens.'[10]

*

1986 was an eventful year for Alf, but also for his old ship the *Discovery*, which had been used by the Sea Scouts and the Royal Naval Reserve since 1946. Now some 30 years later the ship was in danger of being scrapped — there was a major outcry. HRH Prince Philip The Duke of Edinburgh intervened and she was handed over to the Maritime Trust on 2 April 1979. Restored to her 1925 appearance, the *Discovery* was then berthed at St Katharine's Dock near the Tower of London as part of the Historic Ship Collection and opened to the public for the next seven years. In 1985, the Dundee Heritage Trust expressed interest in the old vessel and on 3 April 1986 she returned as precious cargo aboard the floating dock ship *Happy Mariner* to a tumultuous welcome in the city that had built her. The Trust built a dock to accommodate her, with a dedicated exhibition building alongside, where she has been on permanent display to the public since 1992. No longer classed as a Steam Yacht, the RRS *Discovery* is now the centrepiece of Dundee's main visitor attraction 'Discovery Point.'[11]

'It's fair to say that we were all interested in what happened to the old ship,' Alf reminisced. 'The last time I saw her she was somewhere near the Tower of London — would have been the early '80s. Fletcher and I corresponded with each other for some time and we met on a few occasions in Sydney. I believe we all tried to stay in touch with one another, but I suppose, like myself, we all just carried on with different things, and of course some of our companions were no longer around.' In fact, Frank Hurley, James Marr and John King Davis passed away in the 1960s, Eric Douglas, Alexander Kennedy, Karl Oom and Robert Falla during the 1970s and Morton Moyes, William Ingram and Ritchie Simmers by the mid-1980s. By 1986 the only survivors of Mawson's 1929-1931 team were Stuart Campbell, Harold Fletcher and Alf Howard.

*

Sharing BANZARE with schoolchildren

Since returning from Antarctica in the early 1930s Alf had given talks about the BANZAR Expedition at schools in Griffith and in Brisbane, especially after he retired from the CSIRO. When a new subject 'Studies of Society and Environment' — which encompassed Antarctica — was introduced into the Queensland primary school curriculum in the early 1990s, Alf was inundated with requests to talk to schoolchildren about his Antarctic experiences. Like the other members of Mawson's team he was given an album of Hurley's photographs at the end of the expedition and so that he could give students an idea of what it was like to go on a three-masted ship in the Southern Ocean he had a slide made from each image.[12] Over time many Year 3 to Year 7 pupils in central and outer Brisbane schools — such as Churchie, St Joseph's College,

Graceville State School, Jamboree Heights State School and the Brisbane School of Distance Education — had a chance to hear Alf speak alongside his Antarctic slide-show after which he would always encourage as many questions as students wished to fire at him. Alf enjoyed the interaction as he told Shirley: 'This year has been quite an active one for me. As you will see from the enclosed I get involved in talking to primary school classes about Mawson and Antarctica. Fortunately I quite enjoy doing it as the response from the kids is quite interesting.'[13]

Clearly, time spent at each school was just as memorable for Alf as it was for the students. A good example of the importance schools placed on inviting Dr Alf Howard to share his adventures with their pupils is exemplified by his visit to the Jamboree Heights State Primary School in July 1993. A local newspaper reported that after the Year 6 students listened to Alf's talk about his voyages with Mawson 'they interviewed him about his life and then wrote a biography';[14] the 7 to 10-page project had to incorporate a timeline, a short paragraph on such topics as: orientation, childhood, education, expedition, after expedition, and re-orientation, and be supported by photos, illustrations, maps and a bibliography. Once everyone in the class had completed the project a special Antarctic-oriented excursion was arranged for 7 July. First, the Year 6 students took a school bus to South Bank to visit the 'Our World Environment' exhibit and especially the replica of Mawson's base hut; then it was on to the University of Queensland where they proudly presented their biographies to Alf in the Great Court. After a tour of the campus and lunch by the university's lakes they returned to school by bus; it was a memorable day for the students as well as for the 'real-life explorer' they met.

A decade on and Alf was still sharing his stories about Antarctica with schoolchildren. He was 98 when he accepted an invitation to spend a morning at the Brisbane School of Distance Education (BSDE) in West End. The school's teaching reaches students living in the geographically isolated areas of Queensland as well as students travelling overseas. It was a big event for the school and a 'Special Invitation' was circulated: 'Students in Years 4-7 are invited to visit the school on Friday, 8 October, 2004 to listen to a special guest speaker. This speaker will be Dr Alf Howard. Dr Howard accompanied Sir Douglas Mawson on one of his expeditions to Antarctica and will be available to answer students' questions.' When Alf arrived the students had already viewed a video on Antarctica and were involved in a number of related activities. The very large conference room was packed with children and their parents living within a radius of 40 kilometres from the city centre.

Sharing BANZARE with students from the Brisbane School of Distance Education (BSDE)

Before his talk Alf showed great interest in the various Antarctic-related activities by going from table to table and speaking with the students. His talk with accompanying slides was a great success, after which he stood firmly in front of his little admirers answering one question after another for at least 35 minutes. There followed an informal ceremony when Alf was presented with a pen, a stainless-steel coffee mug and a Certificate of Appreciation, after which everyone was invited to a generous morning tea. Alf's talk and question time were filmed so that a DVD could be posted to all students living in remote areas. Before leaving Alf was handed a beautiful hand-made A4 card from Laura, a 12 year-old student, who was unable to attend. The three-dimensional card was decorated with a map of Antarctica cut out of one centimetre thick white polystyrene; to one side of the map on which paper penguins, seals and whales were superimposed, Laura had written a poem about Alf — he was very touched. 'Over the years I've received a fair amount of correspondence and drawings from children thanking me for going to their school and sharing my stories with them. It's all been very gratifying,' reflected Alf. 'Well, I felt it was important that students knew about what the work of Mawson really meant. They certainly had a mixed range of questions — some of them were purely concerned with whether you're cold and others were concerned about what you had to eat so it was a very mixed bag.'

*

Alf beside bronze bust of himself sculptured by Cam Griffin. The plaque reads: IN HONOUR OF DR ALF HOWARD FOR HIS WISDOM INTEGRITY AND VALUED CONTRIBUTION TO THE SCIENTIFIC STUDY OF HUMAN PERFORMANCE
(Photo: Nick Rains)

Correspondence to his niece could at times be rather intermittent if there was 'little to report': 'I am sorry I have not got around to writing to you before this but I am living a rather humdrum existence & there doesn't seem much to write about,' penned Alf in December 1989. 'I am still working with the Human Movement Department at the University but I get rather tired and usually knock off in the early afternoon and after a bit of a feed go straight to bed':

> *The only item of interest has been that the Human Movement Department, which is moving into a new building, decided that they would like to have a bronze head of me stuck up in the foyer. One of the staff has a friend who is an amateur sculptor and arranged that he would do a head of me for just the cost of the casting. I sat for several days a week for 5 or 6 weeks & he produced a job which everyone is very satisfied with. I have got the lad who does the photography for us to take some photos. They have not come back yet but when they do I will send you one. The sitting was quite an exhilarating experience. At first*

> *things did not seem to be going very well but suddenly everything started to go the right way and as I said a very good job resulted.*[15]

Cam Griffin was the sculptor and Doune Macdonald the staff member who arranged Alf's sittings with him. The Griffins enjoyed his visits: 'Somehow or other he got himself out here — he didn't drive — I suppose he came by train':

> Alf came over in the mornings and he'd be here for a few hours, but we didn't work all the time. When you're sculpting someone you've got a lot of time to interact with them. We'd walk about, have a cup of tea, then Alf would usually stay for lunch, and of course he was always an interesting fellow to talk to and I knew that he'd been with Mawson and so on. Alf met most of our children. He was always impressive and everyone liked to talk to him and get him to talk about things. I've got a bit of a workshop down in the garden so Alf was set up there. We did it in clay of course and it was life size. It's a fine line when you're doing a portrait in clay between a caricature and a good likeness, so you've got to get the anatomical details very right to start with. The final process involved creating a negative plaster mould of the clay model, then creating a positive mould from the negative mould, which then made it possible to correct a few little fiddly bits on the nose before we had it cast in bronze by Philip Piperides at his foundry in Lawnton, a 45-minute drive from Brisbane towards the North Coast.[16]

In a follow-up letter to Shirley, Alf was clearly chuffed with the final result: 'I think I mentioned that I had been sitting for a sculptured head. I have received varying comments as to how good an image it is, but I am quite happy with it even if it does make me look a bit severe. The head was unveiled at a do that more or less coincided with the opening of new offices and laboratories for the Department.'[17] Alf was now immortalised in bronze and the unveiling was reported in local and interstate newspapers. Undergraduates still dress Alf's bust on special occasions — with a mortar board at graduation time, and perhaps a scarf and beanie on a HMS sports day.[18] He certainly raised a smile on one of his birthdays when both he and his bronze head sported French berets and other exotic hats for a light-hearted photo shoot.

*

Alf was now well and truly entrenched as a member of the Human Movement Studies family. He would arrive at university soon after 9 am and work five or six hours with only a morning break to go to the staff room and make a pot of tea with real leaves — preferably Russian Caravan. Jobling recalls that when

Alf first went to HMS 'he used to drive an old Datsun until one afternoon he came round the corner from our building and wiped out a BMW, so he said no more driving.'[19] He continued to help many undergraduates, postgraduates and academics devising statistical programs to suit their individual areas of research. Those he supported valued the readiness of his assistance in evaluating their data and for the way 'he was always available for an intrusion into his time.' Some of the postgraduate students he helped returned to the Department years later as lecturers and again sought Alf's advice. A case in point is Robert Neal, who acknowledged Alf in his 1988 doctorate thesis: 'Dr Alf Howard, who at 82 exemplifies the true scholar in search of enlightenment and learning, has provided me with a unique example. His experience, patience and knowledge have made a deep impression on me, and I would like to, by these few words, express my gratitude to him.' In March 2004, when Neal co-authored an article for the *Journal of Biomechanics* with Barry Wilson and Mark Forwood, Alf's help was again sought. They wrote: 'The authors would like to thank Dr Alf Howard for his invaluable statistical advice.'

*

Antarctica revisited

If Alf found life a little 'humdrum' at times that would soon change as the lure of Antarctica became impossible to resist. Early 1990, when the Australian Geographic called for expressions of interest for a 22-day cruise from Hobart to Antarctica Alf jumped at the chance and joined up: 'I've booked for a more or less luxury cruise to the Antarctic,' he wrote to Shirley. 'The cruise comes off next January but I am now getting together the extra warm clothing and other things necessary.'[20]

Six decades had passed since Alf left Hobart on Mawson's second BANZARE voyage bound for Macquarie Island and Commonwealth Bay. It was now 12 January 1991 and Alf was again in Hobart, but this time to board the ice-strengthened M/S *Frontier Spirit* on a nostalgic return visit to the same destinations. He left in excellent company, which included world adventurers Dick and Pip Smith, expedition leader Mike McDowell, and mountaineers Colin Monteath and Greg Mortimer:

> I would say there must have been well over a hundred passengers and double that with crew and officers. We had a number of zodiacs with outboards to get us ashore and Dick Smith had a helicopter strapped to the deck, which brought to mind the old Gipsy Moth on the *Discovery*. Of course it was a hell of a lot more comfortable than the BANZARE voyages. Well it didn't take long before the passengers found out that I'd been down with Mawson and from then on you could say I was given the VIP treatment.

The vessel had two days at Macquarie Island, which gave Alf a chance to reacquaint himself with the local denizens — the King penguins on the beach and in the water at Lusitania Bay, the huge Royal penguin rookery at Sandy Bay, scattered groups of Rockhopper and Gentoo penguins, and massive lumbering Elephant seals lolling on the beaches or wallowing in the mud.

Philip Barnaart, who was stationed at the Australian National Antarctic Research Expedition (ANARE) base on Macquarie Island in 1991, said he had the privilege of meeting Alf when he visited the base at Buckles Bay. The station's log for Wednesday, 16 January noted: 'Guests for lunch were Alf Howard, hydrologist with Mawson's BANZARE 1929-31, Dick Smith and his wife, Pip, Mike McDowell, geophysicist 1971.' Philip recalls how 'Alf impressed everyone with his fitness, interest in everything and his humility. It was an honour to meet him — especially at Macquarie Island with its association with Mawson's expeditions.'[21]

Captain Heinz Aye of the M/S *Frontier Spirit* wrote a letter to Alf soon after leaving Macquarie Island requesting him to write a page in the logbook 'about Antarctica and [his] trip and stay together with the famous Australian Explorer Sir Douglas Mawson' so that his handwritten page could be printed as part of the passenger log book record at the end of the voyage. 'As arranged already you will be in the very first Zodiac going ashore in Commonwealth Bay. I am very happy and proud to have you aboard for this Expedition voyage down to the Australian part of Antarctica.'[22]

From a distance Mawson's 1911-14 base hut appeared the same as on the 1931 visit, but on closer inspection Alf saw a fragile structure seemingly supported by its frozen interior: 'It looked chock-full of ice and badly weathered from the constant katabatic winds and I remember Dick Smith taking his helicopter up to assess the condition of the roof.' 'I was disappointed I couldn't get inside the hut,' Alf told Pip Smith. 'In 1931 we entered it through the roof, and there was lots of material left behind from Mawson's original stay. There were beautiful ice formations beginning to grow then.'[23]

Dick Smith reported that the 'hut was in a shocking state of disrepair' and while in Commonwealth Bay helped 'establish the Mawson's Hut Conservation Committee.' While urgent structural repairs were carried out by the Project Blizzard expeditions in the mid-1980s, the Mawson's Huts Foundation continues to send teams during the Antarctic summer to 'the home of the blizzard' to carry out conservation work on the huts and artefacts.

Alf revisiting Mawson's Hut in 1991

A list of 'Highlights' of the *Frontier Spirit* voyage — besides the landings at Macquarie Island and Commonwealth Bay — included tabular iceberg cruising, Mertz Glacier cruising, area round French Base, Port Martin, Cape Jul and Alf Howard.

*

Revisiting Antarctica revived many memories for Alf and he could not wait to return; he had enjoyed so many aspects of the cruise: congenial company, good food, comfortable cabin and no doubt the special attention accorded to him. 'I got quite a number of good shots and had some of them turned into slides, which I have used in several talks,' he told Shirley. 'The enclosed are among the best. I have put my name down for a cruise to western Antarctica and the [South] Shetland Islands, South Georgia and other sub-Antarctic islands in that area. I hope to know something definite about it in the next few weeks.'[24] Alf's plans for western Antarctica turned into a two-month adventure returning via remote islands in the Pacific Ocean.

Wednesday, 8 January 1992, Alf arrived in Buenos Aires on Aerolineas Argentinas for an overnight stay and took the 06.40 hrs flight to Ushuaia at the southern tip of Argentina; from there he boarded a Russian 38-berth tourist vessel — the *Professor Molchanov* — for a 14-day cruise along the coast of western Antarctica, then continued to the South Orkney Islands, South Georgia and the Falkland Islands. 'The scenery in western Antarctica is quite different from what I've seen before — it's mountainous with glaciers and snowfields, while eastern Antarctica is a continuous ice cliff with the occasional mountain showing through. Both the trips I've been on have been sold out, but the average Australian knows very little about Australia's Antarctic Territory or the rest of the continent,' said Alf in an interview for the *University News* when he returned.[25] 'I was particularly interested to see Elephant Island where Hurley and others were marooned for some months after the *Endurance* went down,' remarked Alf. 'Seeing Shackleton's last resting place at Grytviken also meant something to me, as Marr talked a fair bit about Sir Ernest's final voyage to South Georgia.'

After overnight stopovers in Ushuaia and Buenos Aires Alf arrived in Quito. Basing himself in the Ecuadorian capital for a week he explored the city, had a private tour of the Banco Central Museum of Archaeology, visited the Equatorial Monument and the pre-Inca ruins of Rumichuco, as well as spending a few days in the area around the active, snow-capped 3500-metre-high volcano, Cotopaxi. Back in Quito Alf was ready to take off for the Galapagos Archipelago by San Airlines then board the M/V *Eric* for a five-day cruise, which included time on the islands of Santa Cruz, Isabela, Bartolome and Santiago: 'There was so much to take in; it was like Darwin's natural laboratory. I was fascinated by the piles and piles of marine iguanas on the rocks, the wild tortoises in the forests on one of the larger islands and of course the Galapagos penguins, which I had never seen before; they are even smaller than our Fairy penguins.'

The cruise over, Alf flew to Guayaquil then on to Santiago and boarded a Lan Chile flight the following afternoon to Rapa Nui (Easter Island). His itinerary from the day he left Brisbane to when he returned on 3 March was punishing to the end. During his 24-hour island stopover he was driven in a jeep to the three freshwater crater lakes at Rano Kau, Rano Arol and Rano Raraku; at the Rano Raraku quarry Alf had time to explore some of the 300-odd unfinished moai (statues), the largest of which would have stood 60 feet tall. He also had a chance to look at the sea wall of Ahu Vinapu I at Vinapu, which has been likened to Inca masonry. After a 10-hour break in Papeete and three hours between flights in Sydney, Alf was home.

Alf in front of the wall at Ahu Vinapu on Easter Island in 1992

*

In between Antarctic escapades Alf was back in the Human Movement Studies as an honorary research fellow, undertaking computer programming and statistical work for students and staff. Although he knew he had an appreciative audience at the Department to share his travels with, it was very important to Alf to keep in touch with his only relative — Clarence's daughter:

23.12.92

Dear Shirley

Thanks for your newsy note. I am pleased that you are getting yourself around. I am still doing some of the same. My trip last year to western Antarctica & the Islands near there & then up to Ecuador & the Galapagos & then home by way of Easter Island was very successful & I'm doing another trip this summer towards the end of January down to Commonwealth Bay & then onto Ross Island where I hope to go out to what they call the Dry Valleys. This will be by helicopter from the ship. Then home by way of the New Zealand sub-Antarctic Islands. This will probably keep me quiet for some time.

I have been getting a lot of publicity since the University wrote me up in their Newsletter and from there it got through to the ABC & the local & district papers. The enclosed is one of the best blurbs they produced.

With all the best for Xmas & New Year

Love

Alf

Alf was aboard the world-class Russian icebreaker *Kapitan Khlebnikov* when it left the port of Fremantle on 28 January 1993 for a month-long adventure to Antarctica. The five-day voyage to reach the east coast of the icy continent was taken up with lectures by a team of distinguished polar specialists, which included Robert Headland of the Scott Polar Research Institute, Rod Ledingham and John Splettstoesser. 'I would say we were fairly close to the Magnetic Pole when our icebreaker received an SOS from a French supply ship,' recalled Alf. 'We went off course to see if we could help, but it turned out that the severe gale conditions we were experiencing at the time had triggered their emergency signal.' The French ship was the *Astrolabe*, which had just offloaded supplies at Dumont d'Urville—France's Antarctic base, which the *Khlebnikov* had planned to visit, but now had to bypass because of the detour. Bad weather conditions prevailed in Commonwealth Bay and Alf like the other passengers on board could only look at Mawson's hut through binoculars. However, Alf did take off in a helicopter from the ship on a one-hour flight over the Canada and Commonwealth glaciers and into the snow and ice-free Dry Valleys for a landing. 'We visited Shackleton's hut [at Cape Royds] and Scott's Discovery hut at McMurdo where I tried to picture our old wooden vessel icebound for two years,' ruminated Alf. For John Splettstoesser, the expedition leader, 'Alf was a delight to know and have aboard, remembered for his wit and stamina and enthusiasm to be back in areas that he had visited many decades in the past.'[26]

*

Some time in June 1993, unbeknown to Alf, letters were being sent from his Department supporting him as 'an outstanding candidate for an honorary doctorate.' Alf mentioned the upcoming ceremony along with other news in his Christmas letter to Shirley:

> *... Tomorrow night I have to go along to have a DSc conferred on me. Just why I am not certain but both the Human Movement Department and the University have got quite a bit of publicity out of reference to my being with Mawson & now working for them as an honorary research fellow.*
>
> *I am not going anywhere this Christmas but I have signed up for a trip to the Arctic Ocean & then a tour through Lapland in June-July next year. Whether that will satisfy my roving I am not sure, though I feel that if I do any more travelling it should be nearer home. There is much of Australia I haven't seen yet.*[27]

The ceremony took place on 13 December 1993 in the University of Queensland's Mayne Hall. When it came to Alf's turn to step on stage, a brief summary of his contributions was read out, which included his work on the Mawson expedition, his 'distinguished 40 years with the CSIRO' and his work at the university. 'He requires no legislation to encourage him to work beyond the usual retirement age,' said the speaker, 'and still makes annual trips to Antarctica when most of us would be contemplating Sanctuary Cove as an ambitious project.' Alf was then awarded the Honorary Degree of Doctor of Science 'for outstanding contributions to the advancement of science and dedicated service to The University of Queensland.'

As usual there were plenty of research projects in the Department needing Alf's assistance. In between projects he happily accepted invitations to visit schools as well as talking at a range of functions about his days with Mawson. He was now 88 and crossed the campus most days of the week; no longer driving he either caught a bus or walked — either way it was a fair step from Alf's home in St Lucia to the bus stop and again from the university's Chancellor Place to the Department. Alf was still in very good health and his days of roving were far from over:

> *... My trip to the Arctic was quite successful particularly the trip through the sea to Franz Joseph Land and Spitzbergen. We would not have been able to get through the ice if we had not been able to follow in the tracks of a Russian nuclear-powered icebreaker that had gone through a week or so earlier. The tour along the north coast of Norway up to North Cape was very good but I was a little disappointed in the trip through Lapland. The*

scenery is very good but the Lapps or Sami as they prefer to be called have commercialised the tourism. Also I got the feeling that they are in much the same position as the Australian Aborigines in trying to establish their individual identity. They are spread through Norway, Sweden, Finland, and into Russia & have set up their own parliament but as far as I can see no one recognises it.

I am not going anywhere this summer but at the moment I am negotiating with a crowd in Adelaide to do a cruise on a French ship through the Mediterranean calling at ports in Italy, Greece and Turkey with excursions at most ports. However, the main emphasis is on music and they have their own orchestra with a number of international artists, so there is good music practically all the time.[28]

Alf receiving Honorary Doctor of Science Degree from Sir Llew Edwards at the University of Queensland in 1993

Passionate about the performing arts, Alf was a patron of a number of institutions which included the Queensland Symphony Orchestra and the Australian Ballet. Macdonald remarked that he was constantly difficult to book for anything because he had season tickets for the ballet, opera and concerts. He was very independent in that he would book them himself and usually go by himself. He would thoroughly enjoy it and could give a review on any cultural experience. If two events fell on the same day he would find a chair in the foyer and take a nap between performances. Alf also regularly attended the weekly lunchtime concerts on campus and gave the Music Department his large Beethoven collection of long-playing records when he left his house. Ray

Specht remembers that 'one could always hear classical music coming from Alf's home in Tenth Avenue, St Lucia.'[29]

'Bett was very keen on ballet and that's really how I became hooked and when the Australian Ballet was formed in the early '60s we became Foundation Members.' Alf not only supported the Australian Ballet with his patronage and presence, but was also interested to see the choreographic works of other local, interstate and overseas ballet/dance companies. Sometimes he would go over to Brisbane's Expressions Dance Company to watch a dress rehearsal. In October 1999, he joined a tour to attend performances of leading ballet companies in London, Stockholm, Copenhagen, New York and Toronto. Although *Swan Lake* was, at that time, his favourite ballet, he did not expect to see it performed in four of the five cities he visited: 'I think I've probably seen it too much,' said Alf. 'Just the same I would like to see Graeme Murphy's version one day as I generally like his work.'

The 'musical cruise' was a success according to Alf's letter to Shirley dated 19 December 1995: 'I am afraid that I am not a good corespondent and many of your pleasant letters go unanswered. However, I probably have more news than usual':

> *Back in midwinter I went on a 'musical cruise' to the Mediterranean. We took off from Toulon in France down to Greece and Crete and then to two sites in Turkey and then back to Toulon calling at Naples and Genoa on the way back. As a musical cruise there was the English Chamber Orchestra, which played twice daily either on the ship or at some special site ashore & also made their rehearsals public. There were at least a dozen soloists of varying stages of going up or down the popularity ladder. All together it was a very successful trip with all mod cons including free liquor whenever one wanted it.*
>
> *I am going on another musical cruise in January this time on a much less lavish scale. It is an Australian venture taking the Queensland Philharmonic Orchestra and calling at towns in Vanuatu & New Caledonia with similar arrangements to the Mediterranean trip.*
>
> *However, the highlight of my journeyings is a 2-month circumnavigation of the Antarctic next Xmas. After that I should be quite happy to stay quiet for a long time.*

For weeks before 30 April 1996 the Human Movement Studies Department was holding secret meetings to make sure Alf would have a memorable 90th birthday. Invitations were sent out and a large room with catering facilities was booked. Alf arrived with friends just before 7 pm when pre-dinner drinks and savouries were served. Bruce Abernethy, then Head of Department, welcomed everyone and after the main course Ian Jobling presented a 'This is Your Life' — all about Alf. Slides punctuated his story and either one of the guests or Alf himself would give more details. A few skits were introduced with reference to Alf's early days as a scout, and of course his voyages with Sir Douglas, at which point a look-alike Mawson dressed in polar gear and balaclava made a fleeting appearance. Also recognised were Alf's years at the CSIRO and at the University of Queensland as well as his more recent travels. 'Happy Birthday' was sung as a huge chocolate birthday cake with 90 candles was brought forth; there followed three loud hearty cheers as Alf cut the cake.

Alf with Ian Jobling at his 90th birthday celebration

Alf's letter of 15 May 1996 to his niece clearly indicates that he thoroughly enjoyed both the birthday celebrations and the media attention:

> *Many thanks for your birthday greeting. Being my 90th it turned into quite a dinner with a surprise program of details of my life. Where they got them all I don't know. Some of course I would have told them but others they apparently got from the University data bank on its staff and students. This was on the Saturday night before the anniversary & there was another at work on the 30th. The University got hold of the story and used it as a public relations exercise with sessions on Channels 9 and 2 and the ABC radio. A good time was had by all.*[30]

*

Port Stanley, Falkland Islands, 24 November 1996 — Alf was about to be part of history again as he boarded the *Kapitan Khlebnikov* on the first-ever passenger circumnavigation of Antarctica. Only nine other ships had ever completed such a feat before, the first being the HMS *Resolution* and HMS *Adventure* under the command of Captain James Cook from 1772-1775. Alf was pleased to see some familiar faces on board — Captain Peter Golikov and specialist lecturers Bob Headland and John Splettstoesser.

The ship headed south with a landing in the South Orkney Islands before travelling eastward across the Weddell Sea. As it was Thanksgiving on the 28th turkey with cranberry sauce featured on the dinner menu. By 2 December the *Khlebnikov* was in the pack ice and a 30-minute helicopter ride away from the Rüser-Larsen Rookery where everyone had a chance to see the regal Emperor penguins and their chicks. Two days later the icebreaker dropped anchor at Germany's Neumayer Station, which had never received a passenger ship before. Ever eastward through the tightly packed ice to Japan's Syowa Station, which was reached on 12 December and where a warm welcome awaited those who visited the base. There was also a friendly exchange visit of ship and base personnel at Russia's Molodezhnaya Station on the 14th when fuel was taken on board for the icebreaker's helicopters.

December 15 was particularly significant for Alf as the zodiacs were being prepared for a landing on Proclamation Island — BANZARE claimed territory. The Cruise Log's entry for that day notes:

> At 11.15 a.m., we again assembled in the Lecture Room to hear Alf Howard speak of his experiences with the BANZARE trip with Sir Douglas Mawson. We were indeed fortunate to have Alf amongst the passengers, as he was a member of this expedition and could give us his own personal stories of these voyages, what they did, where they went, and how they travelled more than 60 years ago. We were absolutely fascinated to hear him speak and to share these stories of exploration with someone who was actually there.

'Of course it meant a lot to me to be able to step on to Proclamation Island again. The Adélies were busy gathering pebbles and there were thousands of petrels — it all looked pretty much as I had remembered it when I was last there taking magnetic readings with Simmers. In fact the coastline from that point all the way to Commonwealth Bay was familiar territory from the BANZARE days,' reflected Alf.

December 17, Mawson Station — Australia's first Antarctic base established in 1954 — was ready to welcome all passengers ashore and show them the scientific laboratories, the post office and photos of the dog teams that worked there until 1993. More Emperor penguin rookeries were visited and there were further helicopter shuttles at China's Zhongshan Base and Australia's Davis and Casey stations. A Christmas lunch of roast cherry valley duck in orange sauce with potato strudel followed by coupe 'Santa Claus' was served crossing the Davis Sea. At Casey, a memorable barbecue was prepared with all trimmings when the icebreaker arrived on the 27th. Andrew Brooks was wintering at Casey at the time and well remembers meeting Alf:

> All the passengers onboard had an opportunity to come ashore where they were treated to a tour of the station followed by a BBQ. The hospitality was returned with all of the station's personnel being invited out to tour the ship. It was on this second visit to the ship that I had a chance to have a more detailed discussion with Alf, and I can clearly recall being amazed at his attitude and outlook, as well as being impressed by his physical fitness. Alf acted as a tour guide for the group that I was in and he left us in his wake when climbing all of the stairs to the bridge![31]

New Year's Eve 1996, the ship was lurching and bumping as she forged her way through the heavy pack ice to France's Dumont d'Urville Station on Petrel Island just off Adélie Land; at the same time she was breaking a path through the ice to the station's small supply vessel, *Astrolabe*. Alf and the other passengers were invited ashore for champagne and a tour of the base and were told that 'the 3,000 pairs of Emperor penguins had produced 850 healthy chicks that were due to fledge and go to sea.'[32] 'I was happy to get to the French base at last; there were hundreds of little Adélies all over the place and you had to be careful at times where you stepped.' Gale-force winds and heavy seas at the entrance to Commonwealth Bay once again deprived Alf of another visit to Mawson's Huts on New Year's Day 1997.

Orcas and especially Minke whales were seen regularly; other sightings included Ross seals, the occasional Humpback, Fin and Southern Bottlenose whale as well as a couple of large unidentified species. Continuing her circumnavigation of Antarctica the *Kapitan Khlebnikov* made further stops at Cape Adare, Cape Hallett, and to Ross Island where there was time to enter Shackleton's hut, Scott's Cape Evans hut as well as Scott's *Discovery* hut at America's McMurdo Station, and New Zealand's Scott Base three kilometres further on. Alf again flew into the Dry Valleys and also visited some areas in the Ross Sea region for the first time: 'I enjoyed seeing all the Adélies at Cape Hallett and getting inside Scott's other hut at Cape Evans, which I missed on an earlier trip. The Adélie has always been my favourite penguin and I was lucky to walk around some extremely large rookeries on the trip.' After the long stretch from the Ross Sea, through the Amundsen Sea to the Bellinghausen Sea, the zodiacs were prepared for a landing on Peter I Island with its nesting Adélies, Chinstraps and Gentoo penguins as well as many Elephant seals — it was now 19 January. A couple of days later the Antarctic Peninsula was in sight and a after a few hours exploring Petermann Island the ship entered the deep, narrow and enchanting Lemaire Channel. 'Beautiful blue icebergs glided past us, with groups of penguins porpoising through the water and seals lazily watching us from small ice floes. On each side we had the dark rocky cliffs towering way above us, their peaks rising into a clear blue sky.'[33] In the last days of the voyage visits were made to Deception Island and to other islands near the tip of the Peninsula. Alf was delighted to again have a chance to land on Elephant Island despite the large swell: 'I would say that the last leg of the cruise across the Drake Passage was the worst; it was very rough and the ship rolled like hell. After that it was pretty much smooth sailing to the Falklands.' Alf and his fellow passengers disembarked at Port Stanley on Monday, 27 January 1997 after voyaging 12,565 nautical miles — 23,245.25 kilometres around the entire continent of Antarctica.

'I have just got back from a 2-month cruise circumnavigating the Antarctic on a Russian icebreaker', wrote Alf to Shirley after giving himself a couple of weeks to recuperate. 'We were able to land at one of the spots where we landed in 1930 and saw much of the coast that we discovered on the BANZARE. We also called at the 3 Australian bases on this continent as well as those of several other nations. All in all a very wonderful trip but it has taken me some time to recover from the jet lag flying back from Santiago in Chile.'[34]

*

Many Human Movement staff members and students would have almost certainly selected ABC TV on the evening of 15 March 1997 to see Alf featured in an *Australian Story* episode entitled 'Alf of the Antarctic', introduced by marathon swimmer Tammy Van Wisse. The segment begins with Alf choosing warm undergarments for an upcoming polar voyage. Next, his most recent visit to Antarctica is contrasted with footage from Hurley's *Siege of the South*; he is then seen in the Department giving statistical advice to a postgraduate; the segment closes with Alf reflecting on his life. Jobling recalled that whenever there was anything to do with Antarctica on television he would record it and then watch it with Alf in the Department's lab.

Senator Ian Macdonald, Alf Howard, Charlie Gibbs and Syd Kirkby at the opening of the Queensland Museum ANARE exhibition 'Our Frozen Frontier' on 9 October 1997.

Later in the year Alf was a special guest at the launch of 'Our Frozen Frontier' at the Queensland Museum, a travelling exhibition mounted by the Queensland Branch of the ANARE Club as part of its Jubilee Celebrations in 1997. Before the official opening, Syd Kirkby, then President of the Queensland chapter who 'has explored more territory than anyone living or dead in Antarctica', gave an introductory speech: 'I'd particularly like to welcome today Dr Alf Howard, the Patron of our Club, who is the sole surviving member of Douglas Mawson's 1929-1931 BANZARE — British, Australian and New Zealand Antarctic Research Expedition — which undertook such important exploration and discovery throughout the Australian sector. Welcome Alf, and long may you grace our affairs.'[35] Alf became a regular supporter of the ANARE Club in Queensland when he was introduced to the Club by Michael Bryden at the 1985 Midwinter Dinner in Brisbane and continued to attend all annual winter gatherings until 1997 and the occasional one after that. The Queensland Branch not only requested Alf to be their Patron, but also nominated him for Life Membership of the

Federal ANARE Club. He apparently 'entertained and informed members on numerous occasions and was Guest Speaker at midwinter 1991.'[36]

While Alf was circumnavigating Antarctica in early 1997 letters commending his nomination for recognition through the Order of Australia awards scheme were going to and fro between Government House in Canberra and the Department of Human Movement Studies. A year later Dr Alf Howard AM was awarded the Order of Australia by Queensland's Governor Major General Peter Arnison on 26 January 1998 for his service to science through Antarctic exploration as well as for his work on food technology and preservation, and his contribution to statistical design.

Dr Alf Howard AM being awarded the Order of Australia by Queensland's Governor Major General Peter Arnison on 26 January 1998.

*

Globetrotting

Shirley received news in December 1997 about even more travel plans: 'I am going up to Kamchatka & the Kuril Islands next July but I think this might be my swan song. I find myself getting very tired though this might be because of my work at the uni since I did not feel so tired when I was on my cruise last summer.'[37] The seventeen-day expedition, again on the *Kapitan Khlebnikov*, left Vladivostok on 6 July 1998 to sail north along the coastal section of the Far East Reserve. 'Now passing between Hokkaido & the southernmost Kuril Islands,' wrote Alf in an email from the ship. 'Yesterday was quite interesting. Landed at Terney, Russia. Terney doesn't sound Russian and is actually French as it was discovered by La Perouse before he made his trip to Australia. Yesterday was the 211th anniversary of his discovery and we participated in the local formalities, dancing and singing.'[38]

There was another update in a postcard from Petropavlovsk: 'We have just left the Kamchatka Peninsula & proceeding to the Commander Islands where the animal and bird life is reported to be outstanding. The Valley of Geysers in Kamchatka was absolutely fascinating & I have, I hope, some good photos.'[39] At Commander Bay Alf explored the site where Vitus Bering and his crew were marooned in 1741 en route home from their discovery of Alaska. Stops at other islands were made before a last visit to the Chukotka Peninsula in Russia's eastern Arctic where the passengers encountered Grey whales, guillemots, puffins and other birds. Alf left the *Khlebnikov* in Provideniya from where he flew to Anchorage for an overnight stopover before heading home on July 22.

A chance to visit Mauritius, Seychelles Islands, Reunion and Madagascar in 1999 was irresistible. Alf made a booking. One day, soon after he returned, a neighbour of his, Ray Specht, on his way to the local shops passed Alf sitting on a bench: 'He was still there when I came back and I said, "What's happened, Alf?" and he said, "I've got the flu". Where did you catch it? And he said, "I went to see the night lemurs in Madagascar". Did you get the flu in the plane? "No, we went in a windjammer".'

In front of Dr David Livingstone's statue, Victoria Falls, 2000

To celebrate the new millennium Alf joined a safari tour to Kenya and Tanzania crossing the Serengeti plains then visiting the Oldavai Gorge where some of the earliest fossils of mankind have been found, before continuing to the Ngorongoro Crater. On the same trip he also visited Zanzibar and later spent a few days at Victoria Falls before returning to Australia. 'I went up in a massive balloon over the Serengeti — must have been more than twenty of us on board,' said Alf. 'Looking down on the herds of animals is something I shall never forget. When we landed we were served breakfast with champagne, which was also pretty memorable. I would say that another highlight was seeing the statue of David Livingstone near the Falls.'

*

A Senior Australian of the Year Award was presented to Alf in November 2000 by the then Premier of Queensland, Peter Beattie, and the following year he was one of 12 recipients of the Australian Geographic Society's gold medallion for a lifetime of adventure. 'I don't quite know why I got it,' reflected Alf.

Premier Peter Beattie presenting Alf with a Senior Australian of the Year Award in 2000

Closer to home Alf enjoyed a cruise on the *Coral Princess* in 2002, which took him from the Kimberleys to Darwin. As he still wished to see more of Canada and Alaska he booked a tour that enabled him to cross the Canadian Rockies with a few days in both Banff and Lake Louise. Once in Vancouver he boarded a liner that took him up the west Canadian and Alaskan coasts. 'Well, I did see a few grizzlies here and there, but once we got to Alaska as far as I'm concerned one glacier looked pretty much like the next, and there were plenty of them,' recollected Alf.

As part of Seniors Week 2003, Alf was invited to speak at the State Library of New South Wales where he addressed members of the Australian Storytelling Guild. 'Dr Howard flew from Brisbane yesterday, having scoffed at the offer of a "minder",' noted an article in the *Sydney Morning Herald*: 'He took slides of photographs taken by Frank Hurley and some of his own from a well-preserved 50-year-old leather suitcase to show to his Sydney audience. Now, at 96 he is looking forward to exploring China. Considering he had been to Siberia recently, where would he go after China? "I would like to see more of Asia," Dr Howard said yesterday.'[40]

Alf in the State Library of New South Wales to give a talk as part of Seniors Week in March 2003 (Photo: Rick Stevens)

While Alf did not travel to China or anywhere in Asia again, he helped the postgraduates at Human Movement Studies until the end of 2003 — he was nearly 98. Subscriptions for the ballet and concerts continued and although his eyesight was beginning to deteriorate he persevered with the daily crossword puzzle; in his later years he always had Bertrand Russell's *History of Western Philosophy* close at hand: 'I suppose the point is that you can pick it up any old time and start reading it any old place,' he would say. No longer on campus, Alf still visited schools occasionally and graciously gave interviews when requested. Writing letters was now too tiring, however, he continued to exchange Christmas and birthday cards with Shirley.

From 7 October to 7 November 2004 an exhibition, 'Boroondara 150: celebrating significant people', was on display in the Hawthorn Town Hall Gallery. The exhibition was to showcase '150 Significant People' who have been important to the City of Boroondara, which now incorporates Melbourne's eastern suburbs of Hawthorn, Kew, and Camberwell where Alf grew up. Shirley's nomination for her uncle was immediately accepted and Alf's story was displayed along with the stories of other significant people since 1854.

*

Alf had been with Human Movement Studies more or less since they had their very first computers: 'He was pretty special in those days because he understood computers when many of us didn't,' recalled Macdonald:

> In 2004 Alf very kindly gave the School $80,000, and when a space became available we were able to establish the Alf Howard Computer Lab. His generous gift was used to buy computers for the Lab, as well as to do the furniture fit-out and the wiring. It's been very exciting watching the teaching and learning in the School change because we've been able to have access to tutorials being run in the Computer Lab. It's a busy room. Semester by semester more and more staff use it and more and more students come to enjoy it. That's been a very special legacy of Alf's.[41]

The opening of the new Lab was covered by several newspapers and was an item on a number of TV channels across the country. Asked about the new Lab Alf responded: 'I've always thought the university needed support from the public. From my point of view this was the area in which I was interested, so if I could do anything to help students working in human movement, that's OK.'[42] Alf had turned 99 just days before, so after the official opening of the Lab his birthday was celebrated with a special morning tea.

*

Throughout 2006, Alf was showcased in the media and in a number of exhibitions in Brisbane, interstate and overseas. As he was unable to travel to Melbourne to attend a reception for HRH Prince Philip, The Duke of Edinburgh, hosted by the Royal Society of Victoria on 15 March, ANARE member Graham Pryde took him over to the ABC studios in West End to record a message for the occasion. As recorded in the Club's Journal *Aurora*, 'the Society was able to screen with the assistance of the ABC, a short video message from Dr Alf Howard in Brisbane, the almost 100 year old, sole surviving member of Sir Douglas Mawson's 1929/30 & 1930/31 BANZARE expeditions, which was viewed with great interest by His Royal Highness, who requested that his personal best wishes be conveyed to Dr Howard.'[43]

Celebration for Alf's 100th Birthday at Human Movement Studies, 30 April 2006.
Doune Macdonald and Ian Jobling to Alf's left.

By his 100th birthday on 30 April 2006, Alf had received an avalanche of cards and letters from friends, past colleagues and of course Shirley. There were warm messages from Queen Elizabeth, the Governor-General of the Commonwealth of Australia, the Prime Minister of Australia, the Governor of Queensland, the Premier of Queensland and the Lord Mayor of Brisbane, as well as from a number of Members of Parliament. He also received good wishes from the Vice-Chancellor of the University of Queensland, the Vice-Chancellor of the University of Melbourne and the Scout Association of Australia.

Human Movement Studies celebrated the event with a large gathering of Alf's friends and colleagues for a light luncheon and a slice of Alf's enormous chocolate birthday cake. Jobling, 10 years later, this time presented a shortened version of 'This is your life, Alf.' The room was filled with colourful balloons and reporters' cameras flashing in all directions. The media follow-up went on for some days and Alf enjoyed every minute of it.

During his centenary year there were articles about Alf in the *Australian Geographic* and the *Australian Antarctic Magazine* as well as in various newspapers across the country. By now more people in Australia and overseas were aware that Alf was not only the sole surviving member of Mawson's *Discovery* expeditions, but that he was also the last survivor to have sailed on Scott's old ship the *Discovery*, and was now the last link with the heroic era of Antarctic exploration.

BBC TV Scotland team and author with Alf for Gaelic documentary, *Air an Toir* (In Search Of), June 2006

The Dundee Heritage Trust contacted Alf inquiring if he would record a video message for the official opening of a new gallery at Discovery Point to be named '*Discovery*'s Ocean Odyssey' on 11 May 2006. Alf spoke for seven minutes while the video camera was rolling. His contribution was posted to Dundee and screened at the ceremony. For Niall Cooper, the Trust's curator, the opening of the new gallery was a great success: 'Close to 70 people turned up and everyone really loved Alf's piece, which we showed on the big screen in the auditorium. At the end of the film everyone very warmly applauded. Several people came up to me afterwards to say how interesting and moving they found it.'[44] The event was written up in Dundee's *The Courier and Advertiser* along with an article about Alf the next day. The Trust sent a copy to Alf of the final DVD in a special presentation pack labelled: 'Dr. Alf Howard: The last of *Discovery*'s Antarctic heroes recalls his time on the ship.'

Alf, it must be said, was not adverse to media attention. There is no doubt he was treated at times as a 'celebrity', and especially when he became the sole survivor of Mawson's BANZARE voyages. Whether it was for a photograph, some footage for the evening news or an interview, Alf would be in top form and come alive before a camera or a microphone. Soon after his 100th birthday a team from BBC TV Scotland made arrangements from Glasgow to interview and film Alf for the documentary *Air an Tòir* (In Search Of) about Murdo Morrison from the Isle of Lewis in the Outer Hebrides, who joined the *Discovery*'s crew in Williamstown for the second BANZARE voyage. Interestingly, one of the BBC team — John Morrison — was a distant cousin of Murdo's. The day came when BBC TV flew into Brisbane especially to speak with Alf. They set up cameras, lamps, reflectors and sound booms and in no time at all Alf's living area was transformed into a television studio. Cameras rolled, recording equipment turned on, and Alf was interviewed — he was brilliant. Alf thoroughly enjoyed every moment and had a chat with each of the five-member team. That was in June 2006. The 30-minute documentary in Gaelic, with English sub-titles except for Alf's interview, was shown on Scottish TV nine months later and of course a copy was sent to Alf, which he watched several times.

The year closed with two exhibitions: 'Alf Howard: A Life of Discovery' was mounted in the University of Queensland's main library for most of September and October. Alf stoically visited the display and gave it the 'thumbs up.' In December the Tasmanian Museum and Art Gallery in Hobart prepared a special showcase about Alf as part of their 'Islands to Ice: the Great Southern Ocean and Antarctica' exhibition following the visit of Senior Curator, David Pemberton, who made a special trip to Brisbane to meet him.

*

At the beginning of 2008 Alf was delighted to be asked by the City of Camberwell (Melba's Own) Scout Group to contribute some reminiscences of his scouting days for the foreword to their centenary celebration publication *The Saga of Melba's Own*:

Dear Members of 1st City of Camberwell (Melba's Own) Scout Group,

I started off as a Cub with the First Camberwell Troop during the First World War when I as about ten in 1916. You transferred from the Cubs to the Scouts at about eleven. My brother Clarence (Curly) started as a scout because there weren't any cubs when he was young enough to be one. We met one night during the week and normally on Saturday afternoon. Instruction included knotting, signalling, semaphore and Morse. There was Morse code with flags — a single flag, and semaphore with two flags. Sending Morse by means of a lamp fascinated me. You could be on one hill and on another hilltop, say two miles away, and you could be talking to one another in Morse.

I went camping with the Scouts and can remember one time going by myself to find sites where we could set up camp. It was about twenty miles out of Melbourne and I rode down on my bicycle. At that stage I probably would have been a senior scout. We would have to hire a vehicle, hire the whole show. The hire car would take us down to wherever we could camp, leave us there, and come back for us a week or ten days later. Our main diet was bread and jam and sometimes we'd make ourselves soup. Bread and jam was a good filler but we always had some form of meat for our midday meal, usually sausages. The other thing was to make sure there were sufficient funds to buy extra provisions in a local shop so that you could have a good splash up on the final night.

I wish you many happy memories of your Centenary Celebrations this year.

Alf Howard, AM

King's Scout

1st Registered Cub with 1st Camberwell in 1916

Age in 2008: 102[45]

Every birthday Alf proudly sported a cloth badge sent to him by his old 'Melba's Own' scout troop, a badge of the *Discovery*, and his Order of Australia pin. Friends and colleagues from the ANARE Club, CSIRO and Human Movement Studies as well as other good friends did not forget Alf when he moved from his St Lucia home in late 2003, and Alf was very touched when Sally, the daughter of Eric Douglas — his cabin sharer on the *Discovery* — made a special trip to Brisbane to meet him.

*

Alf Howard lived 104 very fruitful years and believed that a healthy and stress-free lifestyle keeps the mind active and an active mind keeps you young. When asked what other route he may have followed had he not been a scientist he replied: 'Probably a builder of some sort; more the actual carpenter on the job but on the other hand I feel that I've enjoyed everything that I've done.'

'I suppose I'm curious,' he would say. 'I want to know about anything that comes in front of me. I'm honoured in a sense that I've been able to live and work in a scientific milieu and that I've been involved in something that helped someone along the way.'

Mawson's last survivor could be perceived as a modern-day Renaissance man. Alf was a man of universal education, a man who acquired scientific knowledge and had a lifelong passion for the visual and performing arts. 'The Howard story is a celebration of the human spirit, expressed through the resilience of curiosity possessed by us all. We cultivate it or we let it wither. Occasionally, we need an Alf Howard to reinforce that realisation.'[46]

Cheers!

***

NOTES

AAD	Australian Antarctic Division, Kingston, Tasmania
ANZAAS	Australian and New Zealand Association for the Advancement of Science
BZE/ BANZARE	British, Australian and New Zealand Antarctic Research Expedition (BANZARE)
CSIR	Council for Scientific and Industrial Research
CSIRO	Commonwealth Scientific and Industrial Research Organisation
FL	Fryer Library, The University of Queensland
HMS	Department/School of Human Movement Studies
MC	The Mawson Collection, South Australian Museum, Adelaide
ML	Mitchell Library, State Library of New South Wales, Sydney
NLA	National Library of Australia, Canberra
UHS	University High School, Melbourne
UQ	The University of Queensland

JUNE 1929

1 Sir David Orme Masson KBE (1858-1937) was an English scientist who emigrated to Australia to become Professor of Chemistry at the University of Melbourne. He had served Mawson well in a similar capacity for the Australasian Antarctic Expedition (1911-14).

2 Sir (Albert Cherbury) David Rivett, KCMG (1885-1961) was an Australian chemist and science administrator. From 1927 to 1946 he was Deputy Chairman and Chief Executive Officer of the Council for Scientific and Industrial Research (CSIR) and was elected Chairman of the Council of the renamed Commonwealth Scientific and Industrial Research Organisation (CSIRO) from 1946 to 1949. He became Associate Professor at the University of Melbourne in 1921 and succeeded Professor David Orme Masson as Professor of Chemistry in 1924.

3 *Letter* from Dr A.C.D. Rivett to Sir Douglas Mawson dated 17 June 1929, MC 32BZE/34.

4 Letter from Sir Douglas Mawson to Dr A.C.D. Rivett dated 28 June 1929, MC 32BZE/34.

5 Alf Howard, unpublished notes 'British, Australian, New Zealand Antarctic Research Expedition (BANZARE),' nd, Alf Howard papers, FL.

6 The University High School Record, Xmas, 1929, p 38, UHS archives.

7 The University High School Record, Xmas, 1923, pp. 24, 30, UHS archives.

8 Born in Wales Sir Tannatt William Edgeworth David (Edgeworth David) KBE, DSO, RS, (1858-1934) arrived in Australia in 1882. Geologist and Antarctic explorer, his most significant achievements were the discovery of the South Maitland coalfield in New South Wales, leading Douglas Mawson and Alistair Mackay in the first expedition to reach the South Magnetic Pole locality in 1909 and serving with distinction in World War I. He was awarded the Distinguished Service Order in 1918. In T.G. Vallance, D.F. Branagan, 'David, Sir Tannatt William Edgeworth (1858-1934),' *Australian Dictionary of Biography*, Volume 8, MUP, 1981, pp 218-221.

9 Walter Henderson was Head of the External Affairs Branch of the Department of Prime Minister and Cabinet in Canberra from 1926 until 1930.

10 Minutes of Antarctic Committee, Melbourne, 15 June 1929, MC 31BZE/34.

11 'Mr. Alfred Howard,' *Sydney Morning Herald*, 22 June 1929:14.

12 Scott Baty, *Ships that Passed: The Glorious Era of Travel to Australia and New Zealand*. Frenchs Forest, NSW: Reed Books, 1984.

13 De Lesseps statue was badly damaged during the 1956 Suez Crisis; it has only recently been restored by the Paris-based association Friends of Ferdinand de Lesseps and at present stands on the lawns of the Port Fouad shipyard ready to stand on its original pedestal at the entrance to the Suez Canal.

14 Claude Fisher, *The World Jamboree 1929: The Quest of the Golden Arrow*. Foreword by Lord Baden-Powell. Second Edition, London, Boy Scouts Association, 1929.

15 Alf's old Camberwell Scout Group was and is still known as *Melba's Own*. Madame Melba (later Dame Nellie Melba) accepted the office of Patron of the 1st Camberwell Troop in 1912 when she was visited at Coombe Cottage by Sir Robert Baden-Powell and the State Governor, on which occasion the Troop were asked to provide a Guard of Honour for the Chief Scout. In Colin Roche [1968], Gerard Pergual and Ralph Simphendorpher [1983], Jan Black [2008] et. al., 'The Saga of Melba's Own: The Story of First City of Camberwell (Melba's Own) Scout Group 1908-2008' [unpublished], pp. 10 and 17. Dame Nellie was also a Patron of Mawson's 1911-14 expedition.

16 The term 'scout corroboree' appears to have been used less frequently once the first Australian scout jamboree was held in Sydney in 1934.

17 Letter from Fenton Mattingly to Alf Howard dated 25 June 1929.

18 Allen, E.J. and Harvey, H.W., 'The laboratory of the Marine Biological Association at Plymouth,' in *Journal of the Marine Biological Association of the United Kingdom*, Vol. 15 No. 3, 1928:744.

19 Email dated 21 May 2009 from Cathy Broad, Librarian, National Marine Biological Library, Citadel Hill, Plymouth.

Three ships — destination Cape Town

1 'The *Discovery*: Reception on Board,' *Sydney Morning Herald,* 29 July 1929:11.

2 'Mawson Expedition: Scientists Chosen,' *Sydney Morning Herald*. 18 June 1929:10.

3 'The *Discovery*: Departure from London,' *Sydney Morning Herald*, 2 August 1929: 12.

4 Frank Hurley, diary, 1 August 1929, in Papers of Frank Hurley, NLA MS 883, Series 1: Item 15. J.H. Blair was Chief Officer on the *Aurora*, which took Dr Douglas Mawson and his men to Commonwealth Bay on his 1911-1914 Australasian Antarctic Expedition. A.J. Hodgeman was 'entrusted with the details of design [and] was appointed clerk of works on the construction' of the Hut at Commonwealth Bay. In Douglas Mawson, *The Home of the Blizzard*, Kent Town, South Australia: Wakefield Press, 1996: 53-54, 403.

5 Hurley, diary, 3 August 1929.

6 Ibid., 3-4 August 1929.

7 Ibid., 5 August 1929.

8 Ibid., 5-6 August 1929.

9 Ibid., 1-2 August 1929.

10 Ibid., 7-8 August 1929.

11 Ibid., 10 August 1929.

12 Ibid.

13 Ibid., 4 and 11 August 1929.

14 'Voyage from England to Table Bay', *Cape Argus*, 5 October 1929: 11.

15 Ibid.

16 Press release from Captain J.K. Davis to Univalser Fleet Street, London via Portishead Radio, c20 August 1929, MC 44BZE/35.

17 Press release from J.K. Davis to Hearst Newspapers, London, c11 August 1929, MC 44BZE/35.

18 Ibid., 22 August 1929, MC 44BZE/35.

19 Letter from Sir Douglas Mawson to Dr W. Henderson dated 7 August 1929, National Archives of Australia [digital copy, barcode 97235].

20 Simmers, diary, 20 September 1929, David Simmers private collection.

21 Letter from R.G. Casey, High Commissioner for the Commonwealth of Australia in London to the Rt. Hon. S.M. Bruce, Prime Minister of the Commonwealth, Canberra dated 19 September 1929, MC 18BZE/29.

22 Simmers, diary, 21 September 1929.

23 Simmers, diary, 6-7 October 1929.

24 Wireless message from R.G. Casey via the British Wireless Marine Service to Captain J.K. Davis on board the *Discovery* dated 21 September 1929, MC 16BZE/2,

25 Simmers, diary, 7 October 1929.

26 Harold Fletcher, *Antarctic Days with Mawson*, Sydney, Angus & Robertson, 1984, p. 41.

27 'For the South. Party Leaves Melbourne,' *Sydney Morning Herald*, 14 September 1929: 18.

28 Letter from Sir Douglas Mawson to Dr W. Henderson, 7 August 1929, National Archives of Australia [digital copy, barcode 97235].

29 Eric Douglas, BANZARE diary, October 1929, Sally Douglas private collection.

30 'Sports and Entertainment Programme' dated 27 September-7 October 1929, from the Blue Funnel Line steamer *TSS Nestor*. Sally Douglas private collection.

31 Douglas, diary, October 1929.

32 Fletcher, p. 42.

A cargo of infinite variety

1 '*Discovery*'s Lessened Sail Area,' *Cape Times*, 9 October 1929: 1.

2 'Room for Everyone in the Antarctic: Captain Davis of *Discovery* Laughs at Stories of Rivalry,' *Cape Argus*, 9 October 1929: 11. John King Davis was Captain of the *Aurora*–the ship chosen for the Australasian Antarctic Expedition 1911-1914 under the command of Dr Douglas Mawson.

3 Simmers, diary, 11 October 1929.

4 'Mawson departs for Cape Town.' *Sydney Morning Herald*, 25 September 1929: 16.

5 Advertisement, *Table Talk*, September 1929.

6 Advertisement, *Argus*, September 1929.

7 Advertisement, *Cape Times*, 19 October 1929: 26.

8 Hurley, diary, 13 October 1929.

9 'Arrivals for the *Discovery*.' *Cape Times*, 14 October 1929: 10.

10 Simmers, diary, 13 October 1929.

11 A. Grenfell Price, *The Winning of Australian Antarctica*, p. 23.

12 'New Race to the Antarctic Starting.' *Cape Argus*, 8 October 1929: 12.

13 'Norwegian Press Comment: No Secrecy about Aims,' *Cape Argus*, 11 October 1929: 11.

14 Hurley, diary, October 1929.

15 Captain Robert F. Scott, *The Voyage of the Discovery*, Macmillan and Co., Limited, London, 1905, vol. I, p. 71.

16 '*Discovery* Leaves Table Bay,' *Cape Argus*, 19 October 1929: 9.

17 Hurley, diary, October 1929.

18 Ibid, p. 4.

19 Ibid, October 1929, p. 5.

20 William Wilson Ingram, diary, 19 October 1929, ML MSS4120 | Box 2 | Items 3-4.

21 'Saying "So Long" to *Discovery*,' *Cape Times*, 19 October 1929: 15.

22 A barquentine is a vessel with the foremast square rigged, and the main- and mizzen-masts fore-and-aft-rigged.

23 'Discovery leaves Table Bay.' *Cape Argus*, 19 October 1929: 9.

24 While 'actinometer' is the general name for any instrument used to measure the intensity of radiant energy, a 'pyrheliometer' is an actinometer that specifically measures the intensity of direct solar radiation.

25 Samuel Leonard Welsford was the eldest son of Alf's grandfather on his mother's side and was left to run his father's importing business in London. 'The result was that the business was on the rocks almost immediately, and Samuel Leonard felt he would be safer out of the country, and hence his hurried departure for South Africa leaving his wife and three young children in the care of my parents.' From Shirley McKeon's meeting with Alf Howard in 1997 in 'The Welsford Story' written by Shirley McKeon & Cousins.

A stout little ship

1 'Farewell blasts from steamers in dock.' *Cape Argus*, 19 October 1929: 9.

2 Ibid.

3 Hurley, dairy, 19 October 1929.

4 Simmers, dairy, 19 October 1929.

5 Mawson, diary, 19 October 1929 in Sir Douglas Mawson's *Mawson's Antarctic Diaries*, eds. Fred and Eleanor Jacka, Allen & Unwin, Crows Nest, NSW, 1988, pp. 255-256.

6 Ingram, diary, 19 October 1929.

7 'Saying "So Long" to *Discovery*.' *Cape Times*, 19 October 1929: 15.

8 '*Discovery* Departs: Farewell Messages,' *Argus*, 21 October 1929: 7.

9 Scott, vol. I, p. 37.

10 *National Register of Historic Vessels*. Online reference <www.nationalhistoricships.org.uk/ships_register.php?action=ship&id=39>

11 *Discovery Reports* Vol. I, Cambridge, University Press of Cambridge, 1929, p. 152.

12 *National Register of Historic Vessels*. Online reference <www.nationalhistoricships.org.uk/ships_register.php?action=ship&id=39>

13 Mawson, diary, 24 October 1929 in *Mawson's Antarctic Diaries*, p. 257.

14 Ibid., 23 October 1929, p. 256.

15 Ingram, diary, 23 October 1929.

16 Hurley, diary, 1 August 1929.

17 Ibid., October 1929.

18 *Discovery Reports* Vol. I, p.158.

19 Scott, vol. I, p.45.

20 *Discovery Reports* Vol I, pp. 156-157.

21 'Mawson Expedition: The King's Best Wishes,' *Brisbane Courier*, 23 October 1929: 20.

22 The Agulhas current is the second swiftest current in all the world's oceans and is deadlier than the swiftest current, the Gulf Stream, because it flows between land rather than the open ocean.

23 Moyes, BANZARE 1929-30 journal, October 1929, p.4, MC 57BZE/37.

24 Mawson, diary, 20 and 24 October 1929, p. 257.

25 Moyes, BANZARE 1929-30 journal, October 1929, p.4, MC 57BZE/37.

26 List of books for SY *Discovery*'s Library, MC 26BZE/31.

27 Ibid, pp. 4-5.

28 Ingram, diary, 2 November 1929.

29 Mawson, diary, 23 October 1929, pp. 256-257.

30 Simmers, diary, 1 November 1929.

Sailing with legends

1 Hurley, diary, October 1929.

2 Letter of request to join the Australasian Antarctic Expedition (AAE) from James Francis (Frank) Hurley to Douglas Mawson, 29 September 1911, ML Discover Collections Hurley's Antarctica.

3 Moyes, BANZARE 1929-30 journal, October 1929, p.5, MC 57BZE/37.

4 Mawson, diary, 2 November 1929, pp. 258-259.

5 Ibid., p. 259.

6 A 'dip circle' is a measuring instrument for measuring the angle of a magnetic dip or magnetic inclination, which is the angle made by a compass needle with the horizontal at any point on the Earth's surface.

7 Simmers, diary, 2 November 1929.

8 Ibid., 3 November 1929.

9 Hurley, diary, November 1929.

10 Ibid.

11 Mawson, diary, 6 November 1929, p. 260. Clothing itemised on The Jaeger Co. Ltd. London order form dated 4 September 1929. MC 22BZE/31.

12 Hurley, diary, November 1929.

13 Mawson, diary, 5-6 November 1929, p. 260.

14 Ibid., 8 November, p. 260.

15 'The *Discovery*: Report from the Crozets,' *Sydney Morning Herald*, 11 November 1929: 12.

16 Mawson, diary, 7 November 1929, p. 260.

17 Letter from S. Smith & Son Limited, Yalumba Vineyards to Sir Douglas Mawson, 11 September 1929, MC 19BZE/30.

18 Douglas Mawson, *The Home of the Blizzard*, Kent Town, South Australia, Wakefield Press, 1996, p. 201.

19 Ernest Shackleton quoted in John Béchervaise, 'Davis, John King (1884-1967),' *Australian Dictionary of Biography*, Volume 8, MUP, 1981, pp 238-239.

20 Graham Perkin, 'A Red Beard In Frozen Wastes Of Antarctica,' *The Age*, 16 September 1959.

21 John Béchervaise, 'Davis, John King (1884 - 1967),' *Australian Dictionary of Biography*, Volume 8, Melbourne University Press, 1981, pp 238-239.

22 John King Davis, journal, 22 November 1929 in *Trial By Ice: The Antarctic Journals of John King Davis*, ed. Louise Crossley. Bluntisham Books and Erskine Press, Norwich, 1997, p. 127.

23 HMS *Challenger* was the name of the British naval vessel chosen for the first truly scientific Antarctic expedition from 1872-76 under the command of Sir Charles Wyville Thompson. She was the first steamship to cross the Antarctic Circle.

24 Moyes, 'Antarctic Episodes,' pp. 8-9. MC 57BZE/37.

25 Denis Fairfax, 'Moyes, Morton Henry (1886-1981),' *Australian Dictionary of Biography*, Volume 10, Melbourne University Press, 1986, p. 602.

26 Frank Wild quoted in Douglas Mawson, *The Home of the Blizzard*, pp. 271-272.

27 Mawson, diary, 22 November 1929, p. 264.

28 James William Slessor Marr, *Into the Frozen South by Scout Marr of the* Quest *Expedition*, ed. Captain Frank H. Shaw. London: Cassell, 1923, p. 103.

29 B.B.R., 'Obituary: Dr James William Slessor Marr,' *Polar Record*, Vol. 13, No. 82, pp. 94-97.

30 Davis, journal, 23 November 1929, p. 127.

31 Ibid., 25-26 November 1929, p. 128.

32 Mawson, diary, 26 November 1929, p. 265.

On the plank, into the lab

1 Sir Douglas Mawson, 'The B.A.N.Z. Antarctic Research Expedition, 1929-31,' in *The Geographical Journal* Vol. LXXX July to December 1931, pp. 101-131.

2 Fletcher, p. 89.

3 Phillip Garth Law, *Antarctic Odyssey*, Heinemann, Melbourne, 1983.

4 The hexagonal Admiralty Hut was erected by whalers from the *Kildalkey* in January 1929.

5 Simmers, diary, 26 November 1929.

6 Moyes, BANZARE 1929-30 journal, November 1929, p. 10, MC 57BZE/37.

7 Ibid.

8 Davis, journal, 3 and 4 December 1929, p. 132.

9 'The Dux' was the name adopted by BANZARE's scientific team when addressing their leader Sir Douglas Mawson.

10 Simmers, diary, 5 December 1929.

11 Alf Howard, "The Programme of Work and Record of Observations,' in *BANZ. Antarctic Research Expedition 1929-1931*, Reports–Series A, Vol. 3: Oceanography, Part 2: Hydrology, issued through the Barr Smith Library, University of Adelaide. Printed at The Hassell Press, 1940, p. 30.

12 Ibid., Sir Douglas Mawson, 'Hydrology: Introduction,' p. 25.

13 Student card/record for Alf Howard from 1924-1931, Archives, The University of Melbourne.

14 Joan Radford, *The Chemistry Department of the University of Melbourne: its contribution to Australian science, 1854-1959*. Melbourne: Hawthorn Press, 1978, pp. 170-171

15 Howard, *BANZARE. Reports*, Series A, Vol. 3: Oceanography, Part 2: Hydrology, p. 30.

16 Moyes, BANZARE 1929-30 journal, November 1929, p. 11, MC 57BZE/37.

17 Radio communication from Mawson to Henderson, No. 16 dated 10 December 1929, MC 44BZE/35.

18 Alf Howard, 'Polar Waters.' *The Queenslander*, 14 August 1930: 62.

19 Taking water samples the way Alf did from an outboard platform has today been replaced by various modern oceanographic instruments: the shipboard Conductivity, Temperature and Depth (CTD) tool consists of small probes attached to a large metal rosette wheel lowered to the seafloor to determine the essential physical properties of sea water, the results of which are relayed via a conducting cable to a computer onboard ship; the Acoustic Doppler Current Profiler (ADCP) when anchored to the seafloor can measure current speed at equal intervals from the bottom all the way up to the surface; Alace, Palace and Solo floats are drifting instruments that measure ocean temperature and salinity and transmit their data and position to orbiting satellites; and there are also autonomous underwater vehicles (AUVs) such as the two-metre-long Spray glider that carries a variety of sensors giving scientists a clearer understanding of the temperature, salinity and turbidity of specific areas of the oceans. Woods Hole Oceanographic Institution (WHOI); www.whoi.edu/science/instruments/.do?id=1003; www.whoi.edu/science/instruments/.do?id=819; www.whoi.edu/science/instruments/.do?id=1498.

20 Mawson, diary, 8 December 1929, p. 273.

21 Ibid., 10 December 1929, p. 276.

22 Moyes, BANZARE 1929-30 journal, November 1929, p. 11, MC 57BZE/37.

23 Davis, journal, 11 December 1929, p. 135.

Pitching In

1 Davis quoted in 'Famous Ship with a Crew of Young Men,' *The Cape Argus*, 5 October 1929: 11.

2 Radio communication from Sir Douglas Mawson to Prime Minister Henderson, No. 15 dated 8 December 1929, MC 44BZE/35.

3 Mawson, diary, 11 December 1929, p. 276.

4 Ibid., 8 December 1929, p. 273.

5 Reports of B.A.N.Z. Antarctic Research Expedition, 1929-1931–Series B, Vol. I, Part 1, Biological Organization and Station List by T. Harvey Johnston (1937), p. 1.

6 Ibid., pp. 3, 5, and 8.

7 Reports of B.A.N.Z. Antarctic Research Expedition, 1929-1931–Series B, Vol. I, Part 1, Biological Organization and Station List by T. Harvey Johnston (1937), p. 2.

8 T. Harvey Johnston, 'BANZAR Expedition: Zoological and Botanical Operations,' *Cairns Post*, 23 April 1931: 11.

9 Mawson, diary, 17 December 1929, p. 284.

10 Ibid., 9 December 1929, p. 275.

11 Harold Fletcher, diary, 6 December 1929. Ian Fletcher, private collection.

12 Radio communication from Mawson to Henderson, No. 16 dated 10 December 1929, MC 44BZE/35.

13 Ibid., No. 17 dated 13 December 1929, MC 44BZE/35.

14 'The *Discovery*: Heavy Pack Ice,' *Sydney Morning Herald*, 26 December 1929: 8.

15 Minutes of Antarctic Committee, Melbourne, 13 May 1929, MC 31BZE/34.

16 Letter from R.G. Casey to the Rt. Hon. S.M. Bruce dated 19 September 1929, MC 18BZE/29.

17 Simmers, diary, 17 December 1929.

18 Letter from Sir Douglas Mawson to Squadron Leader Drummond, RAAF, Victoria Barracks, Melbourne, 20 June 1929, MC 38-39BZE.

19 Mawson, diary, 19 December 1929, p. 286.

20 Eric Douglas, BANZARE diary, 15 and 18 October 1929, Sally Douglas private collection.

21 Mawson, diary, 22 December 1929, p. 288.

22 Ibid., p. 289.

23 Simmers, diary, 23 December 1929.

24 Mawson, diary, 23 December 1929, p. 290.

Christmas — 66° 28'S, 73° 28'E

1 Davis, journal, 23 December 1929, p. 140.

2 Simmers, diary, 24 December 1929.

3 Mawson, diary, 24 December 1929, p. 291.

4 Ingram, diary, 25 December 1929, MLMSS 4120, Box 2 | Item 5.

5 Scott, vol. II, p. 227.

6 Sir Douglas Mawson, 'Christmas Amid Icefields,' *The Times*, 31 December 1929: 11.

7 Fletcher, *Antarctic Days with Mawson*, p. 131.

8 Mawson, diary, 25 December 1929, p. 291.

9 List of food supplies for SY *Discovery*, MC 26BZE/31.

10 'The domestic side of the *Discovery*.' *Cape Times*, 19 October 1929: 26.

11 Simmers, diary, 25 December 1929.

12 Fletcher, pp. 133-134.

13 List of supplies for SY *Discovery*, MC 26BZE/31.

14 Mawson, diary, 25 December 1929, p. 292.

15 Davis, journal, 26 December 1929, p. 141.

16 Mawson, diary, 27 December 1929, p. 294.

17 Radio communication from Mawson to Henderson, No. 23 dated 31 December 1929, MC 44BZE/35.

18 Eric Douglas interviewed by John Thompson for ABC radio feature 'South with Sir Douglas Mawson' [no date], Sally Douglas private papers.

19 Fletcher, p. 141.

20 In Sally Douglas private collection.

21 Radio communication from Mawson to Henderson, No. 23 dated 1 January 1930, MC 44BZE/35.

22 Simmers, diary, 31 December 1929.

Master versus Commander

1 Mawson, diary, 1 January 1930, pp. 299-300.

2 Davis, journal, 1 January 1930, p. 144.

3 Mawson, diary, 1 January 1930, p. 299.

4 Ernest Shackleton, *The Heart of the Antarctic*, 2 vols. William Heinemann, London 1909. Penguin, London 2002, p. 367.

5 Mawson, diary, 24 December 1929, pp. 290-291.

6 Davis, journal, 24 December 1929, p. 140.

7 Ibid., 30 December 1929, p. 143.

8 Mawson, diary, 1 January 1930, pp. 301-302.

9 Davis, journal, 7 January 1930, p. 147.

10 Mawson, diary, 10 January 1930, p. 311.

11 'Norwegian Expedition,' London *Times*, 31 December 1929: 11.

12 Telegram from the Department of External Affairs in Canberra to Sir Douglas Mawson, dated 17 January 1930, National Archives of Australia/barcode 97235.

13 Mawson, diary, 5 January 1930, p. 306.

14 Ibid., 5 January 1930, p. 307.

15 Ibid., p. 308.

16 Ibid., 7 January 1930, p. 309.

17 Ibid., 12 January 1930, pp. 312-313.

Proclaiming new lands

1 Simmers, diary, 13 January 1930.

2 Fletcher, p. 161.

3 Simmers, diary, 13 January 1930.

4 Mawson, diary, 13 January 1930, p. 314.

5 Fletcher, p. 162.

6 Quoted in A. Grenfell Price, *The Winning of Australian Antarctica*, Sydney, Angus & Robertson Ltd, 1962, p. 71.

7 Simmers, diary, 13 January 1930.

8 Fletcher, p. 164.

9 Mawson, diary, 13 January 1930, p. 314.

10 Davis, journal, 13 January 1930, p. 150.

11 Mawson, diary, 13 January 1930, pp. 314-315.

12 Simmers, diary, 13 January 1930.

13 Ibid., 14 January 1930.

14 MacKenzie, diary, 14 January 1930 quoted in Simmers, diary, 14 January 1930.

15 Davis, journal, 14 January 1930, p. 151.

16 Mawson, diary, 13 January 1930, p. 317.

17 Davis, journal, 14 January 1930, p. 151.

18 Simmers, diary, 14 January 1930.

19 Ibid., 15 January 1930.

20 Davis, journal, 16 January 1930, p. 152.

21 Fletcher, p. 173.

22 Radio communication from Mawson to Casey, No. 33 dated 25 January 1930, MC 44BZE/35.

23 Davis, journal, 20 January 1930, p. 153.

North to Kerguelen

1 Mawson, diary, 18 January 1930, p. 321.

2 Ibid., 22 January 1930, p. 323.

3 Simmers, diary, 22 January 1930.

4 Mawson, diary, 25 January 1930, p. 325.

5 Ibid., 26 January 1930, p. 326.

6 Davis, journal, 26 January 1930, p. 156.

7 Ibid., journal, 27 and 28 January 1930, p. 157.

8 Simmers, diary, 21 January 1930.

9 Davis, journal, 20 January 1930, p. 153.

10 Eric Douglas, BANZARE diary, 27 January 1929, Sally Douglas private collection.

11 Mawson, diary, 26 January 1930, p. 327.

12 Radio communication from Mawson to Prime Minister Henderson, No. 39 dated 7 February 1930, MC 44BZE/35.

13 Fletcher, p. 221.

14 Davis, journal, 28 January 1930, p. 157.

15 Ibid., 31 January 1930, pp. 158-159.

16 Mawson, diary, 29 January 1930, p. 327.

17 Simmers, diary, 29 January 1930.

18 Ibid., 31 January 1930.

19 Mawson, diary, 27 January 1930, p. 327.

20 Ibid., 2 February 1930, p. 328.

21 Davis, journal, 4 February 1930, p. 160.

22 Fletcher, p. 184.

23 Mawson, diary, 6 and 7 February 1930, p. 329.

24 Davis, journal, 8 February 1930, pp. 163-164.

25 Mawson, diary, 8 February 1930, p. 330.

26 'Mawson Expedition Welcomed: Wireless Communication,' *Advertiser*, 2 April 1930: 21.

27 Simmers, diary, 10 February 1930.

28 W.W. Ingram, Medical Report for first BANZARE voyage 1929-1930, MC/43BZE.

29 Ingram, Medical Report 1929-1930, MC/43BZE.

30 Davis, journal, 10 and 13 February 1930, pp. 162 and 164.

31 Simmers, diary, 12 February 1930.

32 Mawson, diary, 9-12 February 1930, p. 330.

33 Simmers, diary, 16 February 1930.

34 Mawson, diary, 15 February 1930, p. 331.

35 Ibid., 13-18 February 1930, pp. 330-332.

36 Ibid., 19 February 1930, p. 332.

37 Ibid., 22-28 February 1930, pp. 332-333.

38 Fletcher, pp. 212-213.

39 Douglas Mawson, 'Antarctic Research Expedition: British, Australian and New Zealand Enterprise,' *Cairns Post*, 2 June 1930: 12.

SS Cathay's surprise barrel drop

1 Davis, journal, 21 March 1930, p. 177.

2 Mawson, diary, 21 March 1930, pp. 344-345.

3 Fletcher, p. 223.

4 Mawson, diary, 22 March 1930, pp. 344-345.

5 Radio message No. 46 from Sir Douglas Mawson to Dr Henderson, 23 March 1930, MC 44BZE/35.

6 Mawson, diary, 27 March 1930, p. 345.

7 Davis, journal, 27 March 1930, p. 178.

8 'Sir Douglas Mawson Home at Last,' *Advertiser*, 1 April 1930: 15.

9 Davis, journal, 31 March 1930, p. 178.

10 'Warm Welcome to Antarctic Research Expedition: Cheering Crowds at Port Adelaide.' *Advertiser*, 2 April 1930: 19.

11 Ibid.

12 'Leader's Story of the Trip,' *Advertiser*, 2 April 1930: 21.

13 'Adelaide Applauds the Work of Mawson Expedition: Great and Historic Occasion,' *Advertiser*, 3 April 1930: 15.

14 Douglas, diary, 3 April 1930.

15 'Mawson Expedition: *Discovery* Reaches Melbourne,' *Argus*, 9 April 1930: 7. Clarence Hare was 21 when he joined Scott's 1901-1904 *Discovery* expedition in New Zealand. He was part of the group that tried to return to the icebound *Discovery* after being caught in the blizzard when Vince lost his life. Amazingly Hare survived being buried in the snow for about 36 hours and suffered no frostbite despite the fact he had not eaten any warm food for nearly two and a half days.

16 '*Discovery* at Melbourne,' *The Queenslander*, 17 April 1930: 47.

On the road with Hurley

1 Howard to Mawson, 7 May 1930, MC 63BZE/38.

2 'Work in Antarctic to be continued,' *Sydney Morning Herald*, 23 May 1930: 118.

3 '*Discovery* in Dock for Overhaul,' *The Register News-Pictorial* [Adelaide], 20 May 1930: 26.

4 'Dry-Dock Report of S.Y. *Discovery*, at Williamstown,' 30 May 1930, MC 30BZE/33.

5 'Thefts from Polar Ship: Food Taken from the *Discovery*,' *Mercury*, 25 June 1930: 8.

6 Mawson to Howard, 9 July 1930, MC 63BZE/38.

7 Ibid., 15 July 1930.

8 Frank Strahan (1886-1976) was appointed Assistant Secretary of the Prime Minister's Department in Canberra from 1921-1935 and then promoted to Secretary.

9 Mawson to Strahan, 28 July 1930, MC 55BZE/37.

10 Advertisement for *Southward Ho! With Mawson*, *Sydney Morning Herald*, 9 August 1930: 2.

11 'New Films: *Southward Ho! With Mawson*,' *Sydney Morning Herald*, 11 August 1930: 5.

12 Howard to Mawson, 16 September 1930, MC 63BZE/38.

13 Mawson to Howard, 17 September 1930, MC 63BZE/38.

14 '*Discovery* Crew Signed On,' *Register News-Pictorial* (Adelaide), 23 October 1930: 9.

15 Simmers, diary, 15 October 1930.

16 Ibid., 1 November 1930.

17 'The *Discovery*: Departure for Hobart,' *Mercury*, 3 November 1930: 6.

18 'Antarctic Expedition: Departure of *Discovery*,' *Argus*, 3 November 1930: 8.

19 Simmers, diary, 6 November 1930.

20 Ibid., 2 November 1930.

21 'The *Discovery*: Hobart reached,' *Brisbane Courier*, 6 November 1930: 12.

South to Macquarie Island

1 Simmers, diary, 7 November 1930.

2 'The *Discovery*,' *Mercury*, 8 November 1930: 18.

3 Simmers, diary, 8 November 1930.

4 'The *Discovery*: Departure on Saturday,' *Mercury*, 18 November 1930: p. 6.

5 'The *Discovery*: Departure To-morrow,' *Mercury*, 21 November 1930.

6 In *The Mercury* dated 12, 18, 14, 20, and 21 November 1930.

7 'The *Discovery*: British Government's Good Wishes,' *Mercury*, 22 November 1930: 8.

8 '*Mercury*, 24 November 1930:

9 Frank Hurley, diary, 22 November 1930.

10 'The *Discovery* Sails for Antarctica,' *Mercury*, 19 November 1930: 6.

11 'Seaman's Surprise: Stowaways on *Discovery*,' *Brisbane Courier*, 11 December 1930: 15.

12 Radio message No. 1 from Sir Douglas Mawson to Strahan, 26 November 1930, MC 44BZE/35.

13 Radio message No. 2 from Sir Douglas Mawson to Strahan, 27 November 1930, MC 44BZE/35.

14 Ingram, Medical Log, SY *Discovery*, 1930-1931, ML MSS4120|Box 2|Items 5.

15 Captain MacKenzie, 'Log of SY *Discovery* 1930-31,' 22-30 November 1930, MC 96BZE/299-44

16 *Macquarie Island*, Published by the Parks & Wildlife Service (PWS) in cooperation with the Nature Conservation Branch (NCB) of the Department of Primary Industries, Water and Environment, Tasmania, 2001, pp. 2, 31.

17 Mawson, diary, 2 December 1930, p. 356.

18 Simmers, diary, 2 December 1930.

19 Mawson, diary, 4 December 1930, pp. 359-360.

20 Ibid., p. 360.

Rendezvous with the *Sir James Clark Ross*

1 Simmers, diary, 7 December 1930.

2 Hurley, diary, 7 December 1930.

3 Ibid.

4 Radio message No. 5 from Sir Douglas Mawson to Strahan, 13 December 1930, MC 44BZE/35.

5 Simmers, diary, 11 December 1930.

6 Hurley, diary, 12 December 1930.

7 Ingram, Medical Log, SY *Discovery*, 1930-1931.

8 Ibid., 14 December 1930.

9 Radio message No. 6 from Sir Douglas Mawson to Strahan, 17 December 1930, MC 44BZE/35.

10 Simmers, diary, 15 December 1930.

11 Radio message No. 6 from Sir Douglas Mawson to Strahan, 17 December 1930, MC 44BZE/35.

12 Hurley, diary, 15 December 1930.

13 Simmers, diary, 16 December 1930.

14 Captain MacKenzie, 'Log of SY *Discovery* 1930-31,' 17-21 December 1930, MC 96BZE/299-44

15 The Danish training vessel *Copenhagen* (*København*) was a five-masted barque that disappeared en route from Buenos Aires to Australia sometime between December 1928 and January 1929. Radio message No. 7 from Sir Douglas Mawson to Strahan, 22 December 1930, MC 44BZE/35.

16 T. Harvey Johnston, BANZARE journal, 22-24 December 1930, MC 15BZE/315-28.

17 Ibid., 25 December 1930.

18 Simmers, diary, 25 December 1930.

19 Johnston, journal, 25 December 1930.

20 Hurley, diary, 25 December 1930.

21 Johnston, journal, 26-27 December 1930.

22 MacKenzie, 'Log of SY *Discovery* 1930-31,' 29 December 1930.

23 Simmers, diary, 29 December 1930.

24 Radio message No. 8 from Sir Douglas Mawson to Strahan, 31 December 1930, 44BZE/35.

25 Simmers, diary, 29 December 1930.

26 Ibid.

27 MacKenzie, 'Log of SY *Discovery* 1930-31,' 30 December 1930, MC 96BZE/299 - 44.

28 Johnston, journal, 31 December 1930.

29 Radio message No. 9 from Sir Douglas Mawson to Strahan, 3 January 1931, 44BZE/35.

30 Johnston, journal, 31 December 1930.

Bound for Commonwealth Bay

1 Stuart Campbell, diary, 4 January 1931. Held in Australian Antarctic Division Library, Special Collection, Kingston, Tasmania.

2 Hurley, diary, 4 January 1931.

3 Campbell, diary, 5 January 1931.

4 Hurley, diary, 5 January 1931.

5 Simmers, diary, 6 January 1931.

6 Mawson, diary, 6 January 1931, p. 367.

7 Campbell, diary, 7 January 1931.

8 Simmers, diary, 8 January 1931.

9 Ibid., 22 January 1931.

10 Hurley, diary, 27 January 1931.

11 Ibid.

12 Radio communication No. 16 from Sir Douglas Mawson to Strahan, 28 January 1931, MC 44BZE/35.

13 Campbell, diary, 8 February 1931.

14 Mawson, diary, 10 February, 1931, p. 376.

15 Radio communication No. 21 from Sir Douglas Mawson to Strahan, 12 February 1931, MC 44BZE/35.

16 Mawson, diary, 13 February, 1931, p. 378.

17 Alf Howard, unpublished notes 'British, Australian, New Zealand Antarctic Research Expedition (BANZARE),' Alf Howard papers, FL.

18 Campbell, diary, 21 February 1931.

19 Ibid., 22, 23, 24 February 1931.

20 Scott, vol. I, pp. 73-74.

21 Mawson, diary, 17 March, 1931, p. 384.

22 Simmers, diary, 18 March 1931.

23 Ibid.

24 'B.A.N.Z. Antarctic Research Expedition: Operations of the 1930-31 Cruise,' *Cairns Post*, 19 May 1931: 11.

25 Ibid.

26 Alf Howard, unpublished notes 'British, Australian, New Zealand Antarctic Research Expedition (BANZARE),' Alf Howard papers, FL.

27 'Shipping,' *Mercury*, 19 March 1931: 4.

28 'The Discovery Returns: Hobart's Enthusiastic Welcome,' *Mercury*, 20 March 1931: 9; 'Research in Antarctic: *Discovery* Returns to Hobart,' *Examiner* (Launceston), 20 March 1931: 10.

29 Campbell, diary, 19 March 1931; Johnston, diary, 19 March 1931.

30 The CSIR (Council for Scientific and Industrial Research) was established in 1926 to carry out scientific research to assist the primary and secondary industries in Australia. It was preceded by the Advisory Council of Science and Industry, which was established in 1916. In 1949 when the CSIR ceased all 'classified' work for the military it was renamed CSIRO, the Commonwealth Scientific and Industrial Research Organisation: www.csiro.au/org/CSIRO HistoryOverview.html.

Melbourne 1931

1 'The *Discovery*: Arrival at Williamstown,' *Mercury*, 28 March 1931: 7.

2 'Sir Douglas Mawson: Entertained at Melbourne,' *Mercury*, 30 March 1931: 6.

3 'Sir Douglas Mawson: Broadcast from 3UZ,' *Argus*, 28 March 1931: 18.

4 Letter from Sir Douglas Mawson to Alf Howard, dated 4 May 1931, MC 63BZE/38.

5 Letter from Sir Douglas Mawson to Alf Howard, dated 8 September 1931, MC 63BZE/38.

6 Letter from Frank Hurley to Eric Douglas, dated 12 September 1931, Sally Douglas private collection.

7 Radiogram from Mawson to Henderson dated 11 February 1930, MC 16BZE/322.

8 Testimonial written by Sir Douglas Mawson for Alf Howard, dated 20 October 1931, MC 63BZE/38.

CSIR Griffith

1 'Twelfth Annual Report of the Council for Scientific and Industrial Research [CSIR] for the Year 1937-38,' p. 46, CSIRO Records.

2 'Eighth Annual Report of the Council for Scientific and Industrial Research [CSIR] for the Year ended 30th June, 1934,' p. 41, CSIRO Records.

3 'Seventh Annual Report of the CSIR for the Year ended 30th June, 1933,' p. 52, CSIRO Records.

4 E.S. West and A. Howard, 'Some Effects of Green Manuring on Citrus Trees and on the Soil,' *Bulletin: Commonwealth of Australia, Council for Scientific and Industrial Research*, No. 120, 1938, p. 7.

5 E.S. West and A. Howard, 'The Design of Overhead Irrigation Systems,' Commonwealth of Australia, Council for Scientific and Industrial Research, Pamphlet No. 50, 1934.

6 A. Howard and G.A. McIntyre, 'A survey, census, and statistical study of the horticultural plantings on the Murrumbidgee Irrigation Areas, New South Wales,' *Bulletin/Commonwealth of Australia, Council for Scientific and Industrial Research*, 168: 1943.

7 Letter from Sir Douglas Mawson to Alf Howard, dated 10 March 1932, MC 63BZE/38.

8 Ibid., 18 May 1932, MC 63BZE/38.

9 Alf Howard, unpublished notes 'British, Australian, New Zealand Antarctic Research Expedition (BANZARE),' Alf Howard papers, FL.

10 'Medal Awards: Antarctic Research Expedition,' *Canberra Times*, 1 May 1934: 2.

11 Letter from Alf Howard to Sir Douglas Mawson, dated 24 October 1934, MC 63BZE/38.

12 Letter from Alf Howard to Sir Douglas Mawson, dated 26 December 1934, MC 63BZE/38.

13 Letter from Alf Howard to Eric Douglas, dated 9 December 1935, Sally Douglas private collection. The expedition in question left Melbourne on 24 December 1935 on the RRS *Discovery II* with two planes: a Wapiti and a Gipsy Moth–bound for Dunedin for refuelling and then on to the Bay of Whales where Lincoln Ellsworth and aviator Hollick Kenyon were reported missing. From the ship in January 1936 Eric Douglas led an RAAF search party for the two adventurers who were eventually both found and returned to the ship.

CSIR Sydney

1 Josephine M. Bastian, D. McG. McBean and M.B. Smith, *Fifty Years of Food Research*, Melbourne: CSIRO, 1979.

2 'Dehydrated Mutton for Civilians Likely,' *Advertiser*, 9 March 1943: 2.

3 Correspondence from Jack Kefford to author dated 19 March 2007.

CSIRO Brisbane

1 A. Howard and J.R. Vickery, 'The Preservation of Beef by Freezing: Co-operative Investigations,' *CSIRO Food Preservation Quarterly*, 10, 1950, pp. 30-31.

2 'Fourth Annual Report of the CSIRO for the Year ended 30th June, 1952,' p. 80, CSIRO Records.

3 E.C. Bate-Smith and M. Ingram 'Forty Years of Research on Meat,' *CSIRO Food Preservation Quarterly*, 27, 1967, pp. 67-72.

4 Kymograph: an instrument for recording variations in pressure, e.g., in sound waves or in blood within blood vessels, by the trace of a stylus on a rotating cylinder.

5 Letter from Professor Ralston Lawrie to author, dated 29 May 2007.

6 Bastian et al, *Fifty Years of Food Research*, p. 164.

7 Tim Cassidy to author, 24 December 2005.

8 Bastian et al., p. 160.

9 Les Brownlie to author, 28 July 2010.

10 Fred Grau to author, 29 July 2010.

11 Robin Shorthose to author, 14 February 2007.

12 Tom Larsen to author, 3 August 2010.

13 Bastian et al., p. 165.

14 Alf Howard, 'The Measurement of Attributes of Eating Quality with Special Reference to Meat,' thesis (PhD), University of Queensland, 1968.

15 Larsen to author.

16 Ibid.

The University of Queensland years

1 Lesley Chase to author, 4 August 2010.

2 Alf Howard, 'A multidimensional scaling study of the perceptual space of vowels,' dissertation (BA Hons), University of Queensland, October, 1979, Archives, School of Languages and Comparative Cultural Studies, The University of Queensland.

3 Ian Jobling to author, 6 July 2004.

4 Margaret Steinberg to author, 29 May 2007.

5 Doune Macdonald to author, 24 January 2006.

6 Craig Engstrom to author, 22 August 2007.

7 Letter from Alf Howard to Shirley Howard, dated 27 July 1986.

8 Ibid., c. October 1986.

9 Jobling to author, 6 July 2004.

10 Ibid.

11 Ann Savours., *The Voyages of the Discovery: The Illustrated History of Scott's Ship*. London: Chatham, 2001, pp. 153, 156.

12 Alf donated his Hurley album of 60 BANZARE photographs to the National Library of Australia in the late 1990s. Identifier: nla.pic-an13751629-1 to nla.pic-an13751629-60. Call number PIC P1963/1-60 LOC Album 923.

13 Letter from Alf Howard to Shirley Howard, dated 12 December 1993.

14 'Students meet real-life explorer,' 4 August 1993, held in Jamboree Heights State School archives.

15 Letter from Alf Howard to Shirley Howard, dated 18 December 1989.

16 Cam Griffin to author, 12 April 2006.

17 Letter from Alf Howard to Shirley Howard, dated 7 May 1990.

18 Macdonald to author, 24 January 2006.

19 Jobling to author, 6 July 2004.

20 Letter from Alf Howard to Shirley Howard, dated 7 May 1990.

21 Email from Philip Barnaart to author, dated 31 July 2010.

22 Letter from Captain Heinz Aye of the M/V *Frontier Spirit* to Alf Howard, dated 18 January 1991.

23 Alf Howard quoted in Pip Smith, 'Cruising in Mawson's Antarctica,' *Australian Geographic*, 25 (Jan-March) 1992, p. 113.

24 Letter from Alf Howard to Shirley Howard, dated 4 August 1991.

25 'Researcher's Antarctic links span 60 years,' *University News* (The University of Queensland), July 1992.

26 Email from John Splettstoesser to author, dated 15 July 2010.

27 Letter from Alf Howard to Shirley Howard, dated 12 December 1993.

28 Letter from Alf Howard to Shirley Howard, dated 18 December 1994.

29 Ray Specht to author, 9 August 2010.

30 Ibid., 14 May 1996.

31 Email from Andrew Brooks to author, dated 30 July 2010.

32 Entry dated 31 December 1996, Log of the *Kapitan Khlebnikov*, November 24, 1996-January 27, 1997.

33 Entry dated 21 January 1997, Log of the *Kapitan Khlebnikov*, November 24, 1996-January 27, 1997.

34 Letter from Alf Howard to Shirley Howard, dated 24 February 1997.

35 Syd Kirkby, Introductory speech at the Launch of the Brisbane ANARE Exhibition, officially opened by Senator the Hon. Ian Macdonald — Parliamentary Secretary to the Minister for the Environment — on 9 October 1997 at the Queensland Museum.

36 *The History of the ANARE Club 1951-2001: The Club for members of the Australian National Antarctic Research Expeditions.* Compiled, written and published by members of the ANARE Club Incorporated, Melbourne, 2002, p. 93.

37 Letter from Alf Howard to Shirley Howard, dated 13 December 1997.

38 Email from Alf Howard to author, dated 13 July 1998.

39 Postcard from Alf Howard to author, dated 16 July 1998.

40 Tony Stephens, 'Mawson survivor still game for discovery, 74 years on,' *Sydney Morning Herald*, 20 March 2003.

41 Macdonald to author, 24 January 2006.

42 'Birthday bash for our Alf,' *UQ University News*, May 2005, p. 6.

43 'Historic Visit of His Royal Highness, Prince Philip, The Duke of Edinburgh to the Royal Society of Victoria on Wednesday 15 March 2006,' *AURORA*, ANARE Club Journal Vol. 25:3, March 2006, p. 2.

44 Letter from Niall Cooper to author, dated 12 May 2006.

45 Foreword, 'The Saga of Melba's Own: The Story of First City of Camberwell (Melba's Own) Scout Group 1908-2008.'

46 Editorial, 'One Man's Crowded Life,' *Sydney Morning Herald,* 27 March 2003.

***

Selected Bibliography

Abernethy, Peter J., Howard, Alf, Quigley, Brian M., 'Isokinetic Torque and Instantaneous Power-Independent Entities?', *Journal of Strength & Conditioning Research*, vol. 10 (4), 1996: 220-223.

Ayres, Philip, *Mawson: A Life*. Carlton South, Vic.: Melbourne University Press, 1999.

Barrett, Noel D., 'Norway and the "winning" of Australian Antarctica', *Polar Record*, vol. 45, n°235, 2009, pp. 360-367.

Bastian, Josephine M., Mc Bean, D. McG, and M.B. Smith, *Fifty Years of Food Research*, Melbourne: CSIRO, 1979.

Bate-Smith, E.C. and Ingram, M. (1967) 'Forty Years of Research on Meat', *CSIRO Food Preservation Quarterly*, 27, 1967: 67-72.

Baty, Scott, *Ships that Passed: The Glorious Era of Travel to Australia and New Zealand*. Frenchs Forest, NSW: Reed Books, 1984.

Bickel, Lennard, *In Search of Frank Hurley*. South Melbourne, Vic.: Macmillan, 1980.

Bouton, P.E., and Howard, A., 'Quality of Pre-Wrapped Frozen Meat Cuts', *CSIRO Food Preservation Quarterly*, vol. 16 (3), 1956: 50-54.

Bowden, Tim, *Antarctica and Back in Sixty Days*, ABC Books, 1991. (Reprinted by Allen & Unwin 1991)

Bowden, Tim, *The Silence Calling — Australians in Antarctica 1947-97*. St. Leonards, NSW: Allen & Unwin, 1997.

Branagan, David, *TW Edgeworth David: A Life*, ed. Paul Cliff. Canberra: National Library of Australia, 2005.

Campbell, Stuart, Diary of the Second Voyage of the British, Australian, New Zealand Antarctic Research Expedition 1929-1931, under the command of Sir Douglas Mawson aboard S.Y. Discovery [typewritten copy made by Stuart Campbell in 1983]. Held in Australian Antarctic Division Library, Special Collection, Kingston, Tasmania.

Collis, Brad, *Fields of Discovery: Australia's CSIRO*. Crows Nest, NSW: Allen & Unwin, 2002.

Dann, Arthur Thurlby., Howard, Alf and Davies, William, 'The Alkaline Hydrolysis of ω-Bromo- and ω-Chloro-nitrostyrenes, *Journal of the Chemical Society*, 1928: 605- 611.

Davis, John King, *High Altitude*, Melbourne: Melbourne University Press, 1962.

Davis, John King, *Trial By Ice: The Antarctic Journals of John King Davis*, Louise Crossley (ed.), Huntingdon: Bluntisham Books, Erskine Press, 1997.

Empey, W.A., and Howard, A., 'Drip Formation in Meat and Fish', *CSIRO Food Preservation Quarterly*, vol. 14 (2), 1954: 33-36.

Ennis, Helen, *Frank Hurley's Antarctica*, Canberra: National Library of Australia, 2010.

Farrer, Keith, *To Feed a Nation: A history of Australian food science and technology*. Collingwood, Vic.: CSIRO Publishing, 2005.

Fisher, Ronald A., *Statistical methods for research workers*. 1925. Edinburgh: Oliver and Boyd, 1958.

Fisher, Ronald A., *The design of experiments*. 1935. Edinburgh: Oliver and Boyd, 1951.

Fletcher, Harold, *Antarctic Days with Mawson: A Personal Account of the British, Australian and New Zealand Antarctic Research Expedition of 1929-31*. Sydney: Angus & Robertson, 1984.

Forwood, Mark R., Baxter-Jones, Adam D., Beck, Tomas J., Howard, Alf, et al., 'Physical Activity and strength of the femoral neck during the adolescent growth spurt: A longitudinal analysis', *Bone*, vol. 38 (4), 2006: 576-583.

Hall, Lincoln, *Douglas Mawson: The Life of an Explorer*. Sydney: New Holland, 2000.

Hardy, Alistair, *Great Waters; A Voyage of National History to study whales, plankton and the waters of the Southern Ocean in the old Royal Research Ship Discovery with the results brought up to date by the findings of the R.R.S. Discovery 11*. London: Collins, 1967.

Hicks, E.W., Howard, A., and Kaess, G., 'The Cooling, Freezing, Storage and Transport of Frozen Meat', *Food Technology in Australia*, vol. 9, 1957: 247-51.

Hooper, Sue L., Mackinnon, Laurel T., and Howard, Alf, 'Physiological and psychometric variables for monitoring recovery during tapering for major competition', *Medicine and Science in Sports and Exercise*. 31:8, August 1999: 1205-1210.

Howard, Alf, *Hydrology (Part 2): The Programme of Work and Record of Observations (Section 1). Series A, Volume III (Oceanography) in Reports of B.A.N.Z. Antarctic Research Expedition 1929-1931 under the Command of Douglas Mawson, Kt., O.B.I., B.E., D.Sc., F.R.S. Reports-Series A Ed. Sir Douglas Mawson*. Adelaide: B.A.N.Z.A.R. Expedition Committee and issued through the Barr Smith Library, University of Adelaide. Printed at The Hassell Press, 1940.

Howard, A., and McIntyre, G.A., 'A survey, census, and statistical study of the horticultural plantings on the Murrumbidgee Irrigation Areas, New South Wales', *Bulletin / Commonwealth of Australia, Council for Scientific and Industrial Research*, N° 168, 1943.

Howard, A., and Vickery, J.R., 'The Preservation of Beef by Freezing: Co-operative Investigations', *CSIRO Food Preservation Quarterly*, 10, 1950: 30-31.

Howard, A., 'Chilling of Beef for Export', *Food Technology in Australia*, vol. 5, 1953: 111, 114, 115, 117, 120.

Howard, A., 'Experimental Shipment of Chilled Beef per *S.S. Jason*', *CSIRO Food Preservation* Cannon Hill, August 1953.

Howard, A., and Kaess, G., 'Preparation of Frozen Packaged Meat', *CSIRO Food Preservation* Cannon Hill, 1955.

Howard, A., 'Some Trends in Meat Research and Practice', *CSIRO Food Preservation* Cannon Hill, 1956.

Howard, A., 'Implications and Conclusions from Investigations on Quality of Frozen Beef', CSIRO Food Preservation, Cannon Hill, 1956.

Howard, A., 'Sensory Tests of the Quality of Meat', *CSIRO Food Preservation Quarterly*, vol. 16, 1956: 26-30.

Howard, A., and Lawrie, R.A., 'Studies on Beef Quality: Part 1. The Effect of Blast-Freezing Hot Beef Quarters', CSIRO Publication, 1956: 1-17.

Howard, A., 'The Measurement of Drip from Frozen Meat', *CSIRO Food Preservation Quarterly*, vol. 16, 1956: 31-35.

Howard, A., 'Carbon Dioxide Anaesthesia for Pig Slaughter', *CSIRO Food Preservation Quarterly*, vol. 17, 1957: 51-52.

Howard, A., 'Preservation of Meat', *The Refrigeration Journal*, vol. 13 (1), 1959: 23, 25.

Howard, A., 'The Chilling, Freezing, and Prepackaging of Beef', *CSIRO Food Preservation Quarterly*, vol. 20, 1960: 2-8.

Howard, A., and Prater, A.R., 'The Effect of Pre-Processing Factors on the Quality of Air-Dried Mutton Mince', *CSIRO Division of Food Preservation Technical Paper No. 23*, 1961.

Howard, A., 'Preservation of Meat Products in the Tropics Without Refrigeration', *Food Technology in Australia*, March 1962.

Howard, A., 'Preservation of Meat', *Meat Industry Bulletin*, August, 1963: 43-56.

Howard, A., 'Wholesale Meat Packaging Halves Butchery Costs', *Packaging Review*, 88 (11), 1968: 28-29.

Howard, Alf, 'The measurement of attributes of eating quality with special reference to meat', thesis (PhD), University of Queensland, 1968.

Howard, A., 'Taste Panel Techniques: I. Reproducibility, Reliability, and Validity', *CSIRO Food Research Quarterly*, vol. 32 (4), 1972: 80-84.

Howard, A., 'Taste Panel Techniques: II. A Validating Technique', *CSIRO Food Research Quarterly*, vol. 33 (1), 1973: 8-14.

Howard, A., Duffy, A., Else, K., and Brown, W.D., 'Possible Substitutes for Nitrite for Pigment Formation in Cured Meat Products', *Journal of Agricultural and Food Chemistry*, vol. 21 (5), 1973: 894-898.

Howard, A., 'Psychometric Scaling of Sensory Texture Attributes', *Journal of Texture Studies*, vol. 7 (1), 1976: 95-107.

Hurley, Captain Frank, *Siege of the South: An Epic of Man's Glorious Struggle with Nature in the Frozen South* [film 1931, 83 mins] Released by Union Theatres Feature Exchange [VHS SoundScreen Australia (tel: 02 6248 2091 — Ruth Hill, Collection Access, ScreenSound Australia, PO Box 2002, Canberra AT 2601.]

Law, Phillip, *Antarctic Odyssey*. Melbourne: Heinemann, 1983.

Marchant, Harvey J., Lugg, Desmond J. and Patrick G. Quilty, eds, *Australian Antarctic Science: The First 50 Years of ANARE*. Kingston, Tasmania: Australian Antarctic Division, 2002.

Marr, J.W.S. *Into the Frozen South by Scout Marr of the Quest Expedition*, ed. Frank H. Shaw. London: Cassell, 1923.

Mawson, Douglas, 'The Antarctic Cruise of the *Discovery*, 1929-30', *Geographical Review* 20 (1930): 534554.

Mawson, Douglas, 'The BANZ Research Expedition, 1929-31', *Geographical Journal*, 80.1932: 1-131.

Mawson, Douglas, 'Presidential address: the unveiling of Antarctica', held in Fryer Library G870.M39 1935, The University of Queensland.

Mawson, Douglas, *Mawson's Antarctic Diaries*, ed. Fred and Eleanor Jacka. Sydney: Allen & Unwin, 1988.

Mawson's huts: the birthplace of Australia's Antarctic heritage, compiled by Mawson's Huts Foundation. Crows Nest, NSW: Allen & Unwin, 2008.

Mawson's Papers: A Guide to the Scientific, Personal and Business Papers of Sir Douglas Mawson, OBE, BE, DSc, FRS, FAA 1882-1958; Professor of Geology and Mineralogy; Antarctic

Scientist and Explorer, compiled by Margaret Innes with additional material compiled by Heather Duff. Adelaide: University of Adelaide Printing Section, 1990.

Moyes, John Layton, *Exploring the Antarctic with Mawson and the men of the 1911-1914 Expedition*. West Gosford, NSW: RSL Leisure Living Ltd, 1996.

Naumann, H.D., Howard, A., and Bouton, P.E., 'Consumer Reactions to Steak Beef', *CSIRO Food Preservation Quarterly*, vol. 26 No. 1, 1966: 12-18.

Price, A. Grenfell, *The Winning of Australian Antarctica: Mawson's B.A.N.Z.A.R.E. Voyages 1929-31, Based on the Mawson Papers*. Sydney: Angus and Robertson, 1962.

Radford, Joan Treasure, *The Chemistry Department of the University of Melbourne: its contribution to Australian science, 1854-1959*. Melbourne: Hawthorn Press, 1978.

Russell, Bertrand., *History ofWestern Philosophy*. 1946. London: Routledge, 1991.

Savours, A., *The Voyages of the Discovery: The Illustrated History of Scott's Ship*. London: Chatham, 2001.

Scholes, A., *Seventh Continent, Saga of Australasian Exploration in Antarctica, 1895-1950*. London: George Allen & Unwin, 1953.

Shackleton, Ernest, *The Heart of the Antarctic: Being the Story of the British Antarctic Expedition, 1907-1909*. London: Heinemann, 1909.

Shackleton, Ernest, *South: The Story of Shackleton's Last Expedition, 1914-1917*. London: Heinemann, 1919.

Swan, R.A., *Australia in the Antarctic*. Melbourne: Melbourne University Press, 1961.

Thomis, Malcolm I., *A Place of Light & Learning: The University of Queensland's First Seventy-five Years*. St Lucia (Qld): University of Queensland Press, 1985.

Tulloch, N.M., Howard, A., Shorthose, W.R., et al, 'Field Techniques for investigation of Pre-Weaning Growth, Post-Weaning Growth, Body Composition, and Meat Studies', *Manual of Techniques for Field Investigations with Beef Cattle*. Canberra: CSIRO, 1973.

Vickery, J.R. *Food Science and Technology in Australia: a review of research since 1900*. Melbourne: CSIRO, 1990.

Weickhardt, Len, *Masson of Melbourne: The Life and Times of David Orme Masson KBE, MA, DSc, LLD, FRSE, FRS Professor of Chemistry, University of Melbourne, 1886-1923*. Parkville, Victoria: Royal Auystralian Chemical Institute, 1989.

West, E.S., and Howard, A., 'The Design of Overhead Irrigation Systems', *Pamphlet / Commonwealth of Australia, Council for Scientific and Industrial Research*, 50: 1934.

West, E.S., and Howard, A., 'Some effects of green manuring on citrus trees and on the soil', *Bulletin / Commonwealth of Australia, Council for Scientific and Industrial Research*, 120: 1938.

Newspapers & Periodicals

Advertiser, Adelaide
Age, Melbourne
Argus, Melbourne
Australasian
Brisbane Courier
Cairns Post, Queensland
Canberra Times
Cape Argus, Cape Town
Cape Times, Cape Town
Examiner, Launceston
Mercury, Hobart
New York Times
Register News-Pictorial, Adelaide
Table Talk, Melbourne
The Queenslander
Times, London
Sydney Morning Herald

Illustration credits

The author gratefully acknowledges that the illustrations in this book have been reproduced by permission and courtesy of the following individuals and institutions:

Front cover photograph: Scientific personnel of BANZARE (1929-30) on deck of the *Discovery*. Mawson Collection, South Australian Museum [R 263]

'The University High School Record', Vol. IX, No. 2, Xmas, 1929, p. 4

'The University High School Record'. Vol. V, No. 1, June 1923, p. 5

Jan Black [2008] et. al., 'The Saga of Melba's Own: The Story of First City of Camberwell (Melba's Own) Scout Group 1908-2008' [unpublished], p. 8

Alf Howard private collection, pp. 17, 20, 60, 122, 135, 139, 143, 172, 189, 191, 203

National Library of Australia, Pictures Collection, pp. 23, 28, 32, 40, 43, 48, 66, 69, 75, 79, 84, 86, 96, 104, 138, 142, 147

Mawson's Papers: A guide to the scientific, personal and business papers of Sir Douglas Mawson, OBE, BE, DSc, FRS, FAA, 1882-1958, Professor of Geology and Mineralogy, Antarctic Scientist and Explorer, compiled by Margaret Innes with additional material compiled by Heather Duff. The Mawson Institute for Antarctic Research, The University of Adelaide, 1990, p. 30

Discovery Reports Vol. I, Cambridge, University Press of Cambridge, 1929, p. 37

BANZ Antarctic Research Expedition 1929-31 Reports - Series A, Vol 1: Geographical Report Based on the Mawson Papers by A. Grenfell Price, Adelaide. Published by the Mawson Institute for Scientific Research 1963, pp. 44, 131, 141

Davis, John King, *Trial By Ice: The Antarctic Journals of John King Davis*, Louise Crossley (ed.), Huntingdon: Bluntisham Books, Erskine Press, 1997, p. 57

Alf Howard, *Hydrology (Part 2): The Programme of Work and Record of Observations (Section 1). Series A, Volume III (Oceanography) in Reports of B.A.N.Z. Antarctic Research Expedition 1929-1931 under the Command of Douglas Mawson, Kt., O.B.I., B.E., D.Sc., F.R.S. Reports-Series A Ed. Sir Douglas Mawson*. Adelaide: B.A.N.Z.A.R. Expedition Committee and issued through the Barr Smith Library, University of Adelaide. Printed at The Hassell Press, 1940, p. 58

Sally Douglas private collection, p. 73, 113, 127

Australasian, 12 April 1930, pp. 93, 107

Shirley Howard private collection, p. 159

Josephine M. Bastian, D. McG. McBean, and M.B. Smith, *Fifty Years of Food Research*, Melbourne: CSIRO, 1979 (CSIRO Archives), pp. 164, 168

Nick Rains, *Australian Geographic*, p. 185

School of Human Movement Studies collection, University of Queensland, pp. 194, 196, 201, 204

The History of the ANARE Club 1951-2001: The Club for members of the Australian National Antarctic Research Expeditions. Compiled, written and published by members of the ANARE Club Incorporated, Melbourne, 2002, p. 200
Rick Stevens/Fairfax Syndication, *Sydney Morning Herald*, 20 March 2003, p. 205
Photographs on pp. 184, 207, 208, 211 by author

Permissions

The author wishes to thank the following for permission to quote from copyright sources:

Allen & Unwin for extracts from *Mawson's Antarctic Diaries*, edited by Fred Jacka and Eleanor Jacka.
Australian Antarctic Division Archives for permission to quote from the diary of Stuart Campbell.
Bluntisham Books & Erskine Press for permission to quote extracts from *Trial by Ice*, edited by Louise Crossley.
Sally Douglas for permission to quote from the diaries of Eric Douglas.
Ian Fletcher for permission to quote from Harold O. Fletcher's *Antarctic Days with Mawson* and from the diaries of Harold O. Fletcher.
Mawson Centre, South Australian Museum, for permission to quote from the Mawson Papers.
Mitchell Library, for permission to quote from the diary of Willaim Wilson Ingram.
David Simmers for permission to quote from the diaries of Ritchie Simmers.

Index

About the Author

Anna Bemrose is an Honorary Researcher in the School of English, Media Studies and Art History at the University of Queensland (UQ). Her research for the present book incorporates many conversations with Alf Howard and with a number of his friends and former CSIRO and UQ colleagues. Her voyage on an icebreaker through the Southern Ocean to Antarctica in 2005, facilitated the task of bringing to life the archival records of Sir Douglas Mawson's 1929-31 British, Australian and New Zealand Antarctic Research Expedition (BANZARE). She is the author of *Robert Helpmann: A Servant of Art*.

Anna Bemrose on Macquarie Island with penquins